OMB Circular A-123 and Sarbanes-Oxley:

Management's Responsibility for
Internal Control in Federal Agencies

OMB Circular A-123 and Sarbanes-Oxley:

Management's Responsibility for Internal Control in Federal Agencies

Cornelius E. Tierney

Edward F. Kearney

Roldan Fernandez

Jeffrey W. Green

Michael Ramos

WILEY

John Wiley & Sons, Inc.

For general information on our other products and services, or technical support,
please contact our Customer Care Department within the United States at 800-762-2974,
outside the United States at 317-572-3993 or fax 317-572-4002.

Wiley also publishes its books in a variety of electronic formats. Some content that
appears in print may not be available in electronic books.

For more information about Wiley products, visit our Web site at http://www.wiley.com.

Library of Congress Cataloging-in-Publication Data:

  Sarbanes-Oxley : complying with OMB Circular A-123, management's
responsibility for internal control in federal agencies / Kearney & Company.
    p. cm.
  ISBN-13: 978-0-471-76813-5 (cloth : alk. paper)
  ISBN-10: 0-471-76813-8 (cloth : alk. paper)
    1. Finance, Public—Auditing—Law and legislation—United States.
  2. Finance, Public—United States—Auditing. 3. Administrative
agencies—United States—Auditing. I. United States. Office of Management
and Budget. II. Kearney & Company (Alexandria, Va.) III. Title.
KF6235.S373   2006
343.73'034—dc22   2006005316

Printed in the United States of America

10 9 8 7 6 5 4 3 2 1

About the Authors

Edward F. Kearney, CPA, CGFM, is the Managing Partner of Kearney & Company. He is a former Senior Manager of Arthur Young & Company (a predecessor firm to Ernst & Young) and a former officer of a public company listed on the NYSE. He also worked for the Department of Housing and Urban Development as an auditor and accountant, and is a co-author of *Federal Government Auditing: Laws, Regulations, Standards, Practices, & Sarbanes-Oxley,* published by Wiley & Sons.

Roldan Fernandez, CPA, CGFM, is a Senior Partner with Kearney & Company. He is a former Principal of Arthur Young & Company and the former CFO of a public company listed in the NYSE. He has over 25 years of diversified experience in all facets of financial management in both the public and private sectors, and is a co-author of *Federal Government Auditing: Laws, Regulations, Standards, Practices, & Sarbanes-Oxley,* published by Wiley & Sons.

Jeffrey W. Green, CPA, is a Senior Partner with Kearney & Company responsible for federal audit engagements and internal control projects covered under the rules of OMB Circular A-123. He is the recipient of the Association of Government Accountants' (AGA) Federal Financial Partnership Award, and is a co-author of *Federal Government Auditing: Laws, Regulations, Standards, Practices, & Sarbanes-Oxley,* published by Wiley & Sons.

Cornelius E. Tierney, CPA, CGFM, is a Director with Kearney & Company, and is the author or co-author of twelve books on governmental accounting and auditing, including *Federal Government Auditing: Laws, Regulations, Standards, Practices, & Sarbanes-Oxley,* published by Wiley & Sons. He served as the Chairman and National Director of Ernst & Young's public sector accounting and auditing practice for nearly 25 years, and was an original member of the Federal Accounting Standards Advisory Board.

Michael Ramos, CPA, is a Consultant and professional writer specializing in auditing matters. He has written numerous successful publications, including practice aids, implementation guides, and authoritative American Institute of Certified Public Accountants (AICPA) Audit and Accounting Guides. This is his fourth book on the internal control requirements of Sarbanes-Oxley.

Kearney & Company is a CPA firm that provides audit, accounting, and consulting services to the Federal government. Additional details on Kearney & Company can be found on the web at *www.kearneyco.com.*

Contents

Preface   ix

1. **Federal Managers' Financial Integrity Act of 1982
   and Sarbanes-Oxley Act of 2002: An Overview**   **1**
   Appendix 1A   Action Plan: Structuring the Project   45
   Appendix 1B   Requirements for Management's Assessment
                   Process: Cross-Reference to Guidance   46

2. **Internal Control Criteria**   **49**

3. **Internal Control Assessment: Project Planning**   **81**
   Appendix 3A   Action Plan: Project Planning   105
   Appendix 3B   Summary of Planning Questions   107

4. **Identifying Significant Control Objectives**   **113**
   Appendix 4A   Action Plan: Identifying Significant Control Objectives   134
   Appendix 4B   Example Significant Control Objectives   136
   Appendix 4C   Map to the COSO *Framework*   138
   Appendix 4D   Map to the Auditing Literature   140
   Appendix 4E   Working with the Independent Auditors:
                   Lessons Learned from the Initial Implementation
                   of Sarbanes-Oxley   140

5. **Documentation of Significant Controls**   **147**
   Appendix 5A   Action Plan: Documentation   174
   Appendix 5B   Evaluating the Design and Implementation
                   of Automated Compliance Tools   176
   Appendix 5C   Linkage of Significant Control Objectives to
                   Example Control Policies and Procedures   183

6. **Testing and Evaluating Entity-Level Controls**   **193**
   Appendix 6A   Action Plan: Testing and Evaluating Entity-Level
                   Controls   213
   Appendix 6B   Survey Tools   215
   Appendix 6C   Example Inquiries of Management Regarding
                   Entity-Level Controls   222
   Appendix 6D   Guidance for Designing a Computer
                   General Controls Review   228

7. **Testing and Evaluating Activity-Level Controls**   **239**
    Appendix 7A   Action Plan: Documentation   256
    Appendix 7B   Example Inquiries   257

8. **Reporting**   **261**
    Appendix 8A   Examples of Current Private Industry Practices   279

Index   **299**

Preface

The Sarbanes-Oxley Act might well be the best known piece of non-tax financial legislation introduced since the depression era–related Securities Exchange Acts of 1933 and 1934. As such, it is not surprising that many federal financial managers have taken an interest in this legislation and are closely monitoring any developments.

The genesis of this book dates back to 2002 and the passage of Sarbanes-Oxley legislation and Securities and Exchange Commission (SEC) financial reporting regulations related to the internal controls of publicly traded corporations. At that time, the authors of this book were commissioned by the Association of Government Accountants (AGA) to research the likely impact of Sarbanes-Oxley on the federal government, including potential future legislation.

Our research supported two observations. First, it reinforced the fact that throughout the years, the federal government and *not* the private sector had been the subject of significant internal control–related legislation. Second, it disclosed that the internal control framework adopted by the Office of Management and Budget (OMB) in earlier years differed from the Sarbanes-Oxley recommended Committee of Sponsoring Organizations of the Treadway Commission's (COSO) framework and the principles and objectives set forth by the SEC and the Public Company Accounting Oversight Board (PCAOB). Today, OMB Circular A-123 has, for all intents and purposes, adopted the COSO framework, and as a result, the federal government approach to internal controls closely parallels that of the private sector.

A Sarbanes-Oxley guided approach to OMB Circular A-123 compliance is relevant for several reasons:

- By emphasizing the similarities with Sarbanes-Oxley, we hope to provide federal financial managers and Congress with sufficient information to prevent the passage of redundant legislation affecting internal controls in federal agencies.
- The adoption of Sarbanes-Oxley by the private sector is already in effect and federal agencies that understand the Act and its similarities to current federal guidance will be able to profit from the lessons learned by industry.
- Existing legislation governing federal financial management can be consolidated, thus eliminating duplication of reporting and adding clarity to all requirements.
- The private sector has already voiced some concern over the additional costs of the implementation of Sarbanes-Oxley, at times questioning the value received in return. It is too early to tell whether the additional requirements are not fully warranted or whether the private sector is simply experiencing "start-up" implementation costs which will benefit future periods. By identifying the similarities between Sarbanes-Oxley and revised Circular A-123 requirements, we hope to facilitate the identification of burdensome requirements to support future changes to the guidance, should these changes appear warranted.

We believe that OMB's initial approach to requiring audits only in cases of continued noncompliance with guidance is sound. While we recognize that this issue will continue to be debated, we believe it is prudent to wait for actual results as well as for "lessons learned" by the private sector before imposing additional requirements.

This book, *OMB Circular A-123 and Sarbanes-Oxley: Management's Responsibility for Internal Control in Federal Agencies,* by Kearney & Company, P.C., is intended to provide an approach to evaluating and testing internal controls which can be adopted by federal managers in their efforts to comply with OMB Circular A-123. This book is the result of consultations with accountants, auditors, financial managers, and systems consultants specializing in both the public and private sectors' systems and internal controls. In developing this book, reliance has been placed on the bodies of knowledge created by Congress, OMB, the Government Accountability Office (formerly the General Accounting Office), the American Institute of Certified Public Accountants, SEC, PCAOB, the Federal Accounting Standards Advisory Board, the Chief Financial Officer's Council, and Offices of Inspectors General. Promulgations of all of these organizations have contributed to the body of knowledge one must possess to efficiently and effectively comply with OMB's Circular A-123 requirements.

Kearney & Company is a certified public accounting firm founded in 1985 that specializes in providing auditing, accounting, and information technology services to the federal government. Additional details on the firm can be found on the web at *www.kearneyco.com.*

This book has been written in a manner which endeavors to assist professionals and nonprofessionals employed by the federal government or other organizations — federal executives, financial and nonfinancial managers, inspectors general, independent public accountants, military comptrollers, legislators, staffs of legislators, budget officers, program and financial analysts, attorneys, systems designers, and systems experts—in short, anyone having responsibility for and/or an interest in federal financial systems and internal controls.

Chapter 1

Federal Managers' Financial Integrity Act of 1982 and Sarbanes-Oxley Act of 2002: An Overview

---

Chapter Summary

Overview of revisions to Office of Management and Budget (OMB) Circular A-123 and Securities and Exchange Commission (SEC) guidance and rules in connection with:

- Management's assessment of the effectiveness of the entity's internal control over financial reporting
- Independent auditor's report(s) on internal control
- Management's required interim (e.g., quarterly) reporting on resolution of deficiencies and the effectiveness of the entity's disclosure controls and procedures
- Summary of the relevant auditing standards relating to internal control
- Description of a structured approach for the evaluation of an entity's internal control
- Suggestions for structuring a project to assist management in evaluating the effectiveness of internal control and preparing for an independent auditor's report on internal controls including an audit of management's internal control assertion

---

SARBANES-OXLEY[1]

On July 30, 2002, with the passage of the Sarbanes-Oxley Act, Congress gave preeminence to internal controls over financial reporting by mandating reporting, disclosures, and independent auditing requirements that, until this Act, had not been much discussed. By this Act, Congress required that:

> Each annual report submitted to the Securities and Exchange Commission by a publicly listed corporation is to contain an internal control report, which shall: 1. State the responsibility of management for establishing and maintaining an adequate internal control structure and procedures for financial reporting; and 2. Contain

an assessment by management of the effectiveness of the internal control structure and procedures of the issuer for financial reporting.—Sec. 404(a) and with respect to the internal control assessment made by management, the public accounting firm that prepares or issues the audit report shall attest to, and report on, the assessment made by the management of the effectiveness of internal control.—Sec. 404(b)

The Sarbanes-Oxley Act changed corporate governance and financial reporting and permanently altered the regulatory environment for publicly listed companies that had prevailed since the 1930s. The Act created a broad, new oversight regime by prescribing specific procedures, steps, and practices to address governance failures. It also codified several new responsibilities of corporate executives, corporate directors, and their lawyers, accountants, and regulators.

Section 404 of the Act underscored the importance Congress placed on having effective internal controls over financial reporting and gave these controls a prominence equal to that of financial statements in all future financial reportings by these companies subject to the Act. The Sarbanes-Oxley Act requires all publicly listed companies to include in their annual report to the SEC a separate auditor's report attesting to management's assessment of the company's internal control. The auditors must independently attest or audit and independently opine on the operational effectiveness of a public company's internal controls.

PUBLIC COMPANY ACCOUNTING OVERSIGHT BOARD

The new priority given to internal controls over financial reporting was made clear in the Public Company Accounting Oversight Board's (PCAOB)[2] Release No. 2004-001, which stated that, in order to achieve reliable financial statements, internal controls must be in place to:

- See that records accurately and fairly reflect transactions in, and dispositions of, a company's assets.

- Provide assurance that the records of transactions are sufficient to prepare financial statements in accordance with generally accepted accounting principles.

- Provide assurance that receipts and expenditures are made only as authorized by management and directors.

- Ensure that steps are in place to prevent or detect theft or unauthorized use or disposition of the company's assets of value that could have a material effect on the financial statements.

PCAOB's stated position is that users will have more confidence in the reliability of a financial statement if management demonstrates that it has exercised adequate internal control over the bookkeeping, the sufficiency and accuracy of books of accounts and records, adherence to rules about the use of the company's assets, and the possibility of a misappropriation of company assets.

MANAGEMENT: ASSESS CONTROLS
OVER FINANCIAL REPORTING

Compliance with the Sarbanes-Oxley Act requires an entity's management to:

- Establish and maintain adequate internal control structure.
- Have and implement policies and procedures for governing financial reporting.
- Annually assess and report to the government on the effectiveness of their internal controls and procedures.

The Sarbanes-Oxley Act requires the independent auditor's report for the financial statements of a publicly listed corporation to be accompanied by a separate auditor's report on controls. In May 2003, the SEC clarified and amplified the provisions of the Act by stating that management's assessment of the internal controls over financial reporting must include:

- A statement of management's responsibilities for establishing and maintaining adequate internal control
- A statement identifying the framework used by management to evaluate the effectiveness of the entity's internal control
- Management's assessment of the effectiveness of the internal control as of the end of the most recent year, including a statement as to whether the internal control over financial reporting is effective
- A statement confirming that the accounting firm that audited the financial statements included in the annual report has issued an attestation report on management's assessment of the entity's internal control
- Any changes in internal control that materially affect or are reasonably likely to affect the entity's internal control
- An attestation report by the registered public accounting firm on management's assessment of the entity's internal control

AUDITOR: AUDIT INTERNAL CONTROLS
OVER FINANCIAL REPORTING

Standards proposed by PCAOB require independent auditors, with respect to a publicly listed company's internal controls over financial reporting, to:

- Review management's assessment of the company's internal control.
- Form an opinion about management's assessment of the effectiveness of internal control.
- Form an audit opinion relative to management's assessment of controls after having:
  - Evaluated the reliability of the process used by management to assess the company's internal control.

- ○ Reviewed the results of tests performed by management, internal auditors, and others during their assessment process.
- ○ Performed his/her own audit tests and attested to and reported on the assessment made by management.

Thus, compliance with the Sarbanes-Oxley Act requires an independent auditor to audit separately the operational effectiveness of internal controls over financial reporting to be satisfied that management's assessment conclusion is correct and fairly stated. This requires the auditor to test and report on the effectiveness of controls over financial reporting separately. To comply, the auditor is to provide a separate audit and reporting of findings resulting from audit tests that includes:

- An evaluation of whether the control structure and procedures are reasonably detailed to reflect the transactions and dispositions of the assets accurately and fairly
- Reasonable assurance that transactions are recorded, as necessary, to prepare financial statements in accordance with generally accepted accounting principles
- Reasonable assurance that receipts and expenditures are made only in accordance with authorizations of management and directors of the entity
- Descriptions of material weaknesses and any material noncompliance found on the basis of testing
- An audit opinion on whether management's assessment of effectiveness of controls is "fairly stated"

ONE INTEGRATED AUDIT, TWO AUDIT OPINIONS

The Sarbanes-Oxley Act and its related implementation standards clearly assert that the required audit of the internal controls over financial reporting is to be integrated with, not separate from, the audit of an entity's financial statements. PCAOB *Auditing Standard No. 2* explains that Congress desires that an *integrated* audit be made of the financial statements and internal controls over financial reporting, further noting that:

> Notwithstanding the fact that the two audits are interrelated, the integrated audit results in two separate objectives: (1) to express an opinion on management's assessment of the effectiveness of the company's internal control over financial reporting, and (2) to express an opinion on whether the financial statements are fairly stated.

Thus, *Auditing Standard No. 2* is a standard that accomplishes both of the following:

1. Addresses the work required to audit internal controls over financial reporting and the relationship of that audit to the audit of the financial statements
2. Refers to the attestation of management's assessment of the effectiveness of internal control as the audit of internal control over financial reporting

PCAOB determined that the audits of controls and financial statements should be integrated because the objectives and work involved in performing an audit of internal controls over financial reporting and an audit of an entity's annual financial statements are so closely related.

CONTROLS STANDARD

The Sarbanes-Oxley Act requires management of a publicly traded company to base its assessment of the effectiveness of internal controls over financial reporting on a "suitable, recognized control framework established by a body of experts that followed due-process procedures to develop the framework." The guidance in PCAOB Standard No. 2 is based on the *Internal Control—Integrated Framework* (the *Framework*) developed by the Committee of Sponsoring Organizations (COSO) of the Treadway Commission in 1992. Sarbanes-Oxley recognizes that other suitable, possibly different, frameworks not containing exactly the same elements as COSO may be used, but the PCAOB cautions that these other frameworks should have elements that encompass all the COSO general themes.

COSO Definition

Since its release in 1992, the COSO *Framework* has become the controls standard for much of the business world. The COSO control concepts have been tested by many, have been applied in thousands of audits, and have been adopted by numerous private and public sector organizations as their own controls framework.

In the COSO *Framework,*[3] *internal controls* are broadly defined as:

A process, effected by the governing board, management, and other personnel of an audited entity, that is designed to provide reasonable assurance regarding the achievement of objectives in the following categories:

- *Effectiveness and efficiency of controls in operations:* relates to the entity's performance and financial goals and safeguarding of entity resources.
- *Reliability of financial reporting:* relates to the preparation of reliable published financial statements, including interim and condensed financial statements, and selected financial data extracted from such statements.
- *Compliance with applicable laws and regulations:* that relate to or apply to the audited entity.

COSO Structural Components

Under the COSO definition, *internal controls* encompass or consist of five interrelated structural components:

- *Control environment:* the environment "sets the tone" of an organization, provides the discipline and structure, and is the foundation for all other components of internal control.
- *Risk assessments:* identification, analysis, and assessment of the relative risks to achievement of entity objectives.

- *Control activities:* the policies, procedures, and practices that help ensure management directives are carried out, including a range of activities such as approvals, authorizations, verifications, reconciliations, reviews of operating performance, security of assets, and segregation of duties.

- *Information and communication:* the information systems that produce reports containing operational, financial, and compliance-related information that make it possible to administer, control, and manage an organization's performance.

- *Monitoring:* the periodic, regular monitoring of systems of internal controls to assess the controls system's performance over a period of time that includes regular management and supervisory activities and other actions personnel take in performing their duties.

With respect to *information technology-related controls,* COSO identified two types of controls:

1. *General controls:* controls over:
   - Data center operations (scheduling, backup, recovery procedures)
   - Systems software controls (acquisition and implementation of operating systems)
   - Access security
   - Application system development and maintenance controls (acquisition and implementation of individual computer software applications)
2. *Application controls:* controls designed to:
   - Control information processing.
   - Help ensure the completeness and accuracy of transaction processing, authorization, and the validity and effectiveness of interface of applications.

INTERNAL CONTROLS IN THE FEDERAL GOVERNMENT[4]

The record of congressional efforts to require the design, implementation, and application of effective systems of internal financial controls over the receipts, expenditures, and fiscal practices of the federal government is one of limited success. However, in some respects, the federal government is already required to follow requirements that only recently were imposed on many companies subject to SEC oversight. It may come as a surprise to those not familiar with the federal government, but even prior to Sarbanes-Oxley, internal control reporting was already an integral part of the federal reporting and auditing model. *Government Auditing Standards* (GAS or "Yellow Book" standards) issued by the Government Accountability Office (GAO; formerly the General Accounting Office) include the issuance of reports on internal controls and compliance with laws and regulations as an integral component of Yellow Book Reporting Standards. Similarly, the Office of Management and Budget (OMB) audit guidance applicable to audit reports issued in compliance with the Chief Financial Officers Act of 1990 (CFO Act) requires the issuance of reports on internal controls and laws and regulations in addition to the report on the financial statements.[5]

A brief history of congressional attempts to improve accountability and internal controls appears below.

The 1800s and 1900s

Although the laws are considerable in number, noting just a few of those that addressed the state of the federal government's internal controls is illustrative of the history.

- The *Act of 1789* founded the U.S. Department of Treasury and established the government's central accounting and reporting system. This is a system that today is still fiscally based, measures cash in and cash out, and has limited value to congressional committees charged with overseeing federal programs or to federal executives charged with operating the programs and monitoring activities in compliance with laws.

- By the *Dockery Act of 1894,* Congress established a federal comptroller concept to implement changes in the federal government's financial management practices, streamline the prior federal financial system, require a system of control checks and balances, and improve the reporting of expenditures by congressional appropriations. Later records indicate that the state of federal controls did not improve.

- Twenty-seven years later, the *Budget and Accounting Act of 1921* established the General Accounting Office and gave the Comptroller General authority to prescribe forms, systems of accounting and internal controls, and procedures for the administrative control and management of federal expenditures. However, the ensuing years revealed that more federal agencies ignored GAO's guidance than complied.

- In 1947, with the *Legislative Reorganization Act of 1947,* Congress again attempted to strengthen federal fiscal controls. Congressional hearings of the 1920s, 1930s, and 1940s are replete with references to reports of commissions and institutes and special studies by Congress and the Executive Branch (e.g., by Hoover, Brownlow, Brookings, and Presidential Executive Orders) that document a continuing concern regarding the deteriorated state of federal financial management. Specifically noted were references to the existence of deteriorated, weak, or no internal financial controls within federal departments and agencies. Comprehensive evaluations of this Act document a general conclusion that the Act of 1947 was not successful in achieving its intended objectives.

- The *Budget and Accounting Procedures Act of 1950* again attempted to promote financial management initiatives, requiring, among many other improvements:
  - More effective controls over receipts, expenditures, funds, property, and other federal assets.

○ Executive agencies to establish and maintain systems of internal controls, accounting, and auditing.

○ Executive agency systems of internal controls, accounting, and auditing to provide full disclosure of the financial results of any agency activities and the effectiveness of its controls.

Throughout the 1950s and 1960s, the GAO repeatedly reported to Congress a less than enthusiastic response by federal agencies to GAO's guidance.

• The *Federal Managers' Financial Integrity Act of 1982* (FMFIA) required that each federal agency establish systems of internal administrative controls and accounting in compliance with standards of the Comptroller General. FMFIA also required that a reporting be made by agency heads to the President and Congress when material weaknesses are identified in an agency's systems of internal administrative controls and accounting.

Seven years later, in a scorecard on FMFIA, the GAO told Congress that a few agencies had had some success in correcting weaknesses in internal controls; however, overall efforts to implement the Act had not produced the results intended, and the federal government did not have the internal controls to manage federal programs effectively.

The 1990s

The number of laws enacted in the single decade of the 1990s, with respect to financial systems and controls, exceeded that of any decade in the preceding 200 years. The CFO Act and the Federal Financial Management Improvement Act (discussed later) were typical of the legislated changes attempted in the 1990s.[6]

Chief Financial Officers Act of 1990.   The CFO Act required for the first time in the country's history that federal agencies prepare annual financial statements and that these statements be independently audited. Other mandates of the CFO Act stated that integrated agency accounting and financial management systems were needed to ensure compliance with internal control standards and policies, to provide consistent control over data entry, transaction processing, and reporting, and to eliminate unnecessary duplication of transaction entries.

A long journey by Congress, numerous Presidents, federal financial executives, and concerned citizens culminated in the CFO Act. For decades, laws had been passed, executive orders issued, regulations released by the Treasury Department and OMB, and hundreds of reports issued by the GAO and offices of federal inspectors general. All of them urged federal agencies to budget carefully, spend frugally, perform efficiently, measure results, report accurately, and have systems of internal controls over the expenditure of public monies. However, a pattern of widespread noncompliance by agencies in the installation and operation of effective systems of internal controls was typical in these years.

The CFO Act required that *integrated* agency accounting and financial management systems be developed and maintained and that they include internal controls to ensure:

- Compliance with applicable accounting principles, standards, requirements, and internal control standards

- Compliance with policies and procedures of OMB relative to accounting, auditing, reporting, internal controls, and other areas of financial management

- Preparation, on a uniform basis, of complete, reliable, accurate, consistent, and timely information that is responsive to the financial information needs of agency management

System requirements of the federal government defined an integrated agency accounting and financial management system as one that coordinates previously unconnected functions to improve overall efficiency and control. To be *integrated*, a system must have four essential characteristics: standard data classifications for recording financial events; common processes for processing similar transactions; consistent control over data entry, transaction processing, and reporting; and a system design that eliminates unnecessary duplication of transaction entries.

Federal Financial Management Improvement Act of 1996.   With the Federal Financial Management Improvement Act of 1996 (FFMIA), Congress emphasized that control standards and systems of control had not been uniformly implemented by agencies and that the financial management systems of federal agencies continued to be seriously deficient.

With the enactment of FFMIA, Congress acknowledged that, although efforts had been devoted to federal internal controls in past years, uniform control standards had still not been implemented as part of an agency's integrated financial management system. Reference was made to the failed fiscal practices of federal agencies, noting specifically that systems of controls were not uniformly implemented and that agency accounting practices did not accurately report financial results of the federal government or full costs of programs and activities. To remedy the long-standing federal agency controls problem, FFMIA required that agencies:

- Implement the federal government's standard general ledger "at the transaction-level."

- Eliminate past practices such as manual cross-walks of data between accounts and systems and working paper and off-the-books adjustments that might never be formally posted to the records.

- Cease overreliance on cash accounting in lieu of the more complete accrual accounting recommended by the Federal Accounting Standards Advisory Board (FASAB).

The objective of the FFMIA was to have periodic federal financial statements and reports routinely flow from underlying transactional documentation, to intermediate journals or registers, then to an agency's ledger accounts, and ultimately into the audited financial statements of an agency. A primary objective was that the audited financial statements required by the CFO Act were to be the routine and automatic byproduct of an effective system of internal controls.

OMB CIRCULAR A-123: MANAGEMENT'S RESPONSIBILITY FOR INTERNAL CONTROL

On December 21, 2004, the OMB issued significant revisions to what is arguably OMB's most significant guidance on internal control. OMB Circular A-123, *Management's Responsibility for Internal Control,* is designed to implement the requirements of the Federal Managers' Financial Integrity Act of 1982. Some notable attributes of the revision include the following:

- OMB acknowledges the passage of Sarbanes-Oxley as a catalyst for the revision.
- The guidance is effective for fiscal year 2006 to provide enough lead time to federal agencies affected by the revision.
- Additional emphasis is placed on the importance of management's role in the process by changing the title from *Management Accountability and Control* to *Management's Responsibility for Internal Control,* thus stressing that internal control is the responsibility of each manager, not the responsibility of a vague or anonymous "management function."
- The COSO *Framework* is effectively incorporated as the OMB standard for internal control.
- New and revised definitions are provided for internal control deficiencies.
- Annual assurance statements by management must be included in CFO Act agency Performance and Accountability Reports (PARs).
- As a subset of the overall FFMIA assurance above, a separate assurance is required specifically addressing the effectiveness of internal control over financial reporting.
- The definitions included in PCAOB's *Auditing Standard No. 2* are adopted for:
  - Control Deficiency
  - Reportable Condition
  - Material Weakness.

For the CFO Act agencies (see Exhibit 1.1), Appendix A to OMB Circular A-123 provides a methodology for these agencies to follow while complying with the Circular. Essentially, Appendix A brings the CFO Act agencies very close to the Sarbanes-Oxley model. The methodology includes:

- A definition of management's scope encompassing controls ensuring:
  - Fair presentation of assets, liabilities, and financial transactions included in the financial statements and accompanying notes
  - Compliance with laws and regulations

Exhibit 1.1   CFO Act Agencies

Department of Agriculture (USDA)	Department of the Treasury (Treasury)
Department of Commerce (DoC)	Department of Veterans Affairs (VA)
Department of Defense (DoD)	Agency for International Development
Department of Education (Education)	(USAID)
Department of Energy (DoE)	Environmental Protection Agency (EPA)
Department of Health and Human	General Services Administration (GSA)
Services (DHHS)	National Aeronautics and Space
Department of Homeland Security (DHS)	Administration (NASA)
Department of Housing and Urban	National Science Foundation (NSF)
Development (HUD)	Nuclear Regulatory Commission (NRC)
Department of the Interior (DoI)	Office of Personnel Management (OPM)
Department of Labor (DoL)	Small Business Administration (SBA)
Department of Justice (DoJ)	Social Security Administration (SSA)
Department of State (State)	
Department of Transportation (DoT)	

- ○ Prevention of fraud and abuse
- ○ Proper documentation of procedures performed in support of management's assertions
- A definition of materiality emphasizing qualitative as well as quantitative considerations
- A definition of the process to guide management's assessment effort, recommending the establishment of a senior assessment team to oversee the process and providing documentation guidance
- Sample/boilerplate statements of assurance
- The setting of June 30 as the assurance statement date; however, agencies opting for an audit opinion may use an assurance date that more closely aligns with the date of the audit opinion (e.g., agency's year-end)
- No requirement for an audit opinion on internal controls; however, leaves the door open for OMB to impose such a requirement on specific agencies (e.g., in the case of noncompliance with requirements or failure to complete corrective actions effectively)

In July 2005, a joint committee of members from the Chief Financial Officers Council (CFO Council) and the President's Council on Integrity and Efficiency (PCIE) issued an *Implementation Guide for OMB Circular A-123, Management's Responsibility for Internal Control, Appendix A, Internal Control over Financial Reporting* (Implementation Guide). The Implementation Guide expands on the internal control assessment process required by OMB Circular A-123 and identifies five component steps of the process:

Step 1. *Planning.* The Implementation Guide strongly recommends the establishment of a Senior Assessment Team during this step. The Senior Assessment

Team, which can be a subset of the Senior Management Council, is primarily responsible for ensuring compliance with the revised OMB Circular. During Planning, the Senior Assessment Team is ultimately responsible for:

- ○ Defining the scope of the assessment
- ○ Identifying materiality thresholds (including both qualitative and quantitative considerations)
- ○ Identifying material line items on financial reports
- ○ Defining testing requirements and schedules
- ○ Coordination of assessment activities (e.g., with agency components or functions affected by the assessment, independent auditors/inspectors general, oversight agencies, and so on)
- ○ Determining key processes
- ○ Execution of risk assessments
- ○ Effective documentation
- ○ Monitoring control efficiency

Step 2. *Evaluating Internal Control at the Entity-Level.* During this step the Senior Assessment Team and/or its designee, if applicable, along with other resources participating in the assessment (referred to as the Project Team), will evaluate organization-wide control considering the five standards of internal control identified in the GAO's Standards for Internal Control in the Federal Government, November, 1999 (also known as the "Green Book"):

- ○ Control Environment
- ○ Risk Assessment
- ○ Information and Communication
- ○ Control Activities
- ○ Monitoring

Step 3. *Evaluating Internal Control at the Process-Level.* Key considerations during this step include:

- ○ Understanding how key business processes affect financial report line items and accounts
- ○ Identification of key controls that allow for the development of accurate, fairly presented data included in the financial statements and accounts
- ○ Identification and understanding of supporting key financial processes and related design of controls
- ○ When applicable, evaluating controls over cross-servicing providers and service organizations
- ○ Documentation of the above processes and related controls

A critical and often specialized procedure requires the evaluation and analysis of information technology applications and related systems. This procedure requires:

- Developing an understanding of electronic data processing (EDP) systems and information technology supporting financial reporting
- Documenting the understanding of systems and controls
- Evaluating information technology risk considering:
  - General Controls
  - Application Controls

Step 4. *Testing Control Design and Operating Effectiveness at the Transaction-Level.* In most respects, the requirements of Steps 1 through 3 were necessary to comply with OMB Circular A-123 prior to its December 2004 revision. Testing, however, is a totally new requirement. This function, which is traditionally associated with auditors, is now also to be performed by management to support its assertions. In traditional terms, testing may consist of:

- Inquiry
- Inspection
- Observation
- Re-performance (e.g., re-computing) of the control procedure

Step 5. *Concluding, Reporting, and Correcting.* During this Step, the Senior Assessment Team will consider the results of its evaluations (Steps 2 and 3) and testing (Step 4).

- *Concluding:* Based on the evaluations and testing, determine whether adequate controls are in place and functioning. Based on the degree of severity, exceptions noted are classified as internal control deficiencies, reportable conditions, and material weaknesses.
- *Reporting* includes:
  - Statement of Assurance of the effectiveness of internal controls over financial reporting as of June 30 or a more suitable date if an opinion is issued on internal controls by the independent auditors (for inclusion in the PAR)
  - Changes in status (e.g., new or resolved material weaknesses)
- *Correcting:* The OMB Circular requires that a summary of the corrective action plan be included in the PAR; however, the Circular also requires that a more detailed plan be kept by the agency to ensure the effective and timely resolution of deficiencies. Of particular note is the fact that OMB reserves the right to require audits of internal controls when agencies are lax in addressing deficiencies within a reasonable period. The Implementation Guide provides additional guidance on correction plans and suggests that the internal documentation of a correction plan include:
  - A description of the deficiency
  - When the deficiency was identified

- A correction deadline
- The individual(s) responsible for monitoring progress
- Metrics and quantifiable/qualitative data that provide information on progress made, as well as the ultimate resolution of the deficiency

In many respects, the Implementation Guide follows the guidance issued by the PCAOB, as well as the OMB. In the chapters that follow, we will propose an implementation approach that is fully compatible with the Implementation Guide.

Additionally, it is important to note that, although Steps 2 and 3 refer to an evaluation of internal control, this evaluation encompasses only an evaluation of the control design at the entity- and process-levels. As such, these are preliminary evaluations, which must be subject to testing in order to conclude on or evaluate the operating effectiveness of internal controls.

Finally, the tests of operating controls encompass entity-level controls as well as process-level controls. Although there appears to be some misunderstanding regarding the scope of testing, it is clear that management cannot assert on the operating effectiveness of controls without also testing entity-level controls.

MANAGEMENT'S REQUIRED ASSESSMENT OF THE ENTITY'S INTERNAL CONTROL

Revised OMB Circular A-123 and the Sarbanes-Oxley Act made significant changes to many aspects of the financial reporting process in the federal government and public company sectors, respectively. A common requirement is that management provide a report on the effectiveness of certain aspects of the entity's internal control over financial reporting. This section summarizes and contrasts some of these requirements. Chapter 8 provides more detailed guidance and examples.

OMB Circular A-123's Definition of Internal Control

Section II of the revised OMB Circular A-123, *Management's Responsibility for Internal Control,* adopts the GAO's internal control definitions/characteristics based on *Standards for Internal Control in the Federal Government,* November 1999. As such, the Circular states that "internal control is an integral component of an organization's management that provides reasonable assurance that the following objectives are being achieved: effectiveness and efficiency of operations, reliability of financial reporting, and compliance with applicable laws and regulations."

The Circular also states that:

Internal control, in the broadest sense, includes the plan of organization, methods, and procedures adopted by management to meet its goals. Internal control includes processes for planning, organizing, directing, controlling, and reporting on agency operations.

The three objectives of internal control are:

1. Effectiveness and efficiency of operations
2. Reliability of financial reporting
3. Compliance with applicable laws and regulations

The Circular adds that the safeguarding of assets is a subset of these objectives and that management is responsible for ensuring that the internal control objectives are met. In addition, the Circular effectively adopts the COSO *Framework* by recognizing the following standards (labeled components by COSO) of internal control:

- Control Environment
- Risk Assessment
- Control Activities
- Information and Communications
- Monitoring.

In addition, Section II, Appendix A of OMB Circular A-123 defines internal control over financial reporting as follows:

Internal control over financial reporting is a process designed to provide reasonable assurance regarding the reliability of financial reporting. Reliability of financial reporting means that management can reasonably make the following assertions:

- All reported transactions actually occurred during the reporting period and all assets and liabilities exist as of the reporting date (existence and occurrence).
- All assets, liabilities, and transactions that should be reported have been included and no unauthorized transactions or balances are included (completeness).
- All assets are legally owned by the agency and all liabilities are legal obligations of the agency (rights and obligations).
- All assets and liabilities have been properly valued, and where applicable, all costs have been properly allocated (valuation).
- The financial report is presented in the proper form and any required disclosures are present (presentation and disclosure).
- The transactions are in compliance with applicable laws and regulations (compliance).
- All assets have been safeguarded against fraud and abuse.
- Documentation for internal control, all transactions, and other significant events are readily available for examination.

Sarbanes-Oxley's Definition of Internal Control

For the purposes of complying with the internal control reporting requirements of the Sarbanes-Oxley Act, SEC rules provide the working definition of the term *internal control over financial reporting*. Rule 13a-15(f) defines internal control over financial reporting as follows:

> A process designed by, or under the supervision of, the issuer's principal executive and principal financial officers, or persons performing similar functions, and effected by the issuer's board of directors, management, and other personnel, to provide reasonable assurance regarding the reliability of financial reporting and the preparation of financial statements for external purposes in accordance with generally accepted accounting principles and includes those policies and procedures that:
>
> 1. Pertain to the maintenance of records that in reasonable detail accurately and fairly reflect the transactions and dispositions of the assets of the issuer
> 2. Provide reasonable assurance that transactions are recorded as necessary to permit preparation of financial statements in accordance with generally accepted accounting principles and that receipts and expenditures of the issuer are being made only in accordance with authorizations of management and directors of the issuer
> 3. Provide reasonable assurance regarding prevention or timely detection of unauthorized acquisition, use, or disposition of the issuer's assets that could have a material effect on the financial statements

In addition, the SEC introduces a new term, *disclosure controls and procedures,* which is different from *internal controls over financial reporting,* just defined. SEC Rule 13a-15(e) defines disclosure controls and procedures as those that are:

> Designed to ensure that information required to be disclosed by the issuer in the reports that it files or submits under the Act is:
>
> - Recorded
> - Processed
> - Summarized
> - Reported
>
> within the time periods specified in the Commission's rules and forms. Disclosure controls and procedures include, without limitation, controls and procedures designed to ensure that information required to be disclosed by an issuer in the reports that it files or submits under the Act is accumulated and communicated to the issuer's management, including its principal executive and principal financial officers, or persons performing similar functions, as appropriate to allow timely decisions regarding required disclosure.

Thus, *disclosure controls and procedures* would encompass the controls over all material financial and nonfinancial information in Exchange Act reports. Management is to include its assertion on disclosure controls and procedures on its quarterly 10Q filings. These assertions are not subject to audit. Information that would fall under this definition that would *not* be part of an entity's internal control over financial reporting might include the signing of a significant contract, changes in a strategic relationship, management compensation, or legal proceedings. Chapter 2 provides additional guidance on disclosure controls and procedures and the effect these might have on management's assessment of the effectiveness of internal control.

Real Differences or Mere Semantics?

When considering the SEC's definition, the following should be noted:

- The term *internal control* is a broad concept that extends to all areas of the management of an enterprise. The SEC definition narrows the scope of an entity's consideration of internal control to the preparation of the financial statements —hence the use of the term "internal control *over financial reporting*."
- The SEC intends their definition to be consistent with the definition of internal controls that pertains to financial reporting objectives that was provided in the COSO *Framework* (see Chapter 2 for a detailed discussion of the COSO *Framework*).
- The rule makes explicit reference to the use or disposition of the entity's assets— that is, the safeguarding of assets.

The SEC narrows the scope of internal control to conform to the requirements of Sarbanes-Oxley, which address internal controls over financial reporting. This narrowing of internal controls to internal controls over financial reporting is compatible with OMB Circular A-123 Appendix A, which addresses internal controls over financial reporting. However, as will be seen in the discussion that follows, the scope of management's assurance included in a federal agency's PAR is broader.

REVISED REPORTING REQUIREMENTS UNDER OMB CIRCULAR A-123

Revised OMB Circular A-123 imposes new reporting requirements on federal agencies and, in addition, may require interim reporting from federal agencies.

Annual Reporting

Pursuant to Section VI of the revised Circular, management is to provide the following assurances in its Performance and Accountability Report:

- *Statement of Assurance.* The statement of assurance represents the agency head's informed judgment as to the overall adequacy and effectiveness of internal control within the agency.
- *Statement of Assurance for Internal Control over Financial Reporting.* Management is required to provide a separate assurance over the effectiveness of the internal controls over financial reporting. This assurance is a subset of the overall Statement of Assurance and is based on the results of management's assessment conducted in accordance with the requirements in Appendix A.

Sample assurances taken from the Implementation Guide are found in Chapter 8.

In addition, federal agencies are required to provide assurance on whether their financial management systems conform to government-wide requirements as set forth in OMB Circular No. A-127, *Financial Management Systems*.

REVISED REPORTING REQUIREMENTS UNDER SARBANES-OXLEY

As was the case with revised OMB Circular A-123, Sarbanes-Oxley imposes additional reporting requirements on management.

Annual Reporting

Section 404 of the Sarbanes-Oxley Act requires chief executive officers (CEOs) and chief financial officers (CFOs) to evaluate and report on the effectiveness of the entity's internal control over financial reporting. This report is contained in the company's Form 10K, which is filed annually with the SEC. The SEC has adopted rules for its registrants that effectively implement the requirements of the Sarbanes-Oxley Act, Section 404.

Under the SEC rules, a company's 10K must include:[7]

- *Management's Annual Report on Internal Control over Financial Reporting*. Provide a report on the company's internal control over financial reporting that contains:

    1. A statement of management's responsibilities for establishing and maintaining adequate internal control over financial reporting.

    2. A statement identifying the framework used by management to evaluate the effectiveness of the company's internal control over financial reporting.

    3. Management's assessment of the effectiveness of the company's internal control over financial reporting as of the end of the most recent fiscal year, including a statement as to whether internal control over financial reporting is effective. This discussion must include disclosure of any material weakness in the company's internal control over financial reporting identified by management. Management is not permitted to conclude that the registrant's internal control over financial reporting is effective if there are one or more material weaknesses in the company's internal control over financial reporting.

    4. A statement that the registered public accounting firm that audited the financial statements included in the annual report has issued an attestation report on management's assessment of the registrant's internal control over financial reporting.

- *Attestation Report of the Registered Public Accounting Firm*. Provide the registered public accounting firm's attestation report on management's assessment of the company's internal control over financial reporting.

- *Changes in Internal Control over Financial Reporting.* Disclose any change in the company's internal control over financial reporting that has materially affected, or is reasonably likely to materially affect, the company's internal control over financial reporting.

The company's annual report filed with the SEC should also include management's fourth-quarter report (see following discussion) on the effectiveness of the entity's disclosure controls and procedures, as described later in this chapter.

Quarterly Reporting

Section 302 of the Sarbanes-Oxley Act requires quarterly reporting on the effectiveness of an entity's "disclosure controls and procedures." Item 307 of SEC Regulation S-K implements this requirement for the company's quarterly Form 10Q filings by requiring management to:

> Disclose the conclusions of the company's principal executive and principal financial officers, or persons performing similar functions, regarding the effectiveness of the company's disclosure controls and procedures as of the end of the period covered by the report, based on the evaluation of these controls and procedures.

In addition to reporting on disclosure controls, the company's quarterly reports must also disclose material changes in the entity's internal control over financial reporting. Note that for these quarterly filings:

- Management is *not* required to evaluate or report on internal control over financial reporting. That evaluation is required on an *annual basis only.*
- The company's independent auditors are *not* required to attest to management's evaluation of disclosure controls.

As noted earlier, with these rules the SEC introduces a new term, *disclosure controls and procedures,* which is different from *internal controls over financial reporting,* defined earlier. Management is required to report on disclosure controls and procedures on a quarterly basis. (However, this assertion is not subject to audit.)

The Disclosure Committee

In relation to its rule requiring an assessment of disclosure controls and procedures, the SEC also advised all public companies to create a disclosure committee to oversee the process by which disclosures are created and reviewed, including:

- Review of 10Q, 10K, and other SEC filings; earnings releases; and other public information for the appropriateness of disclosure
- Determination of what constitutes a significant transaction or event that requires disclosure
- Determination and identification of significant deficiencies and material weaknesses in the design or operating effectiveness of disclosure controls and procedures
- Assessment of CEO and CFO awareness of material information that could affect disclosure

The existence and effective operation of an entity's disclosure committee can have a significant effect on the nature and scope of work to evaluate the effectiveness of the entity's internal control. For example:

- The effective functioning of a disclosure committee may be viewed as an element that strengthens the entity's control environment.
- The work of the disclosure committee may create documentation that internal control teams can use to reduce the scope of their work.

Management Certifications

In addition to providing a report on the effectiveness of its disclosure controls and internal control over financial reporting, the company's principal executive officer and principal financial officer are required to sign two certifications, which are included as exhibits to the entity's 10Q and 10K. These two certifications are required by the following sections of the Sarbanes-Oxley Act:

- Section 302, which requires a certification to accompany each quarterly and annual report filed with the SEC.
- Section 906, which added a new Section 1350 to Title 18 of the United States Code, and which contains a certification requirement subject to specific federal criminal provisions. This certification is separate and distinct from the Section 302 certification requirement.

Exhibit 1.2 provides the text of the Section 302 certification. This text is provided in SEC Rule 13a-14(a) and should be used exactly as set forth in the rule.

Exhibit 1.2   Section 302 Certification, SEC Rule 13a-14(a)/15d-14(a)

I, [identify the certifying individual], certify that:

1. I have reviewed this [specify report] of [identify registrant];
2. Based on my knowledge, this report does not contain any untrue statement of a material fact or omit to state a material fact necessary to make the statements made, in light of the circumstances under which such statements were made, not misleading with respect to the period covered by this report;
3. Based on my knowledge, the financial statements, and other financial information included in this report, fairly present in all material respects the financial condition, results of operations and cash flows of the registrant as of, and for, the periods presented in this report;
4. The registrant's other certifying officer(s) and I are responsible for establishing and maintaining disclosure controls and procedures (as defined in Exchange Act Rules 13a-15(e) and 15d-15(e)) and internal control over financial reporting (as defined in Exchange Act Rules 13a-15(f) and 15d-15(f)) for the registrant and have:
   (a) Designed such disclosure controls and procedures, or caused such disclosure controls and procedures to be designed under our supervision, to ensure that material information relating to the registrant, including its consolidated subsidiaries, is made known to us by others within those entities, particularly during the period in which this report is being prepared;

Exhibit 1.2 Section 302 Certification, SEC Rule 13a-14(a)/15d-14(a) *(Continued)*

    (b) Designed such internal control over financial reporting, or caused such internal control over financial reporting to be designed under our supervision, to provide reasonable assurance regarding the reliability of financial reporting and the preparation of financial statements for external purposes in accordance with generally accepted accounting principles;

    (c) Evaluated the effectiveness of the registrant's disclosure controls and procedures and presented in this report our conclusions about the effectiveness of the disclosure controls and procedures, as of the end of the period covered by this report based on such evaluation; and

    (d) Disclosed in this report any change in the registrant's internal control over financial reporting that occurred during the registrant's most recent fiscal quarter (the registrant's fourth fiscal quarter in the case of an annual report) that has materially affected, or is reasonably likely to materially affect, the registrant's internal control over financial reporting; and

5. The registrant's other certifying officer(s) and I have disclosed, based on our most recent evaluation of internal control over financial reporting, to the registrant's auditors and the audit committee of the registrant's board of directors (or persons performing the equivalent functions):

    (a) All significant deficiencies and material weaknesses in the design or operation of internal control over financial reporting which are reasonably likely to adversely affect the registrant's ability to record, process, summarize and report financial information; and

    (b) Any fraud, whether or not material, that involves management or other employees who have a significant role in the registrant's internal control over financial reporting.

Exhibit 1.3 provides an example of the Section 906 certification. Note that some certifying officers may choose to include a "knowledge qualification," as indicated by the optional language in italics. Officers who choose to include this language should do so only after consulting with their SEC counsel. Unlike the Section 302 certification, which requires a separate certification for both the CEO and CFO, the company can provide only one 906 certification, which is then signed by both individuals.

Exhibit 1.3 Section 906 Certification, 18 U.S.C. Section 1350

In connection with the [annual/quarterly] report of [name of registrant] (the "Entity") on Form [10K/10Q] for the period ended _____ (the "Report"), the undersigned in the capacities listed below, hereby certify, pursuant to 18 U.S.C. ss. 1350, as adopted pursuant to Section 906 of the Sarbanes-Oxley Act of 2002, that *to my knowledge:*

    (i) The Report fully complies with the requirements of Section 12(a) or 15(d) of the Securities Exchange Act of 1934; and

    (ii) The information contained in the Report fairly presents, in all material respects, the financial condition and results of operations of the Entity.

Subcertification

A great deal of the information included in financial statements and other reports filed with the SEC originates in areas of the company that are outside the direct control of the CEO and CFO. Because of the significance of information prepared by others, it is becoming common for the CEO and CFO to request that those individuals directly responsible for this information certify it. This process is known as *subcertification,* and it usually requires the individuals to provide a written affidavit to the CEO and CFO that will allow them to sign their certifications in good faith.

Items that may be the subject of subcertification affidavits include:

- Adequacy of specific disclosures in the financial statements or other reports filed with the SEC, such as *Management's Discussion and Analysis* (MD&A) included in the entity's 10Q or 10K
- Accuracy of specific account balances
- Compliance with company policies and procedures, including the company's code of conduct
- Adequacy of the design and/or operating effectiveness of departmental internal controls and disclosure controls
- Accuracy of reported financial results of the department, subsidiary, or business segment

THE INDEPENDENT AUDITOR'S REPORTING RESPONSIBILITIES

With the passage of Sarbanes-Oxley, and depending on the nature of the auditee (e.g., federal agency, SEC regulated company, privately owned business), the auditor is subject to one of the following requirements:

- Issuance of a report on internal control over financial reporting (audits performed in accordance with *Government Auditing Standards*). This report may contain a disclaimer of an opinion or, as an option, an opinion on internal controls.
- Issuance of a report containing an opinion on management's assurance as well as a separate opinion on internal control over reporting (audits performed pursuant to Sarbanes-Oxley/PCAOB requirements).
- No internal control opinion requirement (audit reports performed in accordance with the generally accepted auditing standards of the American Institute of Certified Public Accountants [AICPA]).

The ensuing discussions will address OMB and PCAOB requirements.

OMB Requirements

Auditor's Report on Internal Controls.   Until the passage of Sarbanes-Oxley, the requirement that internal controls be reported on was only present in audits conducted in accordance with *Government Auditing Standards*. For private sector companies not subject to Sarbanes-Oxley, generally accepted auditing standards only required reportable conditions (including material weaknesses) to be disclosed to an audit committee or, in its absence, the board of directors and/or appropriate management levels. Although generally accepted auditing standards states that written communication is preferable, this is not required as long as the verbal communication is documented in the workpapers.

OMB Bulletin 01-02, *Audit Requirements for Federal Financial Statements,* sets forth the following requirements for the internal control report:

- A statement that, in connection with the financial statement audit of the agency, the auditor:

    o Obtained an understanding of the design of internal controls

    o Determined whether the controls were operational

    o Performed tests of internal controls

- A statement that, with respect to the performance measures included in the MD&A, the auditor obtained an understanding of the design of internal controls related to management's existence and completeness assertions and determined whether they had been placed in operation.

    o A definition of the scope of the tests performed and either an opinion on internal control or (as is the more common practice) a disclaimer of opinion

    o A description of reportable conditions and material weaknesses identified during the audit including the identification (if applicable) of material weaknesses that were not included in the auditee's FMFIA

    o Reference to the issuance of a separate management letter (if applicable)

OMB Bulletin 01-02 provides the following definitions in connection with internal control findings:

> Reportable conditions are matters coming to the auditor's attention that, in the auditor's judgment, should be communicated to management because they represent significant deficiencies in the design or operation of the internal control structure, which may adversely affect the organization's ability to meet the objectives identified in federal regulations, including OMB Bulletin 01-02.

> A material weakness in the internal control structure is a reportable condition in which the design or operation of one or more of the internal control structure elements does not reduce to a relatively low level the risk that errors or irregularities in amounts that would be material in relation to the financial statements being audited may occur and not be detected within a timely period by employees in the normal course of performing their assigned functions.

These definitions and the reporting requirements have been modified somewhat by OMB Circular A-123 as the OMB adopts definitions based on the PCAOB auditing standard. Exhibit 1.4 reproduces the summary exhibit included in OMB Circular A-123.

Exhibit 1.4 OMB Circular A-123 Internal Control Related Definitions and Reporting Requirements

	Definition[a]	Reporting
Control Deficiency (FMFIA Section 2 and internal control over financial reporting)	Control deficiencies exist when the design or operation of a control does not allow management or employees, in the normal course of performing their assigned functions, to prevent or detect misstatements on a timely basis. A design deficiency exists when a control necessary to meet the control objective is missing or an existing control is not properly designed, so that even if the control operates as designed the control objective is not always met. An operation deficiency exists when a properly designed control does not operate as designed or when the person performing the control is not qualified or properly skilled to perform the control effectively.	Internal to the organization and not reported externally. Progress against corrective action plans should be periodically assessed and reported to agency management.
Reportable Condition (FMFIA Section 2 and internal control over financial reporting)	*FMFIA overall*—A control deficiency, or combination of control deficiencies, that in management's judgment, should be communicated because they represent significant weaknesses in the design or operation of internal control that could adversely affect the organization's ability to meet its internal control objectives. *Financial reporting*—A control deficiency, or combination of control deficiencies, that adversely affects the entity's ability to initiate, authorize, record, process, or report external financial data reliably in accordance with generally accepted accounting principles such that there is more than a remote[b] likelihood that a misstatement of the entity's financial statements, or other significant financial reports, that is more than inconsequential will not be prevented or detected.	Internal to the organization and not reported externally. Progress against corrective action plans should be periodically assessed and reported to agency management.
Material Weakness (FMFIA Section 2 and internal control over financial reporting)	*FMFIA overall*—Reportable conditions in which the agency head determines to be significant enough to report outside of the agency. *Financial reporting*—Reportable condition, or combination of reportable conditions, that results in more than a remote[b] likelihood that a material misstatement of the financial statements, or other significant financial reports, will not be prevented or detected.	Material weaknesses and a summary of corrective actions shall be reported to OMB and Congress through the PAR (Management Report for Government Corporations). Progress against

(continues)

Exhibit 1.4 OMB Circular A-123 Internal Control Related Definitions and Reporting Requirements *(Continued)*

	Definition[a]	Reporting
		corrective action plans should be periodically assessed and reported to agency management.
Non-conformance (FMFIA Section 4)	Instances in which financial management systems do not substantially conform to financial systems requirements. Financial management systems include both financial and financially-related (or mixed) systems.	Non-conformances and a summary of corrective actions to bring systems into conformance shall be reported to OMB and Congress through the PAR (Management Report for Government Corporations). Progress against corrective action plans should be periodically assessed and reported to agency management.

Notes

(a) The definition of control deficiency and definitions of reportable condition and material weakness relative to financial reporting are based upon the definitions provided in *Auditing Standard No. 2—An Audit of Internal Control Over Financial Reporting Performed in Conjunction with an Audit of Financial Statements* issued by the Public Entity Accounting Oversight Board (PCAOB).

(b) The term "remote" is defined in SFFAS No. 5, *Accounting for Liabilities of the Federal Government*, as the chance of the future event, or events occurring is slight.

Source: Office of Management and Budget, revised Circular A-123, *Management's Responsibility for Internal Control.*

As noted, there is currently no requirement that an opinion on internal controls be issued. However, as a result of Sarbanes-Oxley, this is an issue that is coming under close scrutiny by federal managers, oversight agencies, Congress, and the executive branch. Currently, there appears to be no consensus on future reporting requirements. As a result, federal financial managers and auditors of federal agencies should be on the lookout for potential major changes regarding reports on internal controls.

Sarbanes-Oxley/Public Company Accounting Oversight Board Requirements

Exhibit 1.5 describes the relationships among the various rule-making bodies, companies, and their auditors regarding reporting on internal control. As described previously, Sections 302 and 404 of the Sarbanes-Oxley Act require management of public companies to report on the effectiveness of the entity's internal control on an annual basis. The company's independent auditors are required to audit this report. The SEC is responsible for setting rules to implement Sarbanes-Oxley Act requirements. Those rules include guidance for reporting by the CEO and CFO on the entity's internal control over financial reporting and disclosure controls, but they do not provide any guidance or set standards for the independent auditors. The PCAOB sets the auditing standards, which will have a direct effect on auditors and how they plan and perform their engagements.

In addition, the auditing standards will have an *indirect effect* on the company as it prepares for the audit of its internal control report. Just as in a financial statement audit, the company should be able to support its conclusions about internal

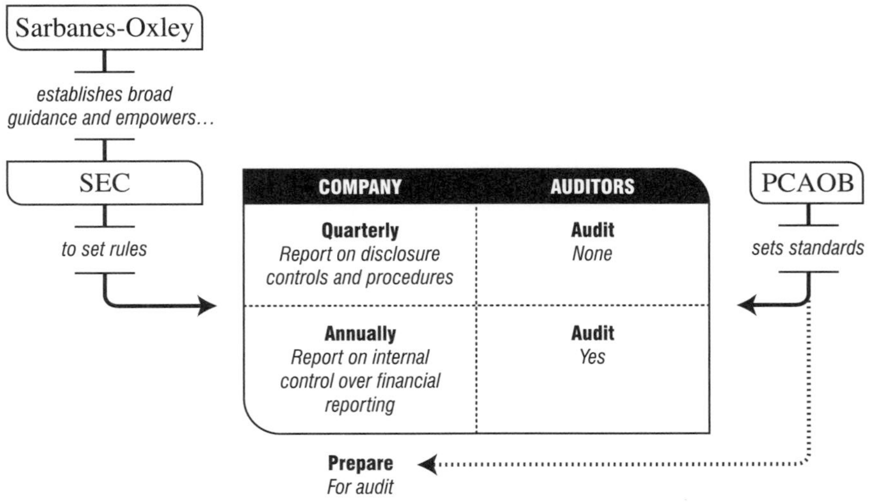

Exhibit 1.5   Relationship of the Rules, Regulations, and Standards

control and provide documentation that is sufficient for the auditor to perform an audit. Thus, in preparing for the audit of its internal control report, it is vital for management and those who assist management to have a thorough understanding of what the independent auditors will require.

The Federal/Private "Audit Gap"

As noted previously, there is no requirement that federal agency internal controls and/or related management assertions be audited. The only reference to an audit is OMB's option to reserve the right to require an internal control audit for agencies that do not appear to be making progress in that area. At this point, the question is whether federal agencies' internal controls should be subject to audit. Many believe that a decision to impose this requirement should, at a minimum, be delayed pending consideration of two important facts:

- Although Sarbanes-Oxley appears to have been favorably received by the private sector, complaints have already been made regarding the cost/benefit of certain requirements, particularly the cost of the audit. As a result, the federal government is well advised to take a "wait-and-see" attitude toward this requirement. "Best practices" in this area have not yet been finalized; there is no need for haste.

- GAO and OMB standards impose a number of requirements on the CFO Act audits of federal agencies, which exceed the requirements found in the AICPA's generally accepted auditing standards (see discussion below).

Important GAO audit requirements not included in the AICPA's audit standards include:

- Reporting on internal controls and on compliance with laws and regulations and (if applicable) provisions of contracts and/or grant agreements
- Reporting in writing to appropriate officials deficiencies in internal control, fraud, illegal acts, agreement violations, and abuse
- Reporting responsible officials' views on the factors listed above

Similarly, OMB Bulletin 01-02, paragraph 6e, imposes the following requirements over and above AICPA standards:

- With regard to internal controls affecting financial reporting and/or compliance with laws and regulations, the auditor shall:
  - ". . . obtain an understanding of the components of internal control . . . and assess the level of control risk relevant to the assertions embodied in the classes of transactions, account balances, and disclosure components of the financial statements. Such controls include relevant EDP general and application controls and controls relating to intra-entity and intra-governmental transactions and balances."
  - "For those internal controls that have been properly designed and placed in operation . . . perform sufficient tests to support a low assessed level of

control risk. . . . Those internal controls that have not been properly designed or placed in operation and those internal controls that are found to be ineffective shall be reported."

- The guidance also provides that:
    - "In obtaining an understanding of the components of internal control, particularly the risk assessment component, and assessing control risk, the auditor shall obtain an understanding of the process by which the agency identifies and evaluates weaknesses required to be reported under FMFIA and related agency implementing procedures."
    - "The auditor shall compare material weaknesses disclosed during the audit with those material weaknesses reported in the agency's FMFIA report that relate to the financial statements of the entity under audit and document material weaknesses disclosed by audit that were not reported in the agency's FMFIA report. The auditor should consider whether the failure to detect and report material weaknesses constitutes a reportable condition or material weakness in the entity's internal control."
    - "With respect to compliance with applicable laws and regulations, the auditor shall perform tests of compliance with laws and regulations that could have a direct and material effect on the Principal Statements and Required Supplementary Stewardship Information, including laws governing the use of budget authority, and any other laws, regulations, and government-wide policies identified by OMB. . . ."
    - "The auditor shall perform tests of the entity's compliance with FFMIA, section 803(a) requirements." The results of these tests are to be reported in connection with compliance with laws and regulations.

The scope of internal control for the auditor in connection with CFO Act audits is significantly expanded by the GAO and OMB. This expansion includes requirements to:

- Test controls
- Compare the auditor's evaluation and testing of internal controls with management's assertion included in their FMFIA reporting
- Issue a report that discloses reportable conditions and material weaknesses and (if applicable) whether management's assertions, which differ from the auditor's conclusions, constitute a reportable condition or material weakness.

Although the scope has been expanded, many believe that the GAO and OMB requirements still fall short of a "full scope" audit of internal controls. The extent of the gap, however, is a subjective matter beyond the scope of this book. It is clear, though, that any decision to increase the auditor's scope to be compatible with Sarbanes-Oxley should take into consideration the requirements already in place and should determine whether the additional cost of a full scope audit can be justified in terms of the potential benefits to be derived.

THE PCAOB AUDITING STANDARD

Although there is no internal control audit requirement for federal agencies, this section is useful in understanding the private sector requirement for auditors, particularly in comparison with the federal requirements summarized in the prior discussion.

PCAOB's *Auditing Standard No. 2, An Audit of Internal Control over Financial Reporting Performed in Conjunction with an Audit of Financial Statements,* is the authoritative guide for auditors engaged by companies subject to the requirements of Sarbanes-Oxley to audit the financial statements and management's assessment of the effectiveness of internal controls over financial reporting. This section provides an overview of the standard. The full text of the standard is posted on the PCAOB website at www.pcaobus.org. The PCAOB standard only directly applies to independent auditors, and *not* to entities that perform their own internal assessment of internal control. In providing guidance to auditors on what is required in an internal control audit, however, the standard will have a significant, *indirect* effect on the work performed by the entity.

Overall Objective of the Auditor's Engagement

The auditor's objective in an audit of internal control is to express an opinion on management's assessment of the effectiveness of the company's internal control over financial reporting. This objective implies a two-step process:

1. Management must perform its own assessment and reach conclusions on the effectiveness of the entity's internal controls.

2. The auditors must perform their own assessment and form an independent opinion as to whether management's assessment of the effectiveness of internal control is fairly stated.

Thus, internal control is assessed twice, first by management and then by the independent auditors. The fact that the auditors will be auditing internal control—and in some cases, re-performing some of the tests performed by the entity—does not relieve management of its obligation to document, test, and report on internal control.

To form an opinion, the auditor will:

- Evaluate the reliability of the process used by management to assess the entity's internal control.

- Review and rely on the results of *some* of the tests performed by management, internal auditors, and others during their assessment process.

- Perform his/her own tests.

Evaluation of Management's Assessment Process

The PCAOB standard provides guidance on the *required* elements of management's process for assessing the effectiveness of internal control. The absence of one or more of those required elements may result in a modification to the standard audit report. For this reason, it is critical that the process comply with all requirements established by the new standard.

The *audit* standard states that the auditor should determine whether management's assessment process has addressed the following elements:

- Determining which controls should be tested, including controls over relevant assertions related to all significant accounts and disclosures in the financial statements. Generally, such controls include:

  ○ Controls over initiating, recording, processing, and reporting significant accounts and disclosures and related assertions embodied in the financial statements

  ○ Controls over the selection and application of accounting policies that are in conformity with generally accepted accounting principles

  ○ Antifraud programs and controls

  ○ Controls, including information technology general controls, on which other controls are dependent

  ○ Controls over significant nonroutine and nonsystematic transactions, such as accounts involving judgments and estimates

  ○ Controls over the period-end financial reporting process, including controls over procedures used to enter transaction totals into the general ledger; to initiate, record, and process journal entries in the general ledger; and to record recurring and nonrecurring adjustments to the financial statements (for example, consolidating adjustments, report combinations, and reclassifications)

- Evaluating the likelihood that failure of the control could result in a misstatement and the degree to which other controls, if effective, achieve the same control objectives.

- Determining the locations or business units to include in the evaluation for a company with multiple locations or business units.

- Evaluating the design effectiveness of controls.

- Evaluating the operating effectiveness of controls based on procedures sufficient to assess their operating effectiveness. To evaluate the effectiveness of the company's internal control over financial reporting, management must have evaluated controls over all relevant assertions related to all significant accounts and disclosures.

- Determining the deficiencies in internal control over financial reporting that are of such a magnitude and likelihood of occurrence that they constitute significant deficiencies or material weaknesses.

- Communicating findings to the auditor and to others, if applicable.

- Evaluating whether findings are reasonable and support management's assessment.

This book provides detailed guidance to aid in compliance with a Sarbanes-Oxley-based management's assessment process that is fully compatible with OMB requirements. Appendix 1B summarizes these requirements and provides a cross-reference to the chapters in this book where you can find the related guidance.

Documentation

The PCAOB standard provides guidance on the nature and extent of the documentation required by the entity to support its assessment of internal control effectiveness. The standard also states that inadequate documentation may be a deficiency in internal control, which could be a material weakness. (Note that OMB Bulletin 01-02 has a similar requirement, as discussed earlier.)

The overall requirement for documentation is that it should provide "reasonable support" for management's conclusion. To attain this threshold, the documentation should include:

- The design of controls over relevant assertions related to all significant accounts and disclosures in the financial statements. The documentation should include the five components of internal control over financial reporting described in the COSO *Framework* (discussed in Chapter 2).

- Information regarding how significant transactions are initiated, recorded, processed, and reported.

- Enough information about the flow of transactions to identify where material misstatements caused by error or fraud could occur.

- Controls designed to prevent or detect fraud, including who performs the controls and the related segregation of duties.

- Controls over the period-end financial reporting process.

- Controls over the safeguarding of assets.

- The results of management's testing and evaluation.

Scope of Testwork

The PCAOB standard also provides guidance on the nature, timing, and extent of the auditor's procedures for a number of situations, including:

- Extent of testing of multiple locations, business segments, or subsidiaries

- Required tests when the entity uses a service organization to process transactions

- Updated testwork required when the original testing was performed at an interim date in advance of the reporting date

To the extent that the PCAOB auditing standard affects management's assessment of internal control, further guidance on these matters is provided in subsequent chapters of this book.

Use of Work of Internal Auditors and Others

The proposed auditing standard provides extensive guidance on the extent to which the independent auditors may rely on the work performed by management (including work performed by internal auditors and others) in their internal control audit. The standard defines categories of controls and the extent to which the independent auditor may rely on the work of others to reach a conclusion.

Determination of Material Weakness

SEC reporting rules require entity management to disclose material weaknesses in internal control. Projects to assess the effectiveness of internal control should be planned and performed in a way that will detect material misstatements. Thus, it is critical to have a working definition of the term. The audit standard provides the following definitions:

- An *internal control deficiency* exists when the design or operation of a control does not allow management or employees, in the normal course of performing their assigned functions, to prevent or detect misstatements on a timely basis.

- A *significant deficiency* is a control deficiency, or combination of control deficiencies, that adversely affects the company's ability to initiate, authorize, record, process, or report external financial data reliably in accordance with generally accepted accounting principles, such that there is more than a remote likelihood that a misstatement of the annual or interim financial statements that is more than inconsequential will not be prevented or detected.

- A *material weakness* is a significant deficiency or combination of significant deficiencies that results in more than a remote likelihood that a material misstatement of the annual or interim financial statements will not be prevented or detected.

The definition of material weakness provided in the auditing standard is different from the traditional definition included in the auditing literature. The standard states that "more than a remote likelihood" is the threshold for determining whether a deficiency is significant. Under previous guidance, the threshold was "a relatively low risk." At this early point in the standards setting and implementation process, it is unclear as to what effect, if any, this change in definition will have on the identification and reporting of material weaknesses. Some auditors are of the opinion that "more than a remote likelihood" is a lower threshold than "relatively low risk." If that is the case, then the adoption of the new auditing standard will result in a greater number of internal control deficiencies being classified as material weaknesses. For this reason, as described in more detail in Chapter 3, it is critical that management reach a consensus on this matter with the entity's independent auditors.

Chapter 8 provides additional guidance on determining the relative magnitude of internal control deficiencies.

A STRUCTURED, COMPREHENSIVE APPROACH FOR EVALUATING INTERNAL CONTROL

This book provides guidance to help entity management:

- Assess the effectiveness of the entity's internal control
- Facilitate the efficient audit or evaluation of the entity's internal control by the independent auditors.

A Structured Approach

There is no one way to structure an assessment project to achieve the above objectives.

Exhibit 1.6 summarizes the approach followed in this book. The approach is discussed in the ensuing chapters. The approach discussed in this book will meet the requirements of Sarbanes-Oxley, and it is also fully compatible with the approach provided in the Implementation Guide issued by the CFO Council. Although it is still too early to determine what impact Sarbanes-Oxley may have on the federal government, the approach proposed in this book satisfies not only existing requirements but also any future changes that may be brought about by Sarbanes-Oxley.

A Top-Down Process[8]

At the outset, it is important to note that this book proposes a top-down approach. In this respect, federal agencies can apply "lessons learned" by industry during their initial efforts to implement Sarbanes-Oxley. Issues particularly relevant to federal agencies are discussed below.

SEC and PCAOB Guidance

On May 16, 2005, in response to information that was gathered about the first year of implementation, both the SEC and PCAOB issued guidance that addressed the most significant problems encountered with the implementation of *Auditing Standard No. 2*. Of the five main areas addressed in the guidance, the need for a top-down approach is of particular relevance to federal agencies.

In its guidance, the PCAOB emphasized that auditors should use a top-down approach and company management would be wise to do so also. A top-down approach begins with an evaluation of entity-level controls and from there moves to the testing of detailed activity-level controls.

Deciding which controls to document and test is based on an assessment of risk. Controls that mitigate significant risks should be documented and assessed. Those that mitigate less significant risks would be subject to considerably less, if any, testing and evaluation.

Exhibit 1.6   Process for Evaluating Effectiveness of Internal Control

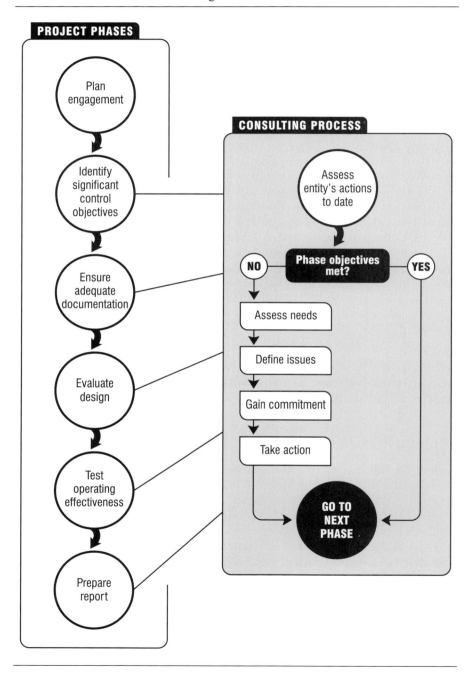

Principles of a Risk-Based, Top-Down Approach

As discussed in further detail in Chapter 2, controls operate at two levels within any organization. Entity-level controls are pervasive and can affect many different financial statement accounts. For example, an entity's hiring and training policies will affect the way in which individual control procedures are performed. Entities that hire qualified people and train them properly will have much greater success when it comes time for those people to perform their jobs. The converse also is true. In that sense, hiring and training policies can have an effect on many different financial statement accounts.

On the other hand, activity-level controls are restricted to one transaction type. For example, controls over cash disbursements will, in general, affect cash disbursements only and will have little or no impact on other accounts, such as the recording of accruals or the depreciation of fixed assets.

In the year of implementation, many companies and their auditors adopted a bottom-up approach in which they began by identifying all of the company's activity-level controls and then documented and tested each of these to determine whether internal control as a whole was effective. As you can imagine, this approach proved extremely time-consuming and costly. Moreover, not only is it not required, it is not even contemplated by *Auditing Standard No. 2*.

The method described by the auditing standard is the exact opposite of this approach. In a top-down approach one begins at the top, at the entity-level. Then the most significant accounts and transaction types at the organization and the control objectives for those accounts and transactions are identified. Once the control objectives are determined, those controls that are in place to meet those objectives should be identified. Those controls, and only those controls, are then tested and evaluated.

This top-down approach should be very familiar to inspectors general, federal financial managers, and external auditors of federal agencies, as it is the approach adopted by GAO in its Financial Audit Manual, proposed by OMB in its revised Circular A-123, and incorporated into the CFO Council's Implementation Guide.

By using a top-down approach, the entity:

- Tests only those controls related to significant accounts and transactions, which eliminates or reduces the need to understand the process and assess controls in those areas that do not affect the likelihood that the agency's financial statements could be materially misstated.

- Tests the minimum number of controls necessary to meet the control objective. Redundant controls (and there are many of these) are not tested (or tested on a rotating basis).

Implementing a top-down approach requires agency management to exercise its judgment. How does management decide which accounts and transactions are "significant" and which are "insignificant"? If not all of the control activities for significant accounts and transactions are going to be tested, how does management determine which ones to test?

To make these and other decisions, it is important to consider the related risk of material misstatement of the financial statements. As described in more detail in Chapter 2, control activities are designed to meet identified risks of misstatement. For example, one of the risks of misstatement is that the agency may fail to record all of its accounts payable as of year-end. To mitigate this risk, management will design and implement procedures at the entity to make sure that all payables are recorded.

Do these controls need to be documented and tested? It depends on the relative significance of the risk of failing to record all accounts payable. What is the likelihood that the failure to record all accounts payable would result in a material misstatement of the entity's financial statements? The answer to this question will help to determine whether to document and test the controls over accounts payable.

Performing an assessment of internal control is not a "paint-by-numbers" exercise. It is a process that requires a great deal of judgment. The primary benchmark for making these judgments is the risk that the financial statements would be materially misstated if the identified control was ineffective. This book provides practical guidance for implementing a risk-based, top-down approach.

Other "Lessons Learned"

In its May 2005 guidance, the SEC and PCAOB identified two additional issues which are relevant to the implementation of revised OMB Circular A-123. These issues/lessons learned are discussed below.

During the first year of compliance, there was a frequent lack of communication between the auditee and the independent auditors. With its May 16 guidance, the PCAOB made it clear that the auditor should be responsive to auditee requests for advice, provided that company management take final responsibility for internal control. As a result, when implementing the revised guidance, it is important that auditors and agency management engage in direct and timely communication with each other.

While there is no current requirement for an audit of internal controls (and/or management's assertion), the fact remains that in the execution of the audit, the auditors will evaluate internal controls and report any reportable condition(s) and material weakness(es) noted. The auditors are in the best position to provide sound advice on the proper approach for an agency to follow in complying with OMB Circular A-123. While there is always the possibility that management and the auditors will disagree on the classification of any given internal control finding (e.g., deficiency, reportable condition, or material weakness), coordinating the effort with the auditors and capitalizing on their expertise will minimize the risk of reaching different conclusions on the effectiveness of internal control.

A second issue addressed the auditor's use of internal control work performed by the auditee. The SEC and PCAOB concluded that auditors should make as much use as possible of the work on internal control performed by the auditee. This guidance should help entities keep down the cost of compliance, but it also means that entities must perform their assessment with qualified individuals in a way that is consistent with the requirements of *Auditing Standard No. 2*. Again, while there is currently no audit requirement, this is an important consideration for agencies opting for an audit on internal controls.

In summary, these two issues are important precedents that federal agencies may refer to in obtaining cooperation from their independent auditors in connection with the agency's implementation of the new requirements, and in their attempts to keep increased costs at a reasonable level.

Distinct Phases and Their Objectives.   The left-hand side of Exhibit 1.6 describes *what* should be done to issue and support management's report about the effectiveness of the entity's internal controls. The diagram depicts six sequential processes, which start with planning and end with reporting. The objective of each of these steps is as follows:

- **Project planning.** The primary objectives of the planning phase are to:
  - Assess information needs and identify sources of information required to perform the assessment of internal control effectively.
  - Determine the overall scope of the engagement.
  - Establish the terms of the working relationship both within the Project Team (whether the team is a contractor, totally internal, or a combination of both) and between the Project Team and the project owner (generally the Senior Assessment Team or the Senior Management Council, depending on the agency's organization and the Project Team's composition).
  - Coordinate the efforts with the independent auditors and/or the Office of Inspector General.

- **Assess internal control effectiveness.** This phase represents the bulk of the project and can be broken down into four separate components or steps:

  Step 1. *Identify significant controls.* [9] Management's assessment is based on the effectiveness of internal control *taken as a whole,* not on the effectiveness of individual components of control or individual controls. This holistic approach to assessing effectiveness recognizes the interdependence of the control components. Implicit in this approach is the notion that some individual controls are more significant to the overall operating effectiveness of internal control than other controls. For example, the effectiveness of an entity's control environment or computer general controls is a prerequisite for the effective operation of an individual control procedure for a specific transaction.

  Additionally, the terms "internal control over financial reporting" and "disclosure controls and procedures" both incorporate the notion of materiality. For example, the attestation standards state that evaluating the effectiveness of the design of a specific control is concerned with whether the control is suitably designed to prevent or detect *material* misstatements.

  For these reasons, the first step in evaluating the effectiveness of internal control *taken as a whole* is to identify significant individual controls, both at the entity and the business process-level. An assessment of internal control effectiveness will focus on these significant controls.

Step 2. *Ensure adequate documentation of significant controls.* The documentation of a control is an important design element of the internal control system. For example, it is difficult for control procedures to be consistently reliable if there is no formal means for communicating the requirements of the procedure. For this reason, management should review the entity's documentation of significant controls to ensure that it is adequate.

Step 3. *Evaluate the design effectiveness of significant controls.* Evaluation of the design of controls requires that procedures be performed to determine whether the control is suitable to prevent or detect material misstatements. The nature of the procedures performed will vary according to the circumstances.

Step 4. *Evaluate the operating effectiveness of significant controls.* Tests of operating effectiveness are concerned with how the control was applied, the consistency with which it was applied, and by whom it was applied.

- **Report.** The process ends with the identification of required corrective actions and the reporting of findings and recommended corrective action plans. This report provides the necessary input for the FMFIA and A-123 required disclosures.

Subsequent chapters in this book provide more detailed guidance on each of these phases in the process.

A Consultative Approach to Achieving Project Objectives.   The right side of Exhibit 1.6 describes a separate process that is repeated continuously for each of the steps required to evaluate the effectiveness of internal control. As the project is undertaken, team members should consider whether the entity may already have taken steps to evaluate the effectiveness of its internal control. For example, the entity may have accumulated evidence to support its assessment of internal control in conjunction with:

- Ongoing systems enhancements/development efforts
- Internal control-related work performed by the Office of the Inspector General (OIG) and/or consultants
- Internal control reporting required by other regulations, such as prior years' compliance with FMFIA requirements

Thus, each step in the evaluation process begins with obtaining an understanding of the actions already taken by the entity to achieve the project objectives. If those steps are adequate and achieve the objective, then no further work is necessary. If those steps are not adequate, then the assessment Project Team is in a position to identify the entity's needs, recommend solutions, gain commitment, and then implement corrective action.

For example, suppose that as part of its prior year FMFIA reporting on internal control, Agency A has formed a disclosure committee to oversee that process. Part of the committee's responsibilities is to identify significant disclosure control policies and procedures. However, the Agency has not taken any steps to identify significant controls over financial reporting. In that situation, the first step in the evaluation process would be to review the work of the disclosure committee related to significant disclosure controls and to assist in the identification of significant internal controls over financial reporting.

CONSIDERATIONS FOR THE ASSESSMENT TEAM

This section provides guidance to the team responsible for the execution of the assessments. Some entities may lack the resources or expertise necessary to conduct a thorough, comprehensive assessment of internal control. In order to comply with the revised reporting requirements, these entities may engage outside consultants to provide the necessary assistance. The guidance in this section also applies to outside consultants.

Although the section is written for Project Team members, it can also be used by federal agencies to monitor effectively the work of consultants who have been engaged in such a capacity.

Pre-Project Execution Considerations

Before beginning a project to help management assess the effectiveness of internal control, information should be gathered and a mutual understanding should be established between the Project Team and the Senior Management Council (if applicable) or appropriate agency executives on the project structure. In this pre-project phase, objectives are to:

- Obtain a commitment from management to move forward with the project.
- Understand management's expectations for the conduct and results of the project.

To achieve the above objectives, one will most likely need to meet with the Senior Management Council or its equivalent/designee. Some suggestions to prepare for the meeting follow.

Obtain a Basic Understanding of the Agency.   The first step in preparing for a meeting prior to entering into the project should be to obtain a basic understanding of the entity. The level of effort required will depend on the team composition (e.g., agency personnel or contractor personnel) and years of experience with the agency (regardless of whether contractor or agency personnel). In any event, the team must have or acquire an understanding sufficient to enable the auditor to:

- Ask insightful questions about the entity and its operations.
- Understand the implications of answers that are provided.
- Identify the most significant issues that will affect project performance.

This preliminary understanding of the agency need *not* be detailed enough to plan the project. Understanding the agency at a greater level of detail can be deferred (if necessary) to the first phase of the project itself. To obtain this understanding one may:

- Read the entity's most recent PAR to gain an understanding of its most significant business processes and the scope and complexity of its operations.
- Review information posted on the entity's website.
- Make inquiries of the entity's independent auditors.

Identify Assumptions and Goals.   Before meeting with the Council or other management executives, it may be helpful to identify any assumptions about proposed work together with the goals of the meeting. By articulating these assumptions and goals, it will be easier to quickly reach a mutual understanding of the nature of the work and the results that can be expected. When preparing for the meeting, consider exploring answers to the following questions:

- What assumptions are being made about the prospective project? For example:
  - Management's understanding of the process that will be followed by the independent auditors in connection with their internal control report (e.g., disclaimer or issuance of opinion)
  - Management's understanding of the depth and quality of documentation required to support management's assessment of internal control effectiveness
  - The entity's existing process for evaluating the effectiveness of internal control
  - The resources the entity has to commit to the project
- What are assumptions being based on? For example:
  - Conversations with management
  - Discussions with the independent auditors
  - Information contained in public documents (PAR, budget submissions) or the entity's own website
- Under what assumptions is management operating? For example:
  - The team's knowledge and expertise
  - The amount of work required to assess the effectiveness of internal control and, if applicable, prepare for an audit of that assessment
  - The urgency of the project
- What is management's planned involvement? For example:
  - Will there be a Senior Assessment Team? (e.g., if the assessment team is responsible for oversight but not project execution)
  - Will members of the Senior Management Council or the Senior Assessment Team actively participate in the project?

○ What communications protocol should be followed to keep top management informed of progress and findings?

Management may be considering several options for how they will conduct their assessment and who they will involve, and their goal for the meeting may be to explore available options with the team.

Identify Key Players.   Prior to meeting with management it is important to consider who should be involved in the meeting. From management, the meeting should include a representative from the Senior Management Council and/or the Senior Assessment Team (if the latter is not participating as an active member of the Project Team). From the Project Team, members with expertise relevant to the agency's situation should also be included. For example, if the agency's business processes are heavily technology dependent, individuals with information technology (IT) auditing experience should be included in the meeting.

Meeting with the Senior Executive Council and/or Members of Top Management

Initial meeting(s) with management can be broken down into two phases:

- Information gathering, in which the team member's primary role is to ask questions, listen, and gather information
- A second phase in which the project members describe the overall approach to the project as a means to obtaining the necessary "buy-in" from top management

During this meeting it is important to refrain from offering solutions, even if those solutions seem obvious. One needs to assess needs thoroughly and understand the agency's mission and current situation before offering a solution. To offer a solution prematurely is to risk proposing the wrong solution or the solution to a different problem.

Gather Information

1. *Assess Entity's Understanding.* The entity's understanding of its own needs can vary widely. On one end of the spectrum, the agency may have already performed a significant amount of work to assess its internal controls (e.g., in connection with prior years' compliance with FMFIA), and as a result of that work, designated the team to oversee the remainder of the process. At the other end of the spectrum, the agency may have made very little progress. It is important to determine where the agency falls along that spectrum of understanding.

2. *Assess the Current Situation.* During the meeting with management, information should be obtained about the current situation. For example, one may wish to make inquiries about:

   ○ The Senior Management Council's or the Senior Assessment Team's overall role and responsibility for the assessment of internal control

- Any known or suspected issues identified to date, including:
  - Scope of work
  - Lack of adequate documentation
  - Means for assessing effectiveness
  - Identified or suspected control deficiencies
  - Other reporting issues
- How management will measure the success of the project

3. *The Team's Role in the Assessment Project.* Whether the person assigned as Project or Team Leader is an agency employee or an outside consultant, it is important that he/she understand management's expectations regarding the team's role in assisting them in the project. The agency may be looking for someone to lead the Project Team and take full responsibility for performing the work necessary for management to make an assessment of the effectiveness of internal control. On the other hand, the agency may simply want the team to help in certain limited matters, such as performing tests of the operating effectiveness of specific controls. Responsibilities should be clarified to ensure that the working relationship (e.g., who should be reported to or decision-making authorities) is aligned with that level of responsibility.

   Additionally, it is important to determine management's understanding of *how the team will add value* to the project. There are several ways in which value can be added, including:

   - *Technical expertise.* Technical expertise can be provided in a number of areas, including internal control design, the design and evaluation of tests of internal controls, and the documentation and support required to support management's assessment and, if applicable, assessment by the independent auditors of internal control.

   - *Problem solving.* Management may look to the team to provide solutions when problems are identified. For example, if internal control deficiencies arise, the team may be asked to design new controls to address the deficiency and develop a remediation plan that complies with A-123 requirements.

   - *Business strategy.* As an understanding is developed of the entity's internal control, there may be opportunities for improvement that fall outside of financial reporting and disclosure. Management may expect the team to identify these areas for improvement in internal control that will help the entity achieve operational goals and strategies. This is particularly applicable to outside consultants who should be in a position to identify broken processes and redundancies, provide insight into best practices, and make recommendations beyond a narrow internal control scope.

   - *Project administration.* Management may expect the team to take the lead in conducting the project, relying on the Project Team Leader to take the initiative to form an effective Project Team, work within the time and budget constraints, provide regular project status reports to management, and coordinate the project with the independent auditors and/or the OIG.

Describe an Overall Approach to the Project.   Once an understanding of the agency's situation and management's expectations is gained, the meeting will invariably shift to how the team will approach the project. This is natural since entities will want to alleviate some of the uncertainty they have about how the project will be performed. Again, it should not be necessary to provide a detailed plan for project performance—sufficient information has not been gathered at this point to provide such a plan in any meaningful way.

However, it is appropriate to discuss the overall approach to the project. In describing that approach, the following should be emphasized:

- *The project will be executed in phases.* Depending on the needs of the agency, the project will start with planning; proceed through an assessment of the documentation, design, and operating effectiveness of significant controls; include a provision for remedial action, if any; and conclude with the preparation of the report including a remediation plan. This phased approach allows management to maintain control of the project, how it proceeds, and whether the team will continue in the role that was originally envisioned. At the conclusion of each phase, the work product will be presented, and management can determine whether and how to proceed to the next phase. Presenting the project in this fashion will alleviate a great deal of the uncertainty management may have about the project.

- *The work builds on what the agency has already done.* Each phase of the project begins by understanding the steps the entity has already taken to achieve the objective of the work. Needs are evaluated, and only the work that is necessary to achieve the stated objective is proposed. Work is not started until there is agreement on the scope of the work, the procedures that will be performed, and the deliverables and their timing. The Project Leader will communicate with the independent auditors during each phase to ensure that the approach and resulting work product will meet their needs.

Clarifying the Project Scope and Work Arrangement

Once the team has been assigned (or contracted) by management to help in their assessment of internal control, then the project scope and understanding with management should be formally documented in internal memoranda or, in the case of outside consultants, in an "engagement letter" (or more likely in a contract between the agency and the consultant). This formal documentation is the best way to ensure that the Project Team and the Senior Management Council and/or top management have an understanding of the services the team will provide. This is the case regardless of the composition of the team. Internal efforts usually only require a formal memorandum distributed and acknowledged by all affected parties.

For consulting services, federal procurement regulations will define the minimum contract documentation requirements. In addition, to ensure a "meeting of the minds," the written agreement should include:

- The main agreement, which describes the general nature of the work and other matters such as fees, limitations of the work, ownership of any resulting intellectual property, confidentiality, and so on.
- An exhibit to the agreement, which describes the work and the related deliverables in more detail. Typically, the work will be done in phases. Ideally, management would retain the control to decide whether and when to move on to the next phase. As the contractor and the client reach an agreement as to the nature and scope of each phase of the agreement, an additional appendix to the engagement letter should be prepared to document this agreement.

Main Agreement.   The main agreement remains unchanged; as the contractor and the client agree to additional phases in the process, additional appendices would be drafted and signed by the client. The contracting firm most likely has a standard engagement letter that can serve as the basis for the main agreement. In modifying this standard letter for an engagement to help in the assessment of the effectiveness of internal control, consider the following:

- *Description of services*. The main agreement should refer to the attachment for a complete description of services.
- *Clarify responsibilities*. The CEO and CFO are responsible for establishing and maintaining adequate internal controls and procedures for financial reporting and for assessing the effectiveness of the agency's internal controls. Working under the direction of the agency's senior management, the contractor's responsibility is to assist them in making their assessment.
- *Guarantees and limitations*. The contractor's agreement should clearly state that no results are guaranteed (e.g., that the independent auditors will issue a "clean opinion" on management's report on internal control). Limitations on what the client can expect from the contractor's work should also be considered. For example, the engagement is not designed to detect occurrences of fraud.
- *Open-ended phrases*. Be careful not to give the impression that the scope of work is open-ended and includes whatever is necessary to "get the job done." Phrases such as "other such services, as necessary" should be avoided.
- *Ownership of work product*. Typically, in a consulting engagement, the work product becomes the property of the client. In some instances, the contractor may wish to retain the ownership or right to future use of certain byproducts of the engagement (i.e., training materials or process methodologies). In either case, be sure to delineate ownership rights clearly in the engagement letter.

Description of Services Exhibit.   In general, the contractor should consider including the following in the exhibit describing the services to be performed at each phase of the engagement.

- *Description of services/objective.* A brief description of the services to be performed and their objectives; for example, "assist in the identification of significant internal controls, which will serve as the basis for testing and evaluating the entity's internal control over financial reporting and disclosure controls."

- *Process.* A summary of the process that will be used to deliver the services.

- *Deliverables.* A description of what will be produced as a result of the work.

- *Fees.* Fees are not part of the main agreement but are determined separately for each phase of the work; thus, the fees should be included in the exhibit.

- *Schedule and timing.* When the product will be delivered and, if appropriate, the timing of significant milestones.

- *Assumptions.* Summarize the assumptions upon which the agreement is based (i.e., that the client will be providing certain resources).

Appendix 1A
Action Plan: Structuring the Project

The following action plan is intended to help with the implementation of suggestions contained in this chapter for structuring a project to assess the effectiveness of internal control.

GENERAL

1. Understand Rules and Standards

Become familiar with the relevant rules and standards pertaining to the assessment of internal control. For example:

- Consider the summary guidance on the following matters discussed in this chapter:
  - FMFIA and OMB Circular A-123 requirements
  - Additional guidance issued by authoritative federal sources (e.g., the CFO Council, PCIE, GAO, OIG)
- Consider similar guidance such as SEC and PCAOB requirements to benefit from the application of developing best practices.
- Stay abreast of developments and new guidance issued by:
  - Congress
  - OMB
  - GAO
  - OIG

- ○ SEC
- ○ PCAOB
- ○ Other standard-setting/development organizations such as the CFO Council, PCIE, and AICPA

2. Choose an Approach

Develop a structured, comprehensive approach for assessing and reporting on the effectiveness of internal control. Possible action steps include:

- Become familiar with the project approach described in this chapter.
- Modify the approach as necessary to meet the needs of the entity, expectations of management, qualifications of potential team members, and so on.

ADDITIONAL CONSIDERATIONS FOR OUTSIDE CONSULTANTS

3. Assess Prospective Clients

Identify and gather information about prospective clients.

4. Meet Prospects

Meet with prospective clients and:

- Gather information about clients' needs.
- Assess their current situation.
- Clarify the clients' expectations about the consultant's role on the Project Team.

5. Reach an Understanding

Obtain a written understanding of the consultant's work arrangement with the client.

Appendix 1B

Requirements for Management's Assessment Process: Cross-Reference to Guidance

---

As indicated in this chapter, the revised OMB Circular A-123 and the PCAOB auditing standard both describe certain elements that should be present in management's internal control evaluation process.

Exhibit 1.7 summarizes those required elements and provides a cross-reference to the chapters in this book where you can find guidance to help you comply with these requirements.

Exhibit 1.7 Cross-Reference to Applicable Guidance

A-123/PCAOB Requirement	Applicable Guidance as noted in Chapter(s)
Determine which controls should be tested	Chapter 4
Controls over initiating, recording, processing, and reporting significant accounts and disclosures and related assertions	Chapter 7
Controls over the selection and application of accounting policies	Chapters 4 and 6
Antifraud programs and controls	Chapters 4 and 6
Controls on which other controls are dependent	Chapters 4 and 6
Controls over significant nonroutine and nonsystematic transactions such as accounts involving judgments and estimates	Chapters 4 and 6
Controls over the period-end financial reporting process	Chapters 4 and 6
Evaluate the likelihood that failure of controls could result in a misstatement	Chapter 8
Determine the locations or business units to include in the evaluation for a company with multiple locations or business units	Chapter 3
Evaluate the design effectiveness of controls	Chapters 6 and 7
Evaluate the operating effectiveness of controls	Chapters 6 and 7
Determine whether the deficiencies in internal control constitute significant deficiencies or material weaknesses	Chapter 8
Communicate findings to the auditor and to others, if applicable	Chapter 8
Evaluate whether findings are reasonable and support management's assessment	Chapter 8

Notes

1. This section was adapted from Kearney & Company's, *Federal Government Auditing: Laws, Regulations, Standards, Practices, and Sarbanes-Oxley.* Chapter 3 — The Federal Government and Sarbanes-Oxley, pp. 43 – 48, John Wiley & Sons, Hoboken, NJ, 2006.
2. The PCAOB was established by Congress to implement the Sarbanes-Oxley Act. Standards proposed by the PCAOB must subsequently be approved by the SEC.
3. Based on a 1992 report by the Committee of Sponsoring Organizations (COSO), a consortium of cooperating organizations that includes the Financial Executives Institute, the American Institute of Certified Public Accountants, the American Accounting Association, the Institute of Internal Auditors, and the Institute of Management Accountants.

4. This section relating to the Sarbanes-Oxley Act of 2002 is an adaptation of the Kearney & Company study, "Audit Federal Financial Controls: Sooner Rather than Later," *Journal of Government Financial Management* (Association of Government Accountants, Alexandria, VA), Winter 2005, pp. 5–7.

5. Although the reports on internal controls and laws and regulations are typically accompanied by an auditor's disclaimer of opinion, the standards do require the auditors to document material weaknesses and reportable conditions as well as events of noncompliance with laws and regulations that come to the auditor's attention.

6. In addition to the CFO Act and the Federal Financial Management Improvement Act of 1996, other noteworthy financial management legislation of the 1990s included the Federal Credit Reform Act, the Government Management Reform Act, the Government Performance and Results Act, and the Clinger-Cohen Act.

7. See Regulation S-K, Item 308 (17 CFR §229.308).

8. The following sections were adapted from Michael Ramos' book, *How to Comply with Sarbanes-Oxley Section 404: Assessing the Effectiveness of Internal Control, 2nd Edition.*

9. As described in more detail in Chapter 2, internal controls should be considered within the context of an entity's overall risk management strategy. To identify and understand an entity's significant controls, it is important to understand the significant risks facing the entity. One may wish to identify and assess these risks as a separate project step. However, the approach described in this book considers this risk assessment to be a component of this process step, the identification of significant controls. See Chapter 4 for additional details.

Chapter 2

Internal Control Criteria

Chapter Summary

Describe the COSO Internal Control — Integrated Framework which is the criterion most widely used by entities in assessing the effectiveness of their internal control.

Summarize the value-chain business activities approach for analyzing activity-level controls.

Provide additional guidance on internal control considerations related to an entity's use of information technology (IT), including:

- The generally accepted IT control objectives contained in the Control Objectives for Information and Related Technology (COBIT) report
- The consideration of controls when an entity uses an outside service organization to process certain transactions

THE NEED FOR CONTROL CRITERIA

A set of criteria is a standard against which a judgment can be made. As described in Chapter 1 of this book, choosing appropriate control criteria is a precondition to performing an assessment of the effectiveness of an entity's internal control. In the United States, the *Internal Control—Integrated Framework* (the *Framework*) published by the Committee of Sponsoring Organizations of the Treadway Commission (COSO) is the most commonly used criteria to assess the effectiveness of internal control. In addition, revised Office of Management and Budget (OMB) Circular A-123 adopts all the key elements of the *Framework* in developing control criteria for the federal government. Therefore, a significant portion of this chapter will be devoted to discussing the COSO *Framework*.

Increasingly, IT has become ingrained into entities' business processes and controls. The consideration of IT-related controls must be integrated with the entity's overall assessment of its internal control—it is no longer acceptable to treat IT controls separately and distinctly from other elements of internal control. The Control Objectives for Information and Related Technology (COBIT) framework, published by the Information Systems Audit and Control Association (ISACA), provides a generally accepted set of IT-related control objectives. This chapter will also describe this guidance, which may be integrated into the COSO *Framework*.

Understanding the criteria used to assess the effectiveness of an entity's internal control is a cornerstone for developing an effective assessment approach.

THE COSO INTERNAL CONTROL — INTEGRATED FRAMEWORK

In 1985, COSO was formed to sponsor the National Commission on Fraudulent Financial Reporting, whose charge was to study and report on the factors that can lead to fraudulent financial reporting. Since this initial undertaking, COSO has expanded its mission to improving the quality of financial reporting. A significant part of this mission is aimed at developing guidance on internal control. In 1992, COSO published the *Framework*, which established a framework for internal control and provided evaluation tools that businesses and other entities could use to evaluate their control systems.[1]

Key Characteristics of the COSO Framework

The COSO *Framework* describes five components of internal control:

- Control environment
- Risk assessment
- Control procedures
- Information and communication
- Monitoring

Before providing a detailed description of each of these five components, it is important to "step back" and provide a discussion of the important characteristics of the COSO approach to internal control.

A Holistic, Integrated View.   The COSO *Framework* contains five components of internal control, and one of the most important characteristics of the *Framework* is understanding how these components relate to each other. COSO envisions these individual components as being tightly integrated with each other in a nonlinear fashion. Each component has a relationship with and can influence the functioning of every other component.

For example, the assignment of authority and responsibility is an important element of an entity's control environment. Suppose that management decides to delegate the authority and responsibility for achieving selected mission objectives to a distinct program office within the agency. The COSO guidance related to the control environment component states that the decision to assign authority and responsibility should involve consideration of the following factors:

- Policies describing appropriate management operating practices
- Knowledge and experience of key personnel
- Resources provided for carrying out duties

However, the control environment component of internal control does not exist in a vacuum. The decision to delegate authority will affect other components to varying degrees. In our example, the decision to assign responsibility for program execution would also affect:

- *Risk assessment.* The program office would want to determine which of their activities affect the entity's accounting and OMB required reporting disclosures, establish objectives for those activities, and identify the risks to achieving those objectives. For example, program expenses must be recorded when incurred (e.g., services and/or goods are received), and procedures must be in place to ensure the timely recognition of expenses for financial statement purposes. The program office will want to assess the risk that its activities are not properly accounted for.

- *Control procedures.* Assume that the program office is responsible for the issuance of federal grants to eligible grantees meeting certain predetermined criteria mandated by Congress. The program office may wish to establish standard grant application and grant agreements in order to reduce the risk that grants are issued to ineligible individuals or entities and/or grantees are free to spend funds for purposes other than those mandated by Congress.

- *Information and communication.* Continuing with the example above, communication channels would need to be opened between the program office and the Accounting Department to ensure that the terms of all grants are known to accounting personnel in order for all relevant accounting implications (e.g., expense recognition) to be properly considered.

- *Monitoring.* Finally, senior management would have to establish a method for monitoring the activities of the program office to ensure that its practices and procedures are consistent with the entity's overall mission objectives.

Thus, when evaluating the effectiveness of internal control, we look at it as an *integrated whole.* Weak controls in one area can be offset by stronger controls in another area.

By Way of Analogy.   Consider your experience when you go to the movies. There may be several things you look for in a good movie—writing, directing, acting, music, cinematography, and so forth. These elements are not related in a linear fashion but in a more complicated, nonlinear way. They play off of each other and come together to form an integrated whole. When we walk out of the theater, we judge the entire experience. We may point to individual elements that were particularly enjoyable, but it is how all the elements come together that serves as the basis for our determination of the quality of the film. This "coming together" is an important characteristic of how we judge internal control.

A Process.   COSO defines *internal control* as a process. When evaluating internal control, one should remember that it is a process that is being evaluated, not an outcome. Certainly, there is a connection between the two. An effective process is more likely to lead to a desired outcome. The existence of undesirable outcomes may indicate that the process itself was flawed. However, that direct connection may not always hold true. It is possible that an internal control failure can be rightly attributed to something other than a flawed process.

A Business/Mission Objective–Driven Approach.   The COSO *Framework* views internal control as "built in" to an entity's overall business processes, as opposed to a separate "built-on" component that attaches itself to the entity's real business. "Building in" internal control requires management to:

1.   Establish business objectives; for our purposes, those objectives relate to financial reporting.

2.   Identify the risks to achieving those objectives.

3.   Determine how to manage the identified risks; the establishment of internal controls is just one of several options.

4.   Where appropriate, establish control objectives as a way to manage certain risks. Individual controls are then designed and implemented to meet the stated control objectives.

Internal controls have no intrinsic value—they are not valuable in and of themselves. Controls have value only to the degree that they allow the entity to achieve its objectives. The effectiveness of internal control is judged according to how well it enables an entity to achieve stated objectives.

Flexible, Adaptable, No "One-Size-Fits-All" Approach.   The COSO *Framework* is not a rigid, prescriptive approach to internal controls. It recognizes that different entities will make different choices regarding how to control their operations. Management will make cost-benefit judgments and choose trade-offs. The result: internal control is not a "one-size-fits-all" proposition.

Moreover, circumstances change at the entity, and so its internal control must be designed in a way to adapt and remain effective in a dynamic environment. In fact, a primary objective of the monitoring component of internal control is assessing the quality of the system's performance over time and recognizing that circumstances will change.

Reasonable Assurance.   COSO recognizes the limitations of internal control (see Exhibit 2.1). No matter how well designed or operated, internal control can provide only reasonable assurance that objectives will be met. Reasonable assurance is a high threshold, but it stops short of absolute assurance. The presence of an internal control failure does not, in and of itself, mean that a system is ineffective. The COSO report states that "even an effective internal control system can experience failure."

The People Factor.   COSO recognizes that internal control is affected by people. Documentation of controls is important, but the effectiveness of internal control depends largely on the people responsible for carrying out individual control elements

Exhibit 2.1   Limitations of Internal Control

Internal control provides reasonable but not absolute assurance that an entity will achieve its financial reporting objectives. Even an effective internal control system can experience a failure owing to the following:

- *Human Error.* The people who implement internal controls may make poor decisions that can lead to control failures. People can also make a simple error or a mistake.

- *Management Override.* Even in a well-controlled entity, managers may be able to override internal controls for illegitimate purposes.

- *Collusion.* Two or more individuals may collude to circumvent what otherwise would be effective controls.

—from the Department Secretary or Agency Chief Executive Officer all the way to rank-and-file employees charged with performing control-related tasks.

Thus, the design of internal control must take into account the human element and must make allowances for human nature. For example, people are greatly influenced by the actions taken by an entity's senior management—more so than they are by what these individuals say. Therefore, the relative strength of an entity's control environment greatly depends on the actions of the entity's leadership. Or consider that the ability of individuals to carry out their responsibilities depends on how well they understand what is required. This need for understanding requires that the entity's internal controls have an effective communication and training element.

Two Levels of Controls.   Implicit in the COSO *Framework* is the idea that controls operate at two levels within an organization—the entity-level and the business process activity-level. Entity-level controls are those that have a pervasive effect on the entity and can influence the effectiveness of internal control in many areas. For example, the entity's hiring policies, or the way that it communicates information across various departments/components, can have an effect on many different transactions. Strengths in entity-level controls will improve the effectiveness of all other controls; weaknesses in these controls can diminish the effectiveness of even the most strongly designed activity-level controls. For example, a timely reconciliation of balances with Treasury may be a very effective control in theory, but if the agency does not hire qualified people to perform the task, then the procedure will not operate as designed.

Activity-level controls are isolated on one transaction. For example, checking to make sure that a vendor is on the list of approved vendors is a control that is isolated to the procurement function. The failure of this control generally affects only procurement transactions and has no effect on other transactions, for example, the recording of payroll expense.

Understanding the difference between entity- versus activity-level is important because the way in which the two are documented, tested, and evaluated varies depending on whether the control operates at the entity-level or activity-level. This concept is reinforced throughout the rest of the book.

Five Components of Internal Control

The COSO *Framework* describes five interrelated components of internal control:

1. *Control environment.* Senior management must set an appropriate "tone at the top" that positively influences the control consciousness of entity personnel. The control environment is the foundation for all other components of internal controls and provides discipline and structure.

2. *Risk assessment.* The entity must be aware of and deal with the risks it faces. It must set objectives integrated throughout all value-chain activities so that the organization is operating in concert. Once these objectives are set, the entity must then identify the risks to achieving those objectives and analyze and develop ways to manage them.

3. *Control activities.* Control policies and procedures must be established and executed to help ensure that the actions identified by management as necessary to address risks are effectively carried out.

4. *Information and communications.* Surrounding the control activities are information and communication systems, including the accounting system. These systems enable the entity's people to capture and exchange the information needed to conduct, manage, and control its operations.

5. *Monitoring.* The entire control process must be monitored and modifications made as necessary. In this way, the system can react dynamically, changing as conditions warrant.

Exhibit 2.2 depicts these five elements of internal control and their interrelationship. As can be seen, the exhibit depicts the elements inside an umbrella. This analogy can be very useful in explaining COSO to those individuals (particularly non-accountants) who have no prior experience with COSO.

Suppose a man is on his way to the train station, and it is raining hard. On the way, he needs to make a call on his cell phone and pick up a paper for the ride home. Without an umbrella, he may or may not be able to perform these tasks effectively. But the umbrella provides a "mini-environment" in which he is protected from the elements and able to accomplish the tasks needed with the best possible chance for success. The control environment shelters him, like the umbrella. Without this overarching protection, he will have a difficult time achieving his goals.

Beneath the umbrella—inside the "mini-environment"—are all of the tasks that need to be performed. In this case, these tasks are the processes that need to function in order to produce reliable financial statements. These are read from top to bottom.

- *Risk Assessment.* Once the overall objective is determined (to produce reliable financial statements), the first thing that needs to be considered is the risks faced to achieving those objectives. Ask the question "what can go wrong?" in preparing the financial statements. For example, the entity may fail to record or accrue all liabilities at year-end.

Exhibit 2.2   COSO Internal Control Components

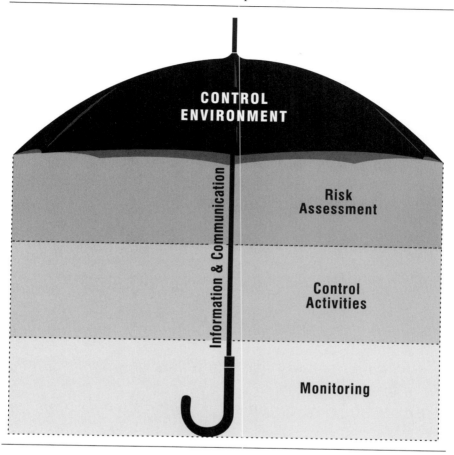

- *Control Activities*. Once what can go wrong has been identified, control objectives and activities can be developed to mitigate those risks. If the risk that needs to be mitigated is the failure to record liabilities at year-end (or at the end of any monthly or quarterly reporting period), then controls specific to those risks should be developed. These controls will vary depending on the characteristics of the organization. For example, capturing all expenses related to federal grants depends largely on the terms of the grants and, in particular, the process controlling grantee expense reporting. Therefore, a control procedure to address the risks of not capturing all expenses would be a control designed to ensure that grantee expense reports are received on a timely basis. For example, an agency with little or no grant issuance responsibility (such as a revolving fund providing services to other federal agencies) may have identified similar risks (e.g., failure to recognize all expenses), but because of the unique characteristics of the revolving fund, the specific control activities will be different than those of an agency with significant grant issuance responsibility.

- *Monitoring.* As controls are performed, they should be monitored to see that they are operating effectively. If the controls are not operating effectively, then the agency needs to take steps to fix the problem.

- *Information and Communication.* Information and communication is required between and among all of the components in order for them to function effectively. For example:
  - o The agency must gather information to understand the job requirements of personnel involved in the financial reporting process in order to communicate these requirements to the Human Resource function responsible for hiring (communication between the control environment and control activities).
  - o Those responsible for identifying risks of financial reporting (e.g., financial managers, including senior management) must communicate these risks to those responsible for designing appropriate controls (communication between risk assessment and control activities).
  - o If supervisors detect problems in the performance of controls, this information needs to be communicated to those responsible for performing the control activities and possibly to those responsible for risk assessment in order to ensure the problem is fixed (communication between monitoring and control activities and risk assessment).

Additionally, controls may affect the entity either pervasively, on an entity-wide basis, or specifically, on an individual activity, account, or class of transactions basis.

THE CONTROL ENVIRONMENT

The control environment sets the tone of the entity. It influences the control consciousness of the people within the organization and is the foundation for all other components of internal control. The following discussion describes the factors highlighted in the COSO report that contribute to an effective control environment.

Integrity and Ethical Values

The effectiveness of internal control cannot rise above the integrity and ethical values of the senior management. Integrity and ethical values are essential elements of the control environment because they affect the design, administration, and monitoring of other internal control components.

Management may tell you a great deal about its integrity and ethical values. Management may even commit its words to a written document. Responses to inquiries and written policies are good, but the COSO report makes it clear that the effectiveness of an entity's control environment depends primarily on management's *actions* and how these actions affect the entity on a day-to-day basis.

In order for management's integrity and ethical values to have a positive impact on the entity, the following must exist:

- Agency management must personally have high ethical and behavioral standards.
- These standards must be communicated to all personnel; in a small agency, this communication is often informal.
- The standards must be reinforced.

Through its actions, management can demonstrate its ethical values in a number of ways, including:

- *Dealing with signs of problems.* Consider how management deals with signs that problems exist, particularly when the cost of identifying and solving the problem could be high. For example, suppose that senior management became aware of a possible environmental contamination on their premises. How would they react? Would they try to hide it, deny its existence, or act evasively if asked about it? Or would they actively seek advice on how to best handle the situation?

- *Removal or reduction of incentives and temptations.* Individuals may engage in dishonest, illegal, or unethical acts simply because the department head or senior level manager gives them strong incentives or temptations to do so. Removing or reducing these incentives and temptations can go a long way toward diminishing undesirable behavior.

  An emphasis on results, particularly in the short term, fosters an environment in which the price of failure becomes very high. *Incentives* for engaging in fraudulent or questionable financial reporting practices include:

  - Pressure to meet unrealistic performance targets, particularly for short-term results
  - High performance-dependent rewards including federally sponsored bonus plans.

  Temptations for employees to engage in improper practices include:

  - Nonexistent or ineffective controls, such as poor segregation of duties in sensitive areas, that offer temptations to steal or conceal questionable financial reporting practices
  - Senior management that is unaware of actions taken by employees
  - Penalties for improper behavior that are insignificant or unpublicized and thus lose their value as deterrents.

- *Management intervention.* In certain situations it is appropriate for management to intervene and overrule prescribed policies or procedures for legitimate purposes. For example, management intervention is usually necessary to deal with nonrecurring and nonstandard transactions or events that otherwise might be handled by the accounting system. The COSO report recommends that management provide guidance on the situations and frequency with which intervention of established controls is appropriate. All occurrences of management intervention should be documented and explained.

Risk of loss has always been present in both private and public sectors because it is easy for individuals in positions of trust to benefit directly through fraud and abuse. However, the more indirect temptation to "window dress" reported financial results is not usually associated with federal financial statement reporting. Ironically, as the federal government becomes more "business-like," adopting best practices in the areas of personnel compensation and financial reporting, the risks associated with a lack of integrity in financial reporting increase proportionately with the emphasis placed on financial operating results. It is important to recognize that a new paradigm is in effect (or evolving) affecting federal financial reporting.

Commitment to Competence

Competence should relate to the knowledge and skills necessary to accomplish the tasks that define an individual's job. Commitment to competence includes management's consideration of the competence levels for particular jobs and how those levels translate into requisite skills and knowledge.

Management's Philosophy and Operating Style

Management's philosophy and operating style encompass a broad range of characteristics. Such characteristics may include:

- Senior management's approach to taking and monitoring business risks
- Attitudes and actions toward financial reporting and legal compliance matters
- Emphasis on meeting budget, profit, and other financial and operating goals

Management's philosophy and operating style have a significant influence on the control environment, regardless of the consideration given to other control environment factors.

Organizational Structure

An entity's organizational structure provides the framework within which its activities for achieving entity-wide objectives are planned, executed, controlled, and monitored.

Significant aspects of establishing an organizational structure include considering key areas of authority and responsibility and appropriate lines of reporting. What is considered "appropriate" will vary according to the size, complexity, and needs of the entity. Small agencies usually have fairly simple organizational structures. A highly structured organization with formal reporting lines and responsibilities may be appropriate and even required for large entities, but for small agencies this type of structure may impede the necessary flow of information.

Assignment of Authority and Responsibility

The assignment of authority and responsibility includes:

- The establishment of reporting relationships and authorization procedures

- The degree to which individuals and groups are encouraged to use initiative in addressing issues and solving problems
- The establishment of limits of authority
- Policies describing appropriate operating practices
- Resources provided for carrying out duties

Alignment of authority and accountability is often designed to encourage individual initiatives, within limits. Delegation of authority means surrendering central control of certain operating and administrative decisions to lower echelons—to the people who are closest to everyday operating transactions.

It is a critical challenge to delegate only to the extent required to achieve objectives. This requires ensuring that risk acceptance is based on sound practices for identifying and minimizing risk, including sizing risks and weighing potential losses versus gains in arriving at good business decisions.

Another challenge is ensuring that all personnel understand the entity's objectives. It is essential that each individual know how his/her actions interrelate and contribute to the achievement of entity objectives.

The control environment is also greatly influenced by the extent to which individuals recognize that they will be held accountable. This holds true all the way to the Secretary or agency head level, who should be accountable to the taxpayers, Congress, and the President, and who has ultimate responsibility for all activities within the organization, including the internal control system.

Human Resource Policies and Practices

Human resource policies and practices affect an entity's ability to employ sufficient competent personnel to accomplish its goals and objectives. Human resource policies and practices include an entity's policies and procedures for hiring, orienting, training, evaluating, counseling, promoting, compensating, and taking remedial action. Federal agencies should strive to formalize human resource policies. Even if they are not formalized, they should, nevertheless, exist and be communicated. For example, in a smaller entity a Senior Manager may verbally make explicit his or her expectations about the type of person to be hired to fill a particular job and may even be active in the hiring process. Formal documentation, although desirable in a federal setting, is not always necessary for a policy to be in place and operating effectively.

Standards for hiring the most qualified individuals (with an emphasis on avoiding conflict of interest, educational background, prior work experience, past accomplishments, and integrity and ethical behavior) demonstrate an entity's commitment to competent and trustworthy people. Hiring practices that include formal, in-depth employment interviews and informative and insightful presentations on the entity's history, culture, and operating style send a message that the agency is committed to its people.

Personnel policies that communicate prospective roles and responsibilities and provide training opportunities indicate expected levels of performance and behavior.

Rotation of personnel and promotions driven by periodic performance appraisals demonstrate the entity's commitment to advancement of qualified personnel to higher levels of responsibility. Competitive compensation programs that include bonus incentives serve to motivate and reinforce outstanding performance. Disciplinary actions send a message that violations of expected behavior will not be tolerated.

Information Technology Considerations

As described later in this chapter, the Information Technology Governance Institute (ITGI) and ISACA have published a document entitled *IT Control Objectives for Sarbanes-Oxley,* which provides extensive guidance on how IT controls should be considered within the context of management's assessment of internal control effectiveness. The document highlights the following important considerations related to an entity's control environment and information technology:

- IT is often mistakenly regarded as a separate organization of the entity and thus a separate control environment.
- IT is complex, not only with regard to its technical components, but also with regard to how those components integrate into the entity's overall system of internal control.
- IT can introduce additional or increased risks that require new or enhanced control activities to be successfully mitigated.
- IT requires specialized skills that may be in short supply.
- IT may require reliance on third parties when significant processes or IT components are outsourced.
- The ownership of IT controls may be unclear.

RISK ASSESSMENT

As indicated previously, the COSO *Framework* considers internal controls within the context of an entity's stated objectives and the risks of achieving those objectives. Exhibit 2.3 describes this risk assessment process. Note that steps 1 through 4 are part of the risk assessment control component, whereas steps 5 and 6 are considered elements of an entity's control activities. Again, what is important is not which control component an individual element "belongs to" but how it relates to internal control taken as a whole.

Objective Setting

The COSO *Framework* considers objective setting (and therefore the risk assessment process) at both the entity-level and the business process activity-level. Setting objectives allows management to identify *critical success factors,* which are the key things that must go right if goals are to be achieved.

Exhibit 2.3   Risk Assessment

STEP 1		
Goals	**Key Questions**	**Examples**
Set objective	What are we trying to achieve?	Produce reliable financial statements

STEP 2		
Goals	**Key Questions**	**Examples**
Identify risks to achieving those objectives	What could happen that would affect our objectives?	A natural disaster could destroy computer systems and data

STEP 3		
Goals	**Key Questions**	**Examples**
Assess risk	What are consequences of risk? What is likelihood event will occur?	Consequences are severe; likelihood is slight

STEP 4		
Goals	**Key Questions**	**Examples**
Manage risk	In light of the assessment, what is the most cost-effective way to manage the risk?	Insure against loss. Develop business recovery plan. Self-insure.

CONTROL ACTIVITIES

STEP 5		
Goals	**Key Questions**	**Examples**
Define control objective	For risks to managed through internal control, what are the control objectives?	Implement recovery plan that reduces the impact of a natural disaster

STEP 6		
Goals	**Key Questions**	**Examples**
Design control	How should control be designed to prevent or detect identified risk?	Design recovery plan. Implement plan. Test on a regular basis.

COSO defines objectives in three broad categories: operations, compliance with laws and regulations, and financial reporting. In relation to reporting on the effectiveness of internal control, as described in this book, the objectives that are relevant for purposes of this discussion are the financial reporting objectives, which COSO defines as addressing:

> The preparation of reliable published financial statements, including interim and condensed financial statements and selected financial data derived from such statements, such as earnings releases, reported publicly.

The term *reliable* means that the financial statements are *fairly presented* in conformity with generally accepted accounting principles (GAAP). In discussing what it means for a "fair presentation," the COSO report cites Statement on Auditing Standards (SAS) No. 69, *The Meaning of "Presents Fairly in Conformity with Generally Accepted Accounting Principles" in the Independent Auditor's Report,* which defines "fair presentation" as considering whether:

- The accounting principles selected and applied have general acceptance
- The accounting principles are appropriate in the circumstances
- The financial statements, including the related notes, are informative of matters that may affect their use, understanding, and interpretation
- The information presented in the financial statements is classified and summarized in a reasonable manner, that is, neither too detailed nor too condensed
- The financial statements reflect the underlying transactions and events in a manner that presents the financial position, results of operations, and cash flows stated within a range of acceptable limits, that is, limits that are reasonable and practical to attain in financial statements.

The concept of materiality is inherent in these judgments related to "presents fairly."

At the activity-level, the people who must take action to achieve the objective must have a good, working understanding of what is required of them. It also is important for management to set priorities for activity-level objectives, recognizing that some objectives are more important than others.

Identify Risks

The COSO report notes that there are many ways in which management can identify risks and that these risks can arise from both internal and external causes. The COSO *Framework* does not endorse any one particular risk identification process, but acknowledges that many can be effective as long as the process is comprehensive and considers all factors that may contribute to or increase risks. Factors to consider include:

- Past experiences of failure to meet objectives
- Quality of personnel

- Changes affecting the entity such as oversight guidance, regulations, personnel, and so on
- The existence of geographically distributed activities (particularly foreign activities when applicable)
- The significance of an activity to the entity
- The complexity of an activity

At the activity-level, management should focus its risk identification efforts on major component agencies, programs, or activities.

Assess and Manage Risks

A commonly acknowledged process for risk analysis includes assessing:

- Consequences of the risk (i.e., asking the question "what would happen if … ?")
- Likelihood of the identified risk occurring (i.e., asking the question "what are the chances that … ?")

Once risks are assessed, management is in a better position to decide on an appropriate way to manage the risk. Risk management techniques include:

- Risk avoidance, for example, by choosing *not* to undertake the activity that gives rise to the risk
- Risk transfer, for example, requiring performance bonds from contractors, hedging on foreign currencies overseas, or the use of financial instruments in a hedging strategy used by Government Sponsored Enterprises (GSEs) such as the Federal National Mortgage Association (FNMA)
- Risk mitigation, for example, by designing and implementing internal control policies and procedures
- Risk acceptance

Manage Change

The mission and operating environment of an entity evolves or changes over time, and change can result in previously well-functioning internal controls becoming less effective. The COSO *Framework* acknowledges that change management should be a part of an entity's regular risk assessment process but goes on to identify those conditions that should be the subject of special consideration within the entity's risk assessment process. These conditions are:

- *Changes in the operating environment.* Changes in the regulatory or operating environment can result in changes in competitive pressures and significantly different risks.
- *New personnel.* New personnel may have a different focus on or understanding of internal control. When people change jobs or leave the agency, management should consider the control activities they performed and who will perform them

going forward. Steps should be taken to ensure that new personnel understand their tasks.

- *New or revamped information systems.* Significant and rapid changes in information systems can change the risk relating to internal control. When these systems are changed, management should assess how the changes will impact control activities. Are the existing activities appropriate or even possible with the new systems? Personnel should be adequately trained when information systems are changed or replaced.

- *Rapid growth.* Significant and rapid expansion of operations can strain controls and increase the risk of a breakdown in controls. Management should consider whether accounting and information systems are adequate to handle increases in volume.

- *New technology.* Incorporating new technologies into production processes or information systems may change the risk associated with internal control.

- *New lines, products, or activities.* Entering into new programs or transactions with which an agency has little experience may introduce new risks associated with internal control.

- *Restructurings.* Agency realignment such as the transfer of one or more agencies to a different department or the creation of a new cabinet-level agency, such as the newly appointed Department of Homeland Security, can seriously impact internal controls. Staff levels may be reduced or reassigned, and segregation of duties potentially compromised, and/or key internal controls eliminated as functions are consolidated.

- *Foreign operations.* Foreign operations and never-ending fluctuations in international relations present a particularly tough challenge to federal agencies with overseas operations. It also constantly introduces new and unique risks that management should address.

- *Accounting changes.* Although not mentioned in the COSO report, SAS No. 55 (as amended), *Internal Control in a Financial Statement Audit,* includes changes in GAAP as a circumstance that requires special consideration in the entity's risk assessment process. GAAP applying specifically to the federal government are relatively new. These principles have been subject to significant change and revision in the recent past, and it is likely that this dynamic trend will continue in the future. An important consideration in evaluating an agency's change management is the mechanism that is in place to stay abreast of developments and implement accounting changes as new pronouncements or revisions become effective.

CONTROL ACTIVITIES

Control activities involve two elements:

1. *Policy.* A policy establishes what should be done.
2. *Procedure.* Procedures are the actions of people to implement the stated policies.

Key Characteristics of Control Activities

The COSO report's discussion of control activities includes several key points, which will affect any entity's evaluation of the effectiveness of its internal control. Some of these key points reiterate the overall concepts described at the beginning of this chapter and include:

- *Link to risk assessment process.* There are many different ways to categorize internal controls (e.g., preventive or detective), and these categories may be useful as a means to organize your understanding of an entity's control activities. However, the category into which a particular control activity falls is not nearly as important as the role it plays in achieving a stated objective. As described in Exhibit 2.2, the establishment of control objectives and related control policies and procedures is linked to the entity's risk assessment process. When evaluating the effectiveness of control activities, it is necessary to consider whether they relate to the risk assessment process and whether they are appropriate to ensure that management's directives are carried out.

- *Agency specific.* Agencies differ in many ways, including their stated objectives, the circumstances of their mission, and the people responsible for managing and controlling their objectives and programs. For these reasons, no two entities should be expected to have the same set of control activities.

- *Documentation of policies.* The COSO report recognizes that oftentimes policies are communicated orally. Although the nature of the federal government usually warrants the formalization and documentation of policies, unwritten policies can be effective:
  ○ When the policy is a long-standing and well-understood practice
  ○ In smaller organizations, in which communication channels involve limited management layers and close interaction and supervision of personnel.

- *Performance of procedures.* More important than the documentation of policy is the performance of the procedures. To be effective, procedures must be performed thoughtfully, conscientiously, and consistently. Additionally, control procedures should include a follow-up component by which conditions identified as a result of the procedures are followed up and appropriate action is taken.

- *Focus on significant activities.* When evaluating control activities, the evaluator should evaluate all significant business activities.

Types of Control Activities

Having said that the category a control is placed in is not as important as how effective the control is at addressing risk, the COSO report then provides examples of types of control activities. These examples do not suggest any hierarchy, structure, or categorizing scheme; instead, they are provided merely to illustrate the wide range of control activities.

- *Top-level reviews.* These control activities include reviews of actual performance versus budgets, forecasts, and prior-period performance. They may also involve relating different sets of data (e.g., operating or financial) to one another, together with analyses of the relationships, investigating unusual relationships, and taking corrective action. Performance reviews may also include a review of functional or activity performance. Note that the control activity is management's analysis and *follow-up* on the matters identified as a result of the review. The control activity is *not* the preparation of a budget or forecast.

- *Information processing.* A variety of control activities are performed to check the accuracy, completeness, and authorization of transactions. The two broad groupings of information systems control activities are general controls and appli-cation controls. General controls commonly include controls over data center operations, system software acquisition and maintenance, and access security. Application controls apply to the processing of individual applications and help ensure that transactions are valid, properly authorized, and completely and accurately processed.

- *Physical controls.* These activities encompass the physical security of assets, including adequate safeguards over access to assets and records such as secured facilities and authorization for access to computer programs and data files and periodic counting and comparison with amounts shown on control records. The extent to which physical controls intended to prevent theft of assets are relevant to the reliability of financial statement preparation depends on the circumstances, such as when assets are highly susceptible to misappropriation. (For example, these controls would ordinarily not be relevant when accountable property losses would be detected pursuant to periodic physical inspection and recorded in the financial statements.) However, if for financial reporting purposes management relies solely on perpetual inventory records, the physical security controls would be relevant to the financial reporting process.

- *Segregation of duties.* Assigning the responsibilities of authorizing transactions, recording transactions, and maintaining custody of assets to different people is intended to reduce the number of situations in which a person might be in a position to perpetrate and conceal errors or irregularities in the normal course of his or her duties. Segregation of duties is often a problem for small agencies.

INFORMATION AND COMMUNICATION

Every entity must identify, capture, and communicate pertinent information in a form and timeframe that allows people to carry out their control and other responsibilities. The COSO report provides a rather broad description of the characteristics of an effective information and communication system. For the purpose of assessing the effectiveness of controls related specifically to financial reporting objectives, the most relevant of these characteristics include the following:

- *Consider all information sources.* The information needed to prepare reliable financial reports is not limited to financial information; nonfinancial information is also important. For example, the information needed to account for Federal

Loan Programs pursuant to Credit Reform requirements and Statements of Federal Financial Accounting Standards (SFFAS) No. 2, *Accounting for Direct Loans and Loan Guarantees*, includes an assessment of current and future economic conditions. Frequently, the assumptions underlying significant accounting estimates rely, to some degree or another, on nonfinancial information.

Additionally, the preparation of financial statements requires that information be gathered from both internal and external sources. In the Federal Loan Program example, the information needed to make the estimate is not limited to internally generated information, such as the face value of the loan. The estimate will also require management to consider externally generated information, such as value of collateral, borrower creditworthiness, default estimates, and so forth.

- *Integration with control activities.* The entity's information and communication systems are closely integrated with its control activities. In order for control activities to be effective, the following must be communicated clearly to individuals who perform control functions:
  - Specific control activity-related duties
  - Relevant aspects of the internal control system, how they work, and their role and responsibility in the system
  - How their activities relate to the work of others (this knowledge will help them recognize a problem or determine its cause or corrective action)
  - Expected behavior—what is acceptable and unacceptable
  - The notion that whenever the unexpected occurs, attention should be given to the event itself and to its cause

  Additionally, management should recognize that information received from *external* sources may indicate control weaknesses. For example, external auditors are required to report internal control deficiencies to the department/agency head, the Office of the Inspector General (OIG), and, where applicable, the agency's audit committee. Oversight agencies (i.e., the OIG, the Government Accountability Office [GAO]) report the results of their examinations, which may highlight control weaknesses. Complaints or inquiries from stakeholders, taxpayers, vendors, or other third parties often point to operating problems. These are just examples of the types of information that originate from outside the entity that may provide feedback about the entity's control activities.

- *Integration with risk assessment and change management process.* As described previously, change management is an integral part of an entity's risk management process, and the COSO report identifies several situations that require "special consideration." Recognize that when the entity undergoes change, its information needs change as well. To be effective, an information system must be flexible and responsive to the constantly evolving needs of the agency.

- *The key role played by senior management.* Senior management plays an important role in the effective functioning of an entity's information and communication system. The COSO report recommends that entities establish an open and effective means of communicating information upstream, one of the key elements of which is management's "clear-cut willingness to listen."

- *Routine and nonroutine information.* An entity's information system is *not* limited to merely capturing the entity's recurring, routine transactions and events but also must include a means for identifying, capturing, and communicating information that is outside the normal course of operations or recorded infrequently.

- *Formal and informal.* The COSO *Framework* recognizes that an entity's information and communication system includes *informal* communications, such as conversations with stakeholders, vendors, and other third parties and between and among employees.

- *Timing is important.* It is not enough to capture and communicate information. The communication must be done in a timely manner that allows it to be useful in controlling the entity's activities.

Additional detailed guidance on an entity's information and communication needs specifically related to financial reporting can be found in SAS No. 55, *Internal Control in a Financial Statement Audit,*[2] and in AU319.47-.53 of *Professional Standards,* Vol. 1, published by the American Institute of Certified Public Accountants (AICPA).[3]

Information System for Financial Reporting

The information system relevant to financial reporting objectives—which includes the accounting system—consists of the methods and records established to record, process, summarize, and report entity transactions (as well as events and conditions) and to maintain accountability for the related assets and liabilities.

The auditing literature describes the necessary elements of an information system for financial reporting, which include the methods and records that:

- Identify and record all valid transactions
- Describe on a timely basis the transactions in sufficient detail to permit proper classification of transactions for financial reporting
- Measure the value of transactions in a manner that permits recording of their proper monetary value in the financial statements
- Determine the time period in which transactions occurred to permit recording of transactions in the proper accounting period
- Properly present the transactions and related disclosures in the financial statements.

MONITORING

Monitoring is a process that assesses the quality of internal control performance over time. It involves assessing the design and operation of controls on a timely basis and taking necessary corrective actions. Monitoring may be performed on an ongoing basis and/or as part of a separate evaluation. Examples of ongoing monitoring activities include the following:

- The regular management and supervisory activities carried out in the normal course of business.

- Communications from external parties, which can corroborate internally generated information or indicate problems. For example, borrowers under Federal Loan Programs implicitly corroborate loan data by paying loan amounts or installments when due. Conversely, complaints about agency-furnished loan data could indicate system deficiencies in loan servicing.

- External auditors regularly provide recommendations on the way internal controls can be strengthened. Auditors may identify potential weaknesses and make recommendations to management for corrective action.

- Oversight agencies such as the GAO and OIG provide recommendations on internal controls on a regular basis.

- Employees may be required to "sign-off" on evidence of the performance of critical control functions. Sign-offs allow management to monitor the performance of these control functions.

Reporting Deficiencies

Providing information regarding internal control deficiencies to the right people is critical if the internal control system is to continue to function effectively. For this reason, the monitoring component of internal controls should include a mechanism for reporting internal control deficiencies and taking appropriate action. COSO uses the term *deficiency* broadly to mean any condition of an internal control system "worthy of attention." Certainly, all deficiencies that can affect the entity's ability to produce reliable financial information should be identified and reported. However, the COSO report notes that even seemingly simple problems with relatively simple and obvious solutions should be carefully considered because they might have far-reaching implications. In all cases, when errors and deficiencies are identified, their underlying causes should be investigated.

Internal control deficiencies should be reported to the individuals who are in the best position to take action. This includes not only the person responsible for the activity involved, but also at least one level of management above the directly responsible person.

BUSINESS PROCESS ACTIVITIES

The COSO *Framework* recognizes that controls exist at two different levels within an organization: the entity-level and the activity-level. For example, employee hiring and training policies affect the control environment at an entity-level — they have a pervasive effect on how controls are implemented and performed. A bank reconciliation (including reconciling Fund Balances with Treasury) is a control procedure performed at an activity-level, namely, the activity of receiving and disbursing cash (or funds with Treasury). Any evaluation of internal controls must consider all significant controls at the entity *and* activity-level. In performing this evaluation, an important issue to consider is how one defines *activity*.

The auditing literature, which is concerned with internal control over financial reporting, takes a financial statement approach to examining activity-level controls. Under this approach, an evaluator would identify activities such as accounts and classes of transactions that are significant to the financial statements. For example, within an entity, the activity-level controls might be assessed as they relate to payroll, purchases, cash receipts and disbursements, and so on. The COSO *Framework* does not take a financial statement approach to analyzing activity-level controls. In the detailed discussion of the *Framework* and in its example evaluation tools, COSO takes a "business process activity" approach to activity-level controls. This approach is based on the value-chain analysis.[4]

The notion behind the value chain is that entities are successful when they provide customers with value. The value chain consists of value activities, which are the physically and technologically distinct activities that an entity performs. The value activities are building blocks used by the entity to create value for its customers. Although the use of the term *customer* in a federal government setting is unusual, thinking of the stakeholders served by any given agency as the agency's customer is very useful in identifying "business processes" and activity-level controls. Value activities can take one of two forms: primary activities and support activities. These are described in the following discussion.

Primary Activities

The primary activities are those involved in the physical creation of the product or service, the delivery of the product or service to the customer (or "sale" as defined by the value-chain methodology), and delivery aftermath activities (or service as defined by the value-chain methodology). Each agency will have its own unique definition of customer/stakeholder (and will often have more than one customer/ stakeholder). Depending on the nature of the agency, "customers" may include all taxpayers (e.g., "customers" served by the Department of Homeland Security) or a subset such as retirees receiving Social Security benefits or farmers and ranchers as defined by the U.S. Department of Agriculture in its "USDA Customer Statement."

Exhibit 2.4 describes the classical depiction of the Value Chain of Primary Activities. The order of events in the value chain are read left to right—an entity starts with inputs; it produces a product or the capacity to deliver a service, ships, sells/ delivers the product or service, and ultimately supports (services) its output. The primary activities in the value chain are described as follows:

- *Inbound logistics.* Inbound logistics for an agency or activity delivering goods or services to related organizations (e.g., a revolving fund) will typically include activities associated with receiving, storing, and disseminating inputs to the product. These include material handling, warehousing, inventory control, vehicle

Exhibit 2.4   Value Chain of Primary Activities

scheduling, and returns to suppliers. In the case of services, inbound logistics also include activities associated with the creation of the capacity to deliver the service.

- *Operations*. Activities associated with transforming inputs into the final product or service. These include employee professional training, packaging, assembly, equipment maintenance, testing, printing, and facility operations.

- *Outbound logistics*. Activities associated with collecting, storing, and physically distributing the product or service to customer/stakeholders. These include service support supplies and/or finished goods warehousing, supplies and materials handling, delivery vehicle operation, order processing, personnel staffing, and scheduling.

- *Marketing and sales*. Activities associated with providing a means by which buyers can purchase the product or service and inducing them to do so. These include advertising, promotion, sales force, quoting, channel selection, channel relations, and pricing. Although many of these activities are not usually associated with federal agencies, the value-chain concept is useful in analyzing the "business processes of a federal agency." For example, the Centers for Medicare and Medicaid Services (CMS) can identify Medicare- and Medicaid-eligible beneficiaries as its customers. The products and services provided can be defined in terms of medical services and related prescription drugs. The sales force encompasses those individuals (whether federal or private employees) disseminating information on available benefits as well as providing CMS's "customers" with information on available options and pricing (e.g., costs to be borne by the beneficiary).

- *Service*. Aftermath activities associated with providing service to enhance or maintain the value of the product or service in the hands of the buyer. In the above CMS example, activities include claims processing (to reimburse providers for the costs to be borne by the federal government) and service/product complaint follow-up (to ensure that beneficiaries are dealt with fairly and in accordance with the wishes of Congress and to prevent fraud, waste, and abuse).

Support Activities

In addition to these primary activities, entities also engage in a set of "support" activities. These activities support the primary activities and each other by providing purchased inputs, technology, human resources, and various entity-wide functions such as cost accounting.

Exhibit 2.5 Overall Value Chain

These support activities can be added to the entity's primary activities to create the overall value chain for the entity, as depicted in Exhibit 2.5. Support activities include:

- *Infrastructure.* Activities involved in general management, budget formulation planning, finance, accounting, legal, and quality management.

- *Human resource management.* Activities associated with recruiting, hiring, training, development, and compensation of all types of personnel.

- *Technology development.* Activities associated with efforts to improve products, services, and processes. Technology development can take many forms, from basic research and product design, to process equipment design and servicing procedures.

- *Procurement.* Activities involved in the purchase of inputs used throughout the entity's value chain, including both primary and support activities. Typically, procurement is spread throughout the entity, which tends to obscure its overall magnitude and may negatively affect internal controls over many purchases.

Different Entities Have Different Value Chains

The way an agency defines the components of its value chain will vary according to its mission. For example, the Department of Education may define the value chain of its Direct Loan Operation in terms of loan origination and the subsequent servicing of the loan or, alternatively, packaging and sale of loan pools on the secondary market. Its definitions of *inputs, operations, outputs,* and *service* will reflect that definition of the value chain. Additionally, the relative importance of each primary activity will depend on the agency's mission. For an entity such as the Defense Logistics Agency, the acquisition, storage, and distribution of inventory will be significant. For the Department of Agriculture's National Finance Center, the marketing and post-sale support of its products and services may be the more significant activity. Some entities may have related, yet different missions. For example, the Department of Health and Human Services (DHHS) encompasses, among others, the Food and Drug Administration, which performs a quality control function; the National Institutes of Health, a research organization; the Centers for Disease Control and Prevention, which combines medical/health-related research with activities designed to prevent diseases and promote the adoption of healthy habits not only in the United States but also worldwide; and the CMS, which provides/subsidizes medical services and products delivered to eligible beneficiaries. Although all these activities are health related, a relevant and thorough evaluation of DHHS must include the identification of control activities based on a separate value-chain analysis for each of these agencies.

Understanding an entity's value chain will help identify the significant business activities for which activity-level controls should be assessed. This value-chain analysis is *not* a replacement for the traditional financial statement approach to identifying the significant activities of an entity that must be controlled or for analyzing those controls; rather, this book treats the value-chain analysis as a *supplement* to these more traditional approaches. Chapter 4 provides guidance on identifying significant controls using a blended approach that includes consideration of an entity's financial statements and its value chain.

CONTROLS OVER INFORMATION TECHNOLOGY SYSTEMS

COSO Guidance

COSO describes a framework for considering IT-related controls that groups these controls into two types: general computer controls and application-specific controls.

- *General controls* include controls over:
    - Data center operations (e.g., job scheduling, backup, and recovery procedures)
    - Systems software controls (e.g., the acquisition and implementation of operating systems)
    - Access security
    - Application system development and maintenance controls (e.g., the acquisition and implementation of individual computer software applications)
- *Application controls* are designed to control data processing and help ensure the completeness and accuracy of transaction processing, authorization, and validity. Application controls also encompass the way different applications interface with each other and exchange data.

The COSO report does not mandate this approach for assessing the effectiveness of internal controls but states that this is one set of groupings of IT-related control activities that can be used.

The COBIT Framework

Since the release of the COSO *Framework,* the ISACA has developed its Control Objectives for Information Technology (COBIT) framework, which provides a generally applicable and accepted standard for IT security and control practices. Among IT audit professionals, COBIT is extensively accepted.

The COBIT framework is similar to that of COSO in that it puts controls within the context of an entity's need to achieve certain business or mission objectives and the risks it faces toward achievement. Within that context, the overall goal of an entity's IT-related control structure is to:

- Ensure the delivery of *information* to the business that addresses the required information criteria.

  This goal is enabled by:

- Creating and maintaining a system of process and control excellence that considers all IT resources.

In defining the goals of IT governance and control, COBIT uses a rather broad brush and does not limit itself to the financial reporting process. COBIT describes the following high-level goals for IT governance:

- IT is aligned with the business/mission, enables the business/mission, and maximizes the benefits to the entity.
- IT resources are used responsibly.
- IT-related risks are managed appropriately.

For our purposes, which relate only to the reliability of financial reporting, only the third COBIT objective, the management of IT-related risks, will be considered.

Information Needs. COBIT emphasizes the "information" portion of "information technology." Given that management needs information in order to achieve the entity's stated objectives, COBIT asks, "what are the necessary qualities of that information to enable that process?" For example, the information that management uses to make decisions must be accurate.

The following summarizes all of the information qualities identified in COBIT. These qualities are then divided into "primary" qualities, which have a direct effect on the reliability of financial information, and "secondary" qualities, which do not affect the financial statements directly but which relate to the purely operational aspects of the business.

Primary Qualities: Direct Effect on the Reliability of Financial Reporting

- *Integrity* relates to the *accuracy* and *completeness* of information, as well as to whether transactions are valid and authorized.
- *Availability* relates to the information's *being available when required by the business* now and in the future. It also concerns the *safeguarding* of necessary resources and associated capabilities.

- *Compliance* deals with *complying with externally imposed business requirements,* such as the preparation of financial statements, tax returns, regulatory requirements, and the like. Compliance relates to the provision of appropriate information for management to exercise its financial and compliance reporting responsibilities.

Secondary Qualities: No Direct Impact on Financial Reporting

- *Effectiveness* deals with information being relevant and pertinent to the business processes, as well as being delivered in a *timely, correct, consistent,* and *usable* manner.
- *Efficiency* concerns the provision of information through the optimal use of resources.
- *Confidentiality* concerns the protection of sensitive information from unauthorized disclosure.

For the purposes of assessing the effectiveness of internal control over financial reporting, consideration of IT-related controls is generally limited only to those that have a direct effect on the reliability of financial reporting. However, one should also be aware of OMB requirements in connection with internal controls designed to promote compliance with laws and regulations (particularly in the area of confidentiality). Finally, in the review of controls, one should also be cognizant of the agency's duty to prevent waste and abuse and be aware of deficiencies in the areas of effectiveness and efficiency.

IT Processes.   COBIT describes a framework whereby IT processes manage IT resources to produce information that has the qualities necessary to manage the business. Within this overall framework, COBIT groups the IT processes into four categories, each of which is critical in delivering information that meets the stated criteria. Exhibit 2.6 summarizes the four main process categories and the key processes within each category.

Note that the delivery and support category of processes is analogous to the COSO category of application controls. The other categories identified by COBIT approximate the general controls described by COSO but are somewhat broader in scope.

You will consider IT-related controls at all stages of the assessment process, from planning to the identification, documentation, and testing of significant controls. At each stage, your work should address each of the four categories of IT processes summarized here.

Recent Developments

In November 2003, the Information Technology Governance Institute (ITGI), in conjunction with ISACA, published *IT Control Objectives for Sarbanes-Oxley.* This publication is intended to help IT professionals understand management's required reporting on the effectiveness of internal control and to plan and perform procedures to help management comply with these requirements. The document also provides

Exhibit 2.6   COBIT IT Processes

Category	Description	Key Processes
Planning and Organization	These processes cover strategy and tactics and concern the identification of the way IT can best contribute to the achievement of stated business objectives, both now and in the future.	• Define a strategic plan • Define the information architecture • Define the IT organization and relationships • Communicate management aims and direction • Manage human resources • Ensure compliance with external requirements • Assess risks • Manage quality
Acquisition and Implementation	To realize the IT strategy, IT solutions need to be identified, developed or acquired, as well as implemented and integrated into business processes.	• Acquire and maintain application software • Acquire and maintain technology infrastructure • Develop and maintain procedures • Install and accredit systems • Manage changes
Delivery and Support	These processes include the actual processing of data by application systems.	• Define and manage service levels • Manage third-party service levels • Manage performance and capacity • Ensure continuous service • Ensure systems security • Educate and train users • Manage the configuration • Manage problems and incidents • Manage data • Manage facilities • Manage operations
Monitoring	All IT processes need to be regularly assessed over time for their quality and compliance with control requirements.	• Monitor the processes • Assess internal control adequacy • Obtain independent assurance

an important bridge between the control components described in the COBIT framework and those described by COSO.

The document can also be used by management or those who assist management in the evaluation process as a means for understanding the overall objectives and general procedures for an IT review of internal control over financial reporting. The document can be downloaded from the ITGI website at www.itgi.org or the ISACA website at www.isaca.org.

DISCLOSURE CONTROLS AND PROCEDURES

This section provides guidance on how to assess and report on the effectiveness of an entity's disclosure controls and procedures.

The Relationship of Disclosure Controls and Internal Controls over Financial Reporting

As described in Chapter 1, *disclosure controls* are broadly defined to include "controls and procedures designed to ensure that information required to be disclosed by the agency and included in the annual Federal Managers' Financial Integrity Act of 1982 (FMFIA) assurance statement (and reported in the agency's PAR) is recorded, processed, summarized, and reported within the time period specified by OMB." Thus, disclosure controls and procedures cover *all* information required to be reported. Internal controls over financial reporting constitute a *subset* of disclosure controls and procedures that covers only the preparation of the financial statements and disclosures required under generally accepted accounting principles. Exhibit 2.7 summarizes this relationship between disclosure controls and internal controls over financial reporting.

With respect to any information required to be disclosed, management should first determine whether the information is included in the consideration of internal controls. If it is, then the evaluation of the entity's internal controls will satisfy the requirement to assess disclosure controls. If the required disclosure information is *not* included within internal controls, then a separate disclosure control should be designed and implemented. It is this group of separate controls that we will refer to as *disclosure controls* going forward.

Disclosure Control Considerations

The objective of disclosure controls is to provide reasonable assurance that all material required disclosure information is captured, evaluated, and, if necessary, reported. There is no equivalent of a COSO *Framework* for establishing control criteria for systems of disclosure controls. However, revised OMB Circular A-123 clearly addresses disclosure controls, and Appendix A of the Circular provides guidance on a process to be followed to ensure that all material information required is captured. Although a revised Circular is in effect and the Chief Financial Officers Council

Exhibit 2.7   Relationship between Disclosure Controls and Internal Controls over Financial Reporting

has issued an implementation guide in "final form," it is anticipated that this guidance (including further revisions to OMB Circular A-123) will likely continue to be expanded or modified, particularly following the close of fiscal year 2006.

Appendix A highlights certain aspects of the assessment that should be considered when evaluating the effectiveness of the disclosure process followed by an agency.

- *Role of the Senior Management Council.* At many federal agencies, a Senior Management Council has been created to assess and monitor deficiencies in internal control. As noted in OMB Circular A-123, members of the Council typically include the Chief Financial Officer (CFO), the Senior Procurement Executive, and the Chief Information Officer (CIO), as well as managers of other functional areas. Many believe that, in addition, the council should also include senior management level personnel involved in the execution of the agency's mission and programs. The inclusion of "line managers" would clearly send the message that the responsibility for internal controls rests on the entire management team, not just on selected staff such as the CFO or CIO.

- *Role of the Senior Assessment Team.* OMB Circular A-123 Appendix A provides for the creation of a Senior Assessment Team responsible for the execution of the assessment. Again, the composition of the team is essential to ensuring that proper disclosure controls are in place. The guidance states that this team should be considered a subset of the Senior Management Council and should include senior executives to emphasize management's commitment to the effort. According to the guidance, the Senior Assessment Team should provide oversight to the assessment process, and the following responsibilities are identified as key:

  o Ensuring that assessment objectives are clearly communicated throughout the agency

  o Ensuring that the assessment is carried out in a thorough, effective, and timely manner

- o Identifying and ensuring that adequate funding and resources are made available
- o Identifying staff and/or securing contractors to perform the assessment
- o Determining the scope of the assessment, i.e., those financial reports covered by the assessment
- o Determining the assessment design and methodology

- *Documentation.* It is important that the assessment team fully document its understanding of internal control over financial reporting. The documentation should be as extensive as warranted by the complexity of the agency's internal controls. In addition, the Senior Assessment Team is responsible for documenting:
  - o The establishment of the Senior Assessment Team, its authority, and members
  - o Contracting actions, if contractors are used to perform or assist in the assessment
  - o Communications with agency management and employees regarding the assessment
  - o Key decisions made by the Senior Assessment Team
  - o Assessment methodology and guide
  - o Assessment of internal control at the entity-level
  - o Assessment of internal control at the process, transaction, or application-level
  - o Testing of controls and related results
  - o Identified deficiencies and suggestions for improvement

- *Quantitative information.* Quantitative information includes both *internally* and *externally* generated information. The entity's disclosure controls should include methods for gathering both types of information reliably and in a timely manner. More time may be required to gather external information than internal information.

- *Qualitative information.* The reliable identification and capture of qualitative information is usually more difficult than the identification and capture of quantitative information. In many respects, the guidance developed by the OMB is similar to that developed by the Securities and Exchange Committee (SEC) for registrants subject to Sarbanes-Oxley. Accordingly, it may be wise to consider the following SEC requirement in the evaluation of agency disclosure controls and procedures. The SEC states that, by definition, disclosure controls should capture "information that is relevant to an assessment of the need to disclose *developments and risk* that pertain to the issuer's business [or in the case of federal agencies, the 'agency's mission']." For example, in the case of an agency issuing grants to eligible grantees, it is not enough to ensure that proper "gatekeeping controls" are in place to ensure eligibility of grantee and appropriateness of grant disbursements. Controls must also be in place to gauge the grantee's performance and ensure that the grantee is in fact furthering the agency's mission.

These types of broad disclosure requirements rely primarily on management's unique insights into the agency's mission and not necessarily from a reading of the financial statements. Thus, it is difficult, if not impossible, to identify this information in advance and to design controls and procedures that ensure its capture and evaluation. Instead, an entity's disclosure "control" may consist of:

- o Identifying those individuals in the entity most likely to spot and assess trends and developments that may require disclosure

- o Making inquiries of these individuals by those with the requisite knowledge of OMB requirements

- *Monitoring internal control effectiveness.* Management is required to disclose material weaknesses and evaluate changes in the entity's internal control; therefore it is important that the Senior Management Council and/or the Senior Assessment Team assume some responsibility for monitoring the continued effectiveness of internal control. In addition, they should be responsible for identifying material weaknesses and changes to internal control.

Notes

1. In 2003, COSO published a draft of a document entitled Enterprise Risk Management Framework, whose purpose was to provide guidance on the process used by management to identify and manage risk across the enterprise. This new framework does not supersede or otherwise amend its earlier internal control framework. Internal control is encompassed within and an integral part of enterprise risk management. Enterprise risk management is broader than internal control, expanding and elaborating on internal control to form a more robust conceptualization focusing more fully on risk. Internal Control—Integrated Framework remains in place for entities and others looking at internal control by itself.
2. SAS No. 55, Internal Control in a Financial Statement Audit.
3. AICPA, AU319.47–53, in *Professional Standards,* Vol. 1 (AICPA).

Chapter 3

Internal Control Assessment: Project Planning

Chapter Summary

- Assess information needs and identify sources of information required to perform a good assessment of internal control effectiveness.
- Determine the overall scope of the project
- Establish the terms of the working relationship, both within the Project Team and between the Project Team and other agency management
- Coordinate the project with the Office of the Inspector General (OIG) and the independent auditors.

THE OBJECTIVE OF PLANNING

There are two main objectives for project planning:

1. *Prepare for key decisions.* During the assessment, important judgments must be made regarding:

   o The focus of the work (e.g., financial statements covered and locations to be included)

   o The types of procedures to be performed

   o The scope of the project

   During the planning phase of the project, information will be gathered to help in making broad, preliminary judgments on the above matters. The knowledge gained from gathering this information will then serve as the background necessary to make informed decisions as the assessment proceeds.

2. *Organize the project team.* Work will need to be performed as effectively and efficiently as possible. To accomplish this, a project team will have to be created that has the required skills, knowledge, and experience to achieve assessment objectives. The work of each team member will also need to be defined and coordinated with other members.

Team composition at the agency level was discussed in Chapter 2. The concepts discussed in this chapter apply regardless of whether the assessment is carried out by agency management or by a contractor hired by the agency.

Planning is an iterative process. The two objectives listed above are *not* performed once at the beginning of the assessment and then remain static. They are rather revisited continuously throughout the project as more information becomes available and the required decisions become more specific and narrowly focused.

INFORMATION GATHERING FOR DECISION MAKING

Several key questions will arise during the assessment that will have to be considered early on in order to gather the necessary information. Broadly, these key questions are:

- Which control objectives are most significant to the entity's overall internal control structure?
- What areas should receive the most attention?
- What is a "significant deficiency" or "material weakness" in internal control?
- What is the overall scope of the project, and what work has already been performed to achieve the assessment objectives?

Significant Control Objectives

As described in Chapter 2, the Committee of Sponsoring Organizations of the Treadway Commission (COSO) *Framework* acknowledges that, within the context of internal control taken as a whole, some controls are more significant than others. For example, one entity may have a highly centralized decision-making and control structure in which management involvement, supervision, and review are more important than many of the individual control procedures performed by entity personnel. In contrast, another entity may have a more decentralized structure whereby senior management relies on others in the entity to make decisions and control certain aspects of the entity's business or mission. In such a situation, the hiring and training of entity personnel and the effective communication of the entity's business/mission and control objectives become much more significant than they would when senior management maintains central control.

As indicated in Chapter 1, one of the first objectives of the project should be to identify significant control objectives. To prepare for that decision, one should consider obtaining an understanding of the following:

- *Key business activities.* Chapter 2 provides a discussion of the value chain as a means to identify an entity's most significant business processes/activities. Typically, significant controls are those related to the value-chain activities that are most critical to the entity's overall success.
- *Mission characteristics.* The entity's business activities can often be understood more completely when considered in the context of the overall mission. A consideration of mission characteristics and the metrics used to gauge performance (both financial and nonfinancial) can help in determining those business activities or reporting processes that require significant control or oversight.

- *Significant risks.* As described in Chapter 2, internal control should be considered within the context of an entity's overall risk management strategy. Significant control objectives are those that help the entity manage its most significant financial reporting risks.

- *Financial reporting considerations.* A primary objective of the assessment is to assess internal control over financial reporting. To assess significant controls, one should have a good understanding of the entity's:
    - Significant financial statement accounts, balances, and classes of transactions
    - Financial reporting processes
    - Critical accounting policies

- *Significant controls.* Office of Management and Budget (OMB) Circular A-123 and implementation guidance emphasize the need for identifying and testing significant or key controls. The Public Company Accounting Oversight Board (PCAOB) is more specific in its discussion of significant controls that should be tested. PCAOB *Auditing Standard No. 2, An Audit of Internal Control over Financial Reporting Performed in Conjunction with an Audit of Financial Statements*, requires independent auditors to evaluate the effectiveness of management's process for evaluating internal control. As part of that evaluation, paragraph 40 of the standard identifies types of controls that should be tested, such as:
    - Controls over initiating, authorizing, recording, processing, and reporting significant accounts and disclosures and related assertions embodied in the financial statements
    - Controls over the selection and application of accounting policies that are in conformity with generally accepted accounting principles
    - Anti-fraud programs and controls
    - Controls, including information technology general controls, on which other controls are dependent
    - Controls over significant, nonroutine, and nonsystematic transactions, such as accounts involving judgments and estimates
    - Company level controls, including:
        - The control environment
        - Controls over the period-end financial reporting process, including controls over procedures used to enter transaction totals into the general ledger; to initiate, authorize, record, and process journal entries in the general ledger; and to record recurring and nonrecurring adjustments to the financial statements (for example, consolidating adjustments, report combinations, and reclassifications)
    - Evaluating the likelihood that failure of the control could result in a misstatement, the magnitude of such a misstatement, and the degree to which other controls, if effective, achieve the same control objectives

- ○ Determining the locations or business units to include in the evaluation for a company with multiple locations or business units
- ○ Evaluating the design effectiveness of controls
- ○ Evaluating the operating effectiveness of controls based on procedures sufficient to assess their operating effectiveness. Examples of such procedures include testing of the controls by internal audit, testing of controls by others under the direction of management, using a service organization's reports, inspection of evidence of the application of controls, or testing by means of a self-assessment process, some of which might occur as part of management's ongoing monitoring activities. Inquiry alone is not adequate to complete this evaluation. To evaluate the effectiveness of the company's internal control over financial reporting, management must have evaluated controls over all relevant assertions related to all significant accounts and disclosures
- ○ Determining the deficiencies in internal control over financial reporting that are of such a magnitude and likelihood of occurrence that they constitute significant deficiencies or material weaknesses
- ○ Communicating findings to the auditor and to others, if applicable
- ○ Evaluating whether findings are reasonable and support management's assessment

Areas of Focus

Like any other project, the focus should be on those areas that are most critical for achieving assessment objectives. As a starting point, one should plan on addressing those control objectives deemed to be significant. In addition, the following matters should be considered:

- Areas of known or suspected control weakness, for example, those that may have been communicated to management by oversight organizations (e.g., the Government Accountability Office [GAO], the Office of Inspector General [OIG]) or the independent auditors as part of their audit of the entity's financial statements.
- Financial statement accounts with a high inherent risk for material misstatement. The term *inherent risk* is defined in auditing literature as the risk of material misstatement in an account irrespective of any internal controls. Many factors can affect inherent risk. For example, account balances that require complex calculations, significant judgment, or estimation usually have a higher inherent risk than other accounts.

Defining Internal Control Deficiencies

There is a presumption that the design and performance of the assessment project will be sufficient to enable the detection of significant deficiencies and material weaknesses in internal control.[1] In order to plan the project, particularly its scope, it is necessary to establish a preliminary understanding of the types and magnitude of internal control weaknesses that will rise to the level of "significant deficiency" or "material weakness." To the extent possible, the assessment team, other agency management, the independent auditors, and possibly the entity's legal counsel should reach a consensus on this preliminary understanding of internal control weaknesses.

Chapter 8 provides detailed guidance on the factors to consider when assessing internal control deficiencies. In general, those factors include:

- The *likelihood* that the internal control deficiency could result in a misstatement of the financial statements. For example, suppose that an entity has both a prevent control and a detect control designed to achieve the same control objective. A deficiency in the prevent control may not result in a misstatement if the detect control is operating effectively. However, absent an effective detect control, a deficiency in the prevent control would be much more likely to result in a misstatement.

- Whether such a misstatement, if it were to occur, would be *material*. In developing a working definition of materiality, one should consider that:
  ○ The auditing and accounting literature, as well as the relevant legal standards, describe materiality *from the user's point of view*. That is, materiality is described as the magnitude of an error or omission that would affect a *user's* decision about the entity.
  ○ Financial statement materiality includes both quantitative *and qualitative* factors.[2]
  ○ Disclosure controls and procedures pertain to both financial and nonfinancial information. Determining materiality related to the disclosure of nonfinancial information will involve a great deal of judgment and may require the input of the entity's legal counsel.

Preliminary judgments about the nature and magnitude of errors that will be considered significant deficiencies or material weaknesses will be greatly influenced by the determination of which controls are considered significant. For example, a weakness in the design or operating effectiveness of a significant control is more likely to be considered a "significant deficiency" than a comparable weakness in a control not considered significant.

PCAOB's *Auditing Standard No. 2* provides definitions for the key terms "control deficiency," "significant deficiency," and "material weakness." OMB Circular A-123, in turn, has generally adopted these definitions. The definitions pursuant to OMB Circular A-123 and applicable reporting requirements are summarized in Exhibit 3.1, which is taken from OMB Circular A-123, *Management's Responsibility for Internal Control.*

These matters are discussed in detail in Chapter 8 and are incorporated into the guidance provided in this and subsequent chapters. When conducting an independent evaluation and assessment of internal controls, procedures should consider obtaining

Exhibit 3.1 OMB Circular A-123 Internal Control Related Definitions and Reporting Requirements

	Definition[a]	Reporting
Control Deficiency (FMFIA Section 2 and internal control over financial reporting)	Control deficiencies exist when the design or operation of a control does not allow management or employees, in the normal course of performing their assigned functions, to prevent or detect misstatements on a timely basis. A design deficiency exists when a control necessary to meet the control objective is missing or an existing control is not properly designed, so that even if the control operates as designed the control objective is not always met. An operation deficiency exists when a properly designed control does not operate as designed or when the person performing the control is not qualified or properly skilled to perform the control effectively.	Internal to the organization and not reported externally. Progress against corrective action plans should be periodically assessed and reported to agency management.
Reportable Condition (FMFIA Section 2 and internal control over financial reporting)	*FMFIA overall* — A control deficiency, or combination of control deficiencies, that in management's judgment, should be communicated because they represent significant weaknesses in the design or operation of internal control that could adversely affect the organization's ability to meet its internal control objectives.	Internal to the organization and not reported externally. Progress against corrective action plans should be periodically assessed and reported to agency management.
	Financial reporting — A control deficiency, or combination of control deficiencies, that adversely affects the entity's ability to initiate, authorize, record, process, or report external financial data reliably in accordance with generally accepted accounting principles such that there is more than a remote[b] likelihood that a misstatement of the entity's financial statements, or other significant financial reports, that is more than inconsequential will not be prevented or detected.	
Material Weakness (FMFIA Section 2 and internal control over financial reporting)	*FMFIA overall* — Reportable conditions in which the agency head determines to be significant enough to report outside of the agency.	Material weaknesses and a summary of corrective actions shall be reported to OMB and Congress through the PAR (Management Report for Government Corporations). Progress against
	Financial reporting — Reportable condition, or combination of reportable conditions, that results in more than a remote[b] likelihood that a material misstatement of the financial statements, or other significant financial reports, will not be prevented or detected.	

(continues)

Exhibit 3.1 OMB Circular A-123 Internal Control Related Definitions and Reporting Requirements *(Continued)*

	Definition[a]	Reporting
		corrective action plans should be periodically assessed and reported to agency management.
Non-conformance (FMFIA Section 4)	Instances in which financial management systems do not substantially conform to financial systems requirements. Financial management systems include both financial and financially-related (or mixed) systems.	Non-conformances and a summary of corrective actions to bring systems into conformance shall be reported to OMB and Congress through the PAR (Management Report for Government Corporations). Progress against corrective action plans should be periodically assessed and reported to agency management.

Notes

(a) The definition of control deficiency and definitions of reportable condition and material weakness relative to financial reporting are based upon the definitions provided in *Auditing Standard No. 2—An Audit of Internal Control Over Financial Reporting Performed in Conjunction with an Audit of Financial Statements* issued by the Public Entity Accounting Oversight Board (PCAOB).

(b) The term "remote" is defined in SFFAS No. 5, *Accounting for Liabilities of the Federal Government*, as the chance of the future event, or events occurring is slight.

Source: Office of Management and Budget, revised Circular A-123, *Management's Responsibility for Internal Control.*

information relating to the following matters during the planning phase of the project:

- Any material weaknesses identified by the entity or its independent auditors during the most recent audit of the entity's financial statements
- Any significant deficiencies that have been communicated to management and (when applicable) the audit committee that remain uncorrected after a reasonable period
- Any restatement of previously issued financial statements to reflect the correction of a misstatement
- The nature of any material weaknesses reported by component agencies of the same cabinet level department or other federal agencies with similar missions/ responsibilities
- Metrics or performance indicators used to evaluate agency performance
- Financial statement materiality, both the quantitative and qualitative aspects
- The existence of any fraud on the part of senior management
- The nature and overall impact of oversight activities affecting the agency

Project Scope and Existing Efforts to Assess Internal Control Effectiveness

As an overall strategy for conducting the assessment is developed, the overall breadth and depth of the project will need to be considered. Both the *Implementation Guide for OMB Circular A-123 Appendix A: Internal Control over Financial Reporting* (Implementation Guide) and PCAOB *Auditing Standard No. 2* provide relevant guidance in this area. Significant factors to consider include:

- Operations in multiple locations
- Internal controls that reside at third parties, such as service organizations
- Recent OIG or other oversight organizations' audits/projects
- Work performed by the disclosure committee and others

Multiple Locations.   When an entity has multiple locations, it is important to determine which of those locations or business units will be included in the scope of the assessment. To make this determination, the following factors should be considered:

- *Relative significance.* To assess the relative significance of the location or agency component, the following should be considered:
  - *Financial significance.* From a financial perspective, it is necessary to consider the locations/components that contribute significantly to material transactions, balances, or classes of transactions. For example, a location/ component that is responsible for a significant portion of the agency's total appropriations or spending authority is more likely to be included in the

scope of the assessment than one that is inactive or is allocated a minor portion of available funds.

- *Operational significance.* A location/component may not be significant from a financial perspective, but may be significant operationally. For example, an entity may have a separate unit responsible for developing and maintaining the technology infrastructure that supports its e-commerce activities. Financially, this business unit may require a small investment in terms of expenditures and assets. However, if the entity's e-commerce activities are significant, then that unit exposes the entity to certain risks, which should be considered when planning the assessment.

- *Risk exposure.* A location or business unit may seem relatively insignificant in terms of assets, expenditures, or other financial statement measures; however, that location may expose the agency to specific significant risks. For example, a specific agency program may require minimum budgetary resources, but is highly visible as a result of presidential initiatives or congressional concerns. Small programs/initiatives that have the potential to expose the agency to additional risk or significant political embarrassment should be considered within the scope of the assessment.

- *Aggregation of several locations or business units.* One should consider whether certain locations, although individually not considered significant, would be considered significant when combined.

- *The entity's approach to controlling its various locations or component units.* The way the entity establishes control over its multiple locations or units will influence the assessment strategy and approach. For example, suppose that Agency A maintains highly centralized processes and financial reporting applications, and the various locations share a common methodology for reporting and controlling activities. Agency B has relatively decentralized processes and, because of mission diversity, component units operate rather autonomously and no two financial reporting systems are alike. For Agency A, one may decide to test the centralized processes and controls together with the common processes at just one or two locations. For Agency B, which lacks common procedures for its component units, it may be more appropriate to expand the scope of the assessment to include the evaluation of controls at more locations and/or units. Other factors one may wish to consider include:

  - Whether the location or business unit could create an obligation on the part of the entity

  - The entity's risk assessment processes

  - The entity's policies and procedures for monitoring the activities of separate locations or component units

  - The effectiveness of other entity-level controls

PCAOB *Auditing Standard* No.2, particularly Appendix B, provides detailed guidance for independent auditors to follow in deciding which locations or units to test. Although the standard's requirements specifically address the auditor's responsibility, it is important to note how closely the audit responsibilities parallel the scope of the self-assessment project, as required by OMB Circular A-123.

- *Specific risks.* Some locations or component units may present specific, significant risks to the entity. The auditor will audit the controls related to these specific risks.
- *Aggregation of locations or business units.* The auditor is required to consider which remaining locations (that is, those that are not individually important or do not pose certain specific significant risks), when aggregated, represent a group with a level of significance that could create a material misstatement. For that group, the auditor will evaluate the effectiveness of entity-level controls. Ineffective entity-level controls will result in the auditor testing controls at some of the locations or component units.
- *No work required.* No work is required on locations or component units that are not able to create, either individually or in the aggregate, a material misstatement.

Service Organizations.   An entity may engage a third-party service organization to perform certain aspects of its information processing. These service organizations, which often consist of federal agencies performing services on behalf of other agencies (i.e., "Centers of Excellence"), may provide a wide variety of services ranging from performing a specific task under the direction of the entity, to replacing entire business processes or functions. The types of services such an organization may provide include:

- *Information processing.* Information processing is a common type of service organization. An information processing service organization may provide standardized services, such as entering the company's manually recorded data and processing it with software that produces computer-generated journals, a general ledger, and financial statements. At the other end of the spectrum, the information processing service organization may design and execute customized applications.
- *Payroll.* Service organizations such as the National Finance Center (NFC) and the National Business Center (NBC) provide a wide range of payroll related services, including periodic payroll disbursements, computation of withholdings, and employee leave recordkeeping.

When an entity uses a service organization to process transactions, the controls over that process reside *outside the entity,* at the service organization. When developing an assessment strategy under these conditions, it is necessary to determine whether the scope of the assessment should be restricted to those controls that remain directly administered by the entity or extended to include the controls at the service organization. In making that determination, the following should be considered:

- Significance of the processing activity
- Degree of interaction between the entity and the service organization

When assessing the significance of the processing activity, one may treat the service organization as if it were a separate business unit or location and follow the guidance discussed previously. For example, one would consider the materiality of the transactions processed relative to the financial statements taken as a whole. In addition, consideration would include whether the nonfinancial or operational information processed by the service organization is significant to the entity and should be subject to disclosure controls and procedures.

Service organizations are addressed in the OMB Circular A-123 implementation guidance. The *degree of interaction* between the entity and the service organization is a term used in Statement on Auditing Standards (SAS) No. 70 (as amended), *Reports on the Processing of Transactions by Service Organizations*. The term refers to the extent to which the entity (the "user organization") is able and elects to implement effective controls over the processing performed by the service organization.

- If the services provided by the service organization are limited to recording user organization transactions and processing related data, and the user organization retains responsibility for authorizing the transactions and maintaining the related accountability, there will be a high degree of interaction. When there is a high degree of interaction between the user and service organizations, then there is a greater likelihood of being able to obtain the information necessary to evaluate internal control by focusing solely on the controls maintained by the user.

- Alternatively, when the service organization is authorized to initiate and execute transactions without prior authorization of each transaction by the user, there will be a lower degree of interaction. Under these arrangements, the user must record activity from information provided by the service organization because the user has no means of independently generating a record of its transactions. In these situations, one would be more likely to *extend* the scope of the assessment to include an assessment of the service organization's controls.

It is not uncommon for the service organization to take action to help its customers gain a better understanding of the design and operating effectiveness of its controls. For example, the service organization might:

- Engage its own auditor to review and report on the systems it uses to process the agency's transactions.

- Engage a service auditor to test the effectiveness of the controls applied to the agency's transactions to enable the company to evaluate controls at the service location as part of management's assessment of its internal control.

In either case, the service organization will produce a report describing the work of the service auditor and his/her findings. That report should be useful when planning the project.

When considering the implications of an outside service organization on the assessment, the guidance contained in SAS No. 70 and the related Audit Guide may be helpful.

Oversight Agency Activities. A fundamental objective of oversight audit activities is to help the entity maintain effective controls by evaluating their adequacy and effectiveness.

Standards established by the Institute of Internal Auditors state that this evaluation should include the:

- Reliability and integrity of financial and operational information
- Effectiveness and efficiency of operations
- Safeguarding of assets
- Compliance with laws, regulations, and contracts

Oversight activities executed by the OIG and, when applicable the GAO, meet and usually exceed the above objectives. In planning the scope of the project, it may be wise to incorporate some of the conclusions reached by the oversight agencies into the findings about the effectiveness of the entity's internal control. However, it is important to remember that the assessments performed by the oversight agencies may not have been performed primarily for the purpose of reporting on internal control within the context of OMB Circular A-123 or the Sarbanes-Oxley Act, Section 404. Therefore, when determining how oversight agency assessments and conclusions affect the scope of an assessment, the following should be considered:

- The scope of the oversight agency's assessments and whether it is sufficient to meet the objectives of the project. For example, the assessment may have evaluated internal controls for only a limited number of component units, excluding one or more of those considered significant. In such a case, it would be wise to include an evaluation of the other significant business units in the scope of the project.

- The timing of the work and whether it is within a timeframe that would permit conclusions being drawn regarding the effectiveness of the entity's internal control as of June 30 of the current fiscal year (or September 30 if an internal control opinion is to be issued by the independent auditors). If a significant amount of time has elapsed since the assessment was executed, additional testing may need to be performed.

- Regarding oversight agencies, it is important to note that PCAOB *Auditing Standard No. 2* states that in the private sector, management and/or the assessment team cannot rely on the work performed by the independent auditor in connection with audit procedures designed to enable the independent auditor to issue his/her opinion on internal controls. In the federal government, although independent certified public accounting firms usually execute the financial statement audits, they do so under the supervision of the OIG. The OIG, in turn, is ultimately accountable for the audit results and related opinion. In addition, for selected agencies, the GAO is responsible for the direct execution of the audit. Under these circumstances, it is not clear whether the assessment team can rely on some of the work performed by the oversight agency (particularly if an opinion on internal controls is being issued) and no specific guidance is available on the subject. The assessment team should reach an agreement with the OIG and, when applicable, the independent auditors and GAO, regarding this matter prior to placing reliance on oversight agency audits. This issue does not mean that the assessment team will ignore oversight agency findings that are relevant to its assessment of internal controls.

Senior Management Council and Disclosure Committee. Both the OMB and the PCAOB provide for the creation of a committee of high-level managers (Senior Management Council and Disclosure Committee, respectively) that is responsible for overseeing the process by which internal controls are reviewed and reported by management. When planning the assessment, one should consider the policies and processes of these management bodies and the extent to which their work product can be used to support the entity's evaluation of its internal control. Policies and processes of the Senior Management Council and/or the Disclosure Committee that may affect the planning of the project include:

- Areas of the entity's business that should be monitored for disclosure issues
- Individuals within each monitored area who are best able to identify potential disclosure issues
- Methods for communicating identified disclosure issues to the council or committee
- If applicable, the impact of any significant changes to the entity on the entity's disclosure controls and procedures, for example:
  - New information systems
  - Revisions to agency objectives
  - New and/or terminated programs
  - Geographic expansion
  - Changes in personnel with significant control responsibilities

INFORMATION SOURCES

With few exceptions, because of the public nature of the federal government and the overriding need for departments and agencies to be accountable to the taxpayers, a great deal of information exists about an agency, its finances, composition, mission, goals, and programs. When one is planning the project, it is likely that problems will be encountered relating to having too much, rather than too little, information. For that reason, the information-gathering strategy should focus on selectivity.

The scope of and need for data gathering largely depends on the composition of the assessment team (e.g., in-house management or contractor personnel). The approach discussed in this section assumes limited knowledge of the agency and may not be required in its entirety if an experienced financial management team or a contractor with prior agency experience is conducting the assessment. However, the assessment team is well advised not to trust everything to memory. Most federal agencies are too dynamic to justify minimal data gathering at the outset of the assessment effort.

Chances are that most of the information needed to plan an assessment can be provided by just a few sources. An important and readily available source of information on a federal agency is its annual Performance and Accountability Report (PAR). The following is a discussion of the information sources that are most likely to provide the information needed to achieve the planning objectives described earlier in this chapter.

Performance and Accountability Report

All executive-level agencies subject to the Chief Financial Officers Act of 1990 (CFO Act), the Government Management and Reform Act of 1994 (GMRA), and/or the Accountability of Tax Dollars Act are required to be audited annually. Currently, these agencies must submit their PAR no later than November 1 (in draft form) and November 15 (final). The PAR provides a great deal of narrative information about the entity, its mission, goals, programs, and performance measures, in addition to its most recent financial statements. An in-depth reading of the PAR can provide a sound background for understanding key elements of the entity and its mission that affect risk and the design of internal control. An agency's PAR should be considered the primary source of information needed for planning. When reading the entity's PAR, keep in mind that the main objectives are to:

- Learn about the characteristics of the entity and its mission.
- Highlight possible areas of focus.

It is unlikely that one single area or item of disclosure would be sufficient to provide all the information needed for planning. Instead, look for patterns and recurring themes about the agency, its mission, and likely business processes supporting mission execution and, where applicable, the delivery of services. OMB guidance provides that the PAR be presented in three parts. The first of these parts provides an overview of the agency's operations, its mission, and performance highlights. It also includes an assessment (positive or negative) by the department head of the agency's controls and the reliability of the financial and performance information provided. This section is followed by a discussion of agency performance (Part II), including performance indicators, followed by the financial section (Part III). The following is a brief summary of the information contained in the PAR that is typically most valuable to understanding and planning an evaluation of an entity's internal control.

Part I: Management's Discussion and Analysis.   Management's Discussion and Analysis (MD&A) generally provides an overview of the agency. It includes an introductory letter from the department head and is followed by an overview of the PAR. Current OMB guidance requires that this overview address important matters that:

- May lead to significant actions or proposals by top management
- Are significant to the managing, budgeting, and oversight functions of Congress and the administration

- Significantly affect the judgment of citizens about the efficiency and effectiveness of their federal government

In addition, the guidance states that the MD&A (often referred to as Overview) must include the following:

- A brief mission statement and organizational structure or overview
- Highlights of "most important" performance goals and results (positive and negative) for the applicable year, including trend data, where available
- Actions being taken or planned where "most important" goals are not yet being met
- If appropriate, forward-looking information regarding significant demands, risks, uncertainties, events, conditions, and trends
- A brief analysis of financial statements
- A brief description of systems, controls, and legal compliance
- A summary description of Federal Managers' Financial Integrity Act of 1982 (FMFIA) material weaknesses action taken and other significant control non-compliance issues
- Other "most important" information identified by the agency head

A thorough review of the MD&A can provide a sound initial understanding of an agency, major ongoing initiatives, and an initial "feel" for the control environment in which the agency operates.

Part II: Performance Section.   Each federal agency is responsible for developing a strategic plan that outlines its future strategic direction (usually five years). The plan identifies specific strategic goals that generally guide the agency in the execution of its mission.

Goals not only guide mission execution, but just as importantly, assist in the development of quantifiable performance measurements that enable the agency, the President, Congress, and taxpayers to gauge performance. Part II addresses the agency's mission and whether it successfully accomplished these goals.

Considering the size of many federal agencies and the diversity and variety of agency missions, it should be clear that evaluating performance in the federal government is a daunting task. This section, however, can be very illuminating in developing a sound understanding of the agency. For example:

- Whether or not the PAR effectively reports performance is usually a good indication of the agency's internal control environment.
- The section usually describes the major programs the agency is involved in to support the execution of its mission(s) and the achievement of related goals. This information is invaluable in understanding the "business" of the agency and the different activities for which it is responsible.

- The section usually identifies major initiatives that will affect the assessment of internal control.
- Usually, the discussion will provide information on the different locations that may be relevant to the assessment.
- Finally, the section clearly sets forth what management considers important and therefore, the areas on which the assessment team should focus.

This discussion is usually quite informative about the characteristics of the agency and the dynamics of the environment in which operates. It also contains information about the key financial and nonfinancial measures that will generally be used to judge the agency's performance, and this knowledge can help make preliminary determinations about materiality and, in particular, qualitative aspects of materiality. Qualitative materiality judgments are critical for determining which accounts, balances, and classes of transactions are significant, regardless of dollar amounts, and which internal control deficiencies may be considered material weaknesses.

Other information in this section that may provide additional insight into the entity, its stakeholders, its operating environment, or its internal controls includes:

- The extent to which the entity's business is seasonal (e.g., agencies in health maintenance or disease prevention activities will probably be affected by seasonality, with potential increases in workload, which may tax internal controls)
- Areas of potential risk (e.g., property management, credit, and collection risk)
- Information about key stakeholders
- Susceptibility to fraud, waste, and abuse

Part III: Financial Section.   The financial section should include the following:

- A letter from the agency CFO containing the following elements:
  - A brief discussion of audit weaknesses and noncompliance including progress made in correcting such instances and related timetables, as well as potential impediments to remediation
  - Integrity Act information (unless included in the overview)
- Agency financial statements and related auditor's reports
- An Inspector General summary addressing:
  - The most serious management and performance challenges facing the agency
  - A brief assessment of the agency's progress in addressing those challenges

If required, the section may also include agency-specific statutory reports.

This section will disclose significant information affecting the assessment, including:

- Critical accounting policies
- Major accounts and group of accounts

- Estimation processes supporting the development of account balances
- Contingencies including legal proceedings

In addition, this section provides essential information affecting the assessment, such as:

- Whether the auditor was able to issue a "clean" opinion on the financial statements, and in the case of qualified, disclaimed, or adverse opinions, the reasons behind the departure from the standard auditor's report.

- If an opinion on internal controls was forthcoming, whether a clean or qualified opinion on internal controls was issued.

- Whether the auditor issued a formal opinion or disclaimer (because it was not within his/her scope); the auditor's report on internal control will, if applicable, list conditions that in the opinion of the auditor are reportable conditions including material weaknesses.

- The IG's views on significant management issues.

The PAR expresses the views of both the CFO and oversight parties such as the OIG and independent auditors. Although this is not the rule, it is not necessarily uncommon for the PAR to indicate that disagreements (even serious disagreements) exist between financial managers such as the CFO and oversight agencies (usually the OIG, but may include the GAO and the independent auditors). It is important to be aware of these issues to ensure that areas of disagreement are objectively analyzed. It is equally important to try to avoid increasing any friction that may be present. Finally, although there are often very valid reasons for disagreement among the parties above, it is important to note that these disagreements may also be the result of a poor or ineffective internal control environment.

Other Information Sources

In general, the PAR should be the primary source of information about an agency and its operating environment. However, there are other significant sources of information that should not be ignored. A review of other sources can help to confirm the knowledge gained through reading the PAR and possibly update or identify other conditions that were not included in the PAR. Other helpful sources of information include:

- *Annual Budget.* Budgeting is the lifeblood of most agencies because they can only operate within the restrictions imposed by the funds appropriated by Congress and, if applicable, restrictions imposed by Congress on the use of the appropriated funds. Except as dictated by national security or similar considerations, an agency's budget and the related congressional hearings are well documented and available to the public. This is an invaluable source of information because, in addition to providing additional information on available financial resources, an agency's budget provides:

- ○ Information on congressional concerns and areas that Congress considers to be of high importance (and that are thus critical in the determination of qualitative materiality)

- ○ Often a more "frank" discussion on internal controls than that available in the PAR, including existing disagreements (if applicable) between organizations within the agency such as the CFO and OIG

- ○ Additional information on agency programs, performance measures, and congressional evaluation of the agency's performance

- ○ Budgetary actions such as budget cuts and personnel reductions, which may impact the effectiveness of internal controls

- ○ Future agency plans

- ○ The potential state of the agency's internal control environment

- *OIG Reports.* The OIG issues semiannual audit reports on matters and issues affecting the agency. In addition, the OIG regularly reports on the projects and limited audits in which they are involved. These reports are an invaluable source of information on the status of internal controls and other issues of significance to the assessment.

- *GAO Reports.* At a minimum, one should determine whether the GAO has recently issued reports on the agency. Almost without exception, GAO reports will impact the assessment (either because they comment on or identify control weaknesses or because they address areas of concern to Congress).

- *Website.* A wealth of information, particularly pertaining to recent developments, which would not appear in the most recent PAR, can be obtained from an agency's website.

- *Policies and Procedures Manuals and Other Formal Documentation.* Although this type of research would most likely be conducted at a later stage in the assessment, it may be useful to consult these sources whenever clarification is needed regarding some of the information obtained, as discussed above.

- *Agency Personnel.* It goes without saying that making inquiries of key personnel at the initial planning stage of the project is an excellent way to probe deeper into issues identified during the review of the PAR and other written documentation. Also, personnel interviews can confirm one's understanding of information already gathered and help to establish a relationship with individuals from the agency who will be closely involved with the assessment. In addition to senior management, inquiries should also be made of operating and OIG personnel.

Additional Guidance

Appendix 3B provides detailed guidance on the questions that should be considered when one is performing research and gathering the information needed to plan the assessment.

STRUCTURING THE PROJECT TEAM

During the planning phase of the project, the overall responsibilities of the project team and how the team will be configured to achieve its objectives should be described.

Establishing Responsibilities and Lines of Reporting

The project team should have the responsibility for overseeing and coordinating all the activities relating to the evaluation and reporting on the effectiveness of the entity's internal control. As a condition for assuming this responsibility, the team should have the authority to conduct the evaluation in a way that is appropriate given the nature, size, and complexity of the organization. Exhibit 3.2 shows an example of how a project team for evaluating internal control fits into an entity's overall financial reporting structure. As described in Chapter 2, internal controls over financial reporting are a subset of an entity's disclosure controls and procedures. Thus, Exhibit 3.2 describes the internal control evaluation assessment team (possibly a contractor) as reporting to the Senior Assessment Team, which in turn reports to the agency head and the Senior Management Council.

The creation of a Senior Management Council and a Senior Assessment Team is recommended, but not required by, the OMB guidance and the Implementation

Exhibit 3.2   Example Project Team Organization

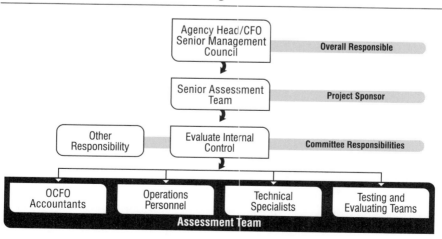

Guide. However the lines of reporting are configured, it is important to ensure that the assessment team reports to one of the senior committees or executives at the entity in order to emphasize that:

- The successful completion of the evaluation is important for the entity.
- Communications and requests from the assessment team should be given a high priority.

Assessment Project Team Members

The project team should be comprised of individuals with the knowledge, skills, and authority within the entity to oversee a successful assessment. Collectively, the group should have a high-level knowledge of the entity's operations and strategies and should also have the authority to make important decisions and obtain and allocate the necessary resources. Exhibit 3.2 describes an example project team consisting of accountants, key operating personnel, technical specialists, and one or more testing and evaluation teams.

OCFO Accountants.   Accountants in the Office of the Chief Financial Officer (OCFO) can be a valuable resource in helping an entity to identify significant accounting cycles and to gather and develop the information necessary to document internal controls.

Operations Personnel.   Operating personnel from the agency's major programs or activities should be involved with the project team. These individuals will contribute an in-depth understanding of the entity's operations, the business/program risks of various activities, and existing controls. Having these individuals on the project team will also help establish important communication channels between the team and entity employees who will be responsible for providing information to the team or implementing its recommendations. The presence of operating personnel sends a clear signal that internal controls are everyone's responsibility, not just that of the chief financial officer.

Technical Specialists.   The project team may need technical expertise in order to meet its objectives successfully. In some agencies it is typical to establish certain quality control groups. For example, agencies issuing a significant amount of grants will have grant specialists and often evaluation committees whose responsibilities include setting grantee qualification criteria and developing aftermath procedures to ensure the proper use of grant funds. Individuals with this type of expertise can be invaluable to project teams seeking to understand an agency's operations and internal control structure.

Given the scope and size of many federal agencies, IT specialists will almost invariably be required to assess controls. An IT specialist is essential for helping the project team to:

- Identify risks related to IT systems.

- Document and test IT controls.

- Design and implement missing IT controls, if any.

- Monitor the continued effectiveness of IT controls.

As described in Chapter 2, the Information Technology Governance Institute (ITGI) and the Information Systems Audit and Control Association (ISACA) have published *IT Control Objectives for Sarbanes-Oxley*, which provides guidance to IT auditors who assist management in the testing and evaluation of internal controls. In addition, the GAO's Federal Information System Controls Audit Manual (FISCAM) provides even more intensive guidance on internal controls and IT auditing.

In addressing the planning of these projects, the authors of *IT Control Objectives for Sarbanes-Oxley* note the following:

> To meet the demands of Sarbanes-Oxley, most organizations will require a change in culture. More likely than not, enhancements to IT systems and processes will be required, most notably in the design, documentation and evaluation of IT controls. Because the cost of noncompliance can be devastating to an organization, it is crucial to adopt a proactive approach and take on the challenge early.[3]

The above observation is equally as relevant to the federal government; however, with the enactment of numerous federal financial management improvement efforts, including the Federal Information Security Management Act (FISMA), it is arguable that this change in culture is already under way at many federal agencies. As a first step toward planning the IT component of the project, the document recommends the following:

- Management and the project leader should obtain an understanding of the risks inherent in IT systems and the effect these risks have on the project.

- IT management should obtain an understanding of the financial reporting process and its supporting systems.

- The chief information officer should have an advanced knowledge of the types of IT controls necessary to support reliable financial information processing.

Testing and Evaluation Teams. Depending on the size and complexity of the entity, the organization/composition of the assessment team, and whether contractors are employed in any capacity, the project team may conduct the testing and evaluation of internal controls itself. Alternatively, the team may act in more of a supervisory capacity and delegate the performance of the procedures to one or more testing and evaluation teams. If the assessment requires the use of multiple project teams, steps should be taken to ensure the consistency and quality of the procedures performed. For example, training (either formal or informal) on the evaluation process and control documentation tools may be required.

COORDINATING WITH THE OFFICE OF THE INSPECTOR GENERAL AND THE INDEPENDENT AUDITORS

Given the role of the OIG in the execution of audits pursuant to the CFO Act and OMB guidance, it is important that the OIG remain independent of the assessment. However, the guidance suggests that the OIG be involved in a consulting capacity throughout the execution of the assessment. The OIG is in an excellent position to assist the project in a consulting capacity by:

- Enhancing the understanding of entity operations, significant risks, and controls
- Providing insight into the relative strengths and weaknesses of each component of internal control
- Providing technical expertise and advice in areas such as IT auditing
- Providing advice on the design or testing of controls

In addition to coordinating with the OIG, coordination with the entity's independent auditors is vital. This coordination process begins with the planning phase of the project and continues with each subsequent phase. Proper coordination between the team and the independent auditors will facilitate an effective and efficient audit. A lack of coordination with the auditors could result in a variety of negative, unforeseen consequences, including:

- Duplication of effort
- Unnecessary expansion of the assessment scope, including the performance of additional tests that are not warranted by the circumstances
- Misunderstandings relating to the definition or reporting of material weaknesses
- Lack of agreement on what constitutes an effective assessment of internal controls when the auditors have been retained to express an opinion on management's assertion

As a starting point for understanding the auditors' expectations related to the assessment, one should have a working knowledge of the standards the independent auditors are required to follow when auditing an entity's internal control. It is important that the assessment team understand existing audit requirements and closely follow developing audit and other guidance issued by the GAO and OMB as well as developments within the PCAOB.

Reaching a Consensus on Planning Matters

It is important to reach a consensus with the entity's independent auditors on key planning decisions. These should include:

- The overall assessment process and approach
- The scope of the project, including locations or business units to be included
- Preliminary identification of significant controls

- The nature of any internal control deficiencies noted by the auditors during their most recent audit of the entity's financial statements

- Tentative conclusions about what will constitute a significant deficiency or material weakness

- The nature and extent of the documentation of controls

- The nature and extent of the documentation of tests of controls

- Whether the auditors will rely (and to what extent) on the results of initial test-work to reach their conclusion

Additionally, some firms have developed guidance on the factors to consider when determining whether internal control, as a whole, is effective. If the independent auditors have developed such guidance, it is important to obtain that guidance, as it will help in the design and subsequent evaluation of the effectiveness of significant controls. For example, Chapter 6 describes the Internal Control Reliability Model as a tool that can help evaluate overall effectiveness of internal control. Some audit firms may have similar models.

During the early phases of the project, it may not be possible to obtain a definitive understanding with the auditors on all significant planning matters. In such situations, it is still important to work with the auditors to reach a consensus regarding:

- A clear understanding of the issue(s) needing resolution

- The additional information required to reach a resolution

- The process(es) to be followed to resolve the matter

- An estimated timeframe for the process(es) to be completed and the issue(s) to be resolved

DOCUMENTING YOUR PLANNING DECISIONS

Planning decisions should be documented. Having a written record of these decisions can help to:

- Clarify and confirm an understanding of the assessment with management, the entity's independent auditors, and others. Circulating this planning document and receiving feedback on it can greatly improve the communications process among all those affected by the assessment.

- Establish a concise record of significant facts and circumstances that influenced the design of the assessment, which can be used by others who review the entity's internal control going forward.

- Provide a permanent record of the entity's compliance with the requirement to review the effectiveness of its internal control.

The documentation should discuss key planning considerations and conclusions. Items that ought to be documented include the following elements.

Background Information

- Sources of written information considered in planning the assessment.

- Excerpts of key passages from those documents, for example, the description of the entity's programs and related performance indicators as set forth in the PAR.

- Any discussions with management, the entity's auditors, or others. Include a general description of what was discussed and when the discussions were held.

Tentative Conclusions

- Significant controls

- Definitions of materiality, significant internal control deficiencies, and material weaknesses

- Considerations for determining the effectiveness of internal control

- Project scope, including the effects of:

  o Responsibilities and activities of the assessment team, the Senior Assessment Team (if different), and the Senior Management Council

  o Coordination with the OIG and the extent to which the OIG will participate in a consulting capacity

  o The use of an outside service organization to process certain transactions

  o Multiple locations and component units

Project Team Organization and Project Administration

- Lines of reporting (i.e., to whom the project team will report)

- Timetable for completion of key phases of the project

- Plans for coordinating with the Senior Management Council, external auditors, legal counsel, and others, as appropriate

- The involvement of specialists

Discussions with Independent Auditors

- Project matters discussed with the independent auditors

- Conclusions reached on key planning matters

- Open items and any issues that remain to be resolved

Before finalizing any documentation, it would be advisable to consult with the entity's legal counsel regarding the nature and extent of the documentation.

Appendix 3A
Action Plan: Project Planning

The following action plan is intended to help in implementing the suggestions contained in this chapter for planning the project.

1. Information Sources

Identify and obtain sources of information about the entity that will be useful for planning purposes. For example:

- Consider published sources of information, including:

    - The agency's most recent PAR

    - Budgetary submissions and records of Congressional hearings

    - OIG semiannual reports

    - OIG and GAO reports

- Identify key individuals to be the subject of inquiries that will help in supplementing the knowledge gained through reading written materials.

2. Preliminary Understanding of Significant Control Objectives and Areas of Focus

Based on research, develop a preliminary understanding of the agency's significant control objectives and areas of emphasis for the assessment. For example:

- Identify possible significant control objectives by considering:

    - The entity's mission and key programs/activities

    - Agency operating environment

    - Agency stakeholders

    - Financial reporting matters

    - Preliminary evaluation of the internal control environment

- Identify other areas of focus, including those that:

    - Have a known or suspected control weakness

    - Possess a high risk for material misstatement regardless of any controls

3. Preliminary Definition of Material Weakness

Project scope and procedures must be designed to detect material misstatements. Therefore, in planning the assessment, a preliminary definition of what will constitute a material weakness should be developed. For example:

- Consider the definition of material weakness provided in the auditing literature.

- Describe how this definition will be applied to the specific circumstances of the entity. Consider:

  - Factors that will affect the *likelihood* that an internal control deficiency will result in a misstatement of the financial statements

  - How the entity will determine materiality, including the qualitative factors that affect materiality

  - The nature of any material weakness reported by other agencies with similar missions and/or in the same operating environment

4. Project Scope

Determine the overall scope of the project. Consider:

- Financial reports

- The locations, business units, or reporting segments that will be subject to documentation and testing

- The effect, if any, of information processing performed by third-party service organizations

- How the work already performed by internal auditors may be used to achieve project objectives

- How the policies, processes, and work product of the disclosure committee may be used in the project

5. Project Team

A project team will need to be formed to carry out the plan. Forming this team may require:

- Establishment of the overall responsibilities of the assessment team and obtaining the concurrence of the agency head, the CFO, and (if applicable) the Senior Management Council, who have the ultimate responsibility for forming an opinion and reporting on the effectiveness of the entity's internal control.

- Establishment of the lines of reporting for the team to ensure that it has the proper stature and authority in the organization to achieve its objectives.

- Identification of the knowledge and skills required by the team as a whole. Choose individual team members based on these requirements.

6. Coordinate with Independent Auditors/Office of Inspector General

Reach a consensus with the independent auditors/Office of Inspector General regarding key planning decisions. For example, it is important to communicate and reach agreement with the auditors on matters such as:

- The overall assessment process and approach
- The scope of the project, including locations or component units to be included
- Preliminary identification of significant controls
- The nature of any control deficiencies noted by the auditors, the OIG, and (if applicable) the GAO
- Tentative conclusions about what will constitute a significant deficiency or material weakness
- The nature and extent of the documentation of controls
- The nature and extent of the documentation of tests of controls
- Whether the auditors will rely on the results of testwork (and to what extent) to reach their conclusions

7. Documentation

In documenting planning decisions, consider the following:

- Consult with legal counsel regarding the nature and extent of possible documentation of planning decisions.
- Prepare documentation of key matters, including:
  - Information used to make decisions
  - Tentative conclusions on significant planning matters
  - Project team organization, composition, and so forth
  - Discussions with independent auditors and the OIG

Appendix 3B
Summary of Planning Questions

Exhibit 3.3 summarizes some of the questions that should be considered when one is planning a project to assess the effectiveness of an agency's internal control. The second column provides guidance on how the answers to the questions are relevant for planning purposes. The third column offers suggestions on the most likely sources for obtaining the information.

Exhibit 3.3 Summary of Planning Questions

Planning Questions to Consider	Relevance for Project Performance	Potential Information Sources
Entity Operations and Operating Environment Characteristics What are the primary characteristics of the entity's operating environment? Consider the effect of: • Financial reporting practices • Economic conditions • Laws and regulations • Technological changes	• Determine significant controls • Establish materiality thresholds • Understand vision, goals, programs, business processes, performance indicators, and financial reporting risks	• Performance Accountability Report (PAR) • Inquiries of management or auditors/OIG • Oversight agency reports (e.g., GAO, OIG) • Budgetary submissions • Agency websites • Agency publications • Congressional actions
What are the fundamental operating characteristics of the entity?	• Develop a preliminary understanding of the entity's value chain (including significant business processes and related subprocesses and activities)	• Same as above
Which financial statement accounts, balances, or disclosures possess one or more of the following attributes? • Subjective in nature • Complex accounting • Accounting rules subject to interpretation • Dependent on external information	• Make judgments about inherent risk, which will help identify those areas where strong controls are important	• Financial statements • Inquiries of management or auditors/OIG
Assessment Project Scope Which business processes or locations: • Are financially most significant? • Are operationally most significant? • Have the potential to expose the entity to significant risk or obligation (including political risk)? • Lack adequate available information?	• Determine scope of project	• PAR • Budgetary submissions • Inquiries of management • Oversight agency reports
Does the entity use a service organization to process significant information?	• Determine scope of project	• Inquiries of management

(continues)

Exhibit 3.3 Summary of Planning Questions *(Continued)*

Planning Questions to Consider	Relevance for Project Performance	Potential Information Sources
What is the nature and extent of the entity's: • OIG function? • Internal review function? • Disclosure committee (if applicable)?	• Determine scope of project	• Inquiries of management
Internal Control Considerations What processes does the entity currently have in place to perform a self-assessment of its internal control?	• Determine scope of project • Plan the nature of the procedures to be performed	• Inquiries of management • PAR • FMFIA reporting process
What have been the most significant recent changes to the agency and its internal controls?	• Identify potential problem areas and set the focus for the project • Determine significant controls	• Inquiries of management and auditors/OIG • PAR • Budgetary submissions
What is the nature and extent of the entity's existing documentation of its internal control?	• Determine scope of the project • Assess needs	• Inquiries of management • PAR • Oversight agency reports
What are management's current views regarding: • The most important policies, procedures, and practices it uses to control the business? • Areas of potential weakness in internal control?	• Determine significant controls • Determine scope of project	• Inquiries of management • Management responses to internal control findings
Has management received communications from oversight agencies and/or its independent auditors regarding control deficiencies observed during audits of the entity's operations, programs, financial statements, etc.? What was the nature of these deficiencies?	• Determine significant controls • Determine scope of the project	• Internal control reports • Other third-party reports (e.g., independent auditors, consultants, OIG, GAO)

(continues)

109

Exhibit 3.3 Summary of Planning Questions (*Continued*)

Planning Questions to Consider	Relevance for Project Performance	Potential Information Sources
Has the entity or its external auditors established guidance for: • Defining "effective," for the purposes of assessing internal controls? • Defining "deficiency" and "material weakness?"	• Design procedures • Establish scope of procedures • Evaluate effectiveness of internal controls	• Inquiries of management and auditor/OIG
If no guidance has been provided on defining a significant deficiency or material weakness, then— • What are the most significant financial and nonfinancial metrics used by stakeholders to evaluate the entity? • What qualitative (i.e., disclosure) information would be most relevant to stakeholders?	• Make preliminary judgments about materiality	• Inquiries of management, auditors/OIG, and attorneys • PAR • Oversight agency reports • GPRA submissions
Existence of Significant Deficiency and Possible Material Weakness In the past year, has there been a restatement of a previously issued financial statement to reflect the correction of a misstatement?	• Identify significant deficiency and possible material weakness	• Inquiry of management • Independent auditor's report on financial statements
In the past year, have the independent auditors identified a material misstatement in the financial statements that was not initially identified by the agency's internal control?	• Identify significant deficiency and possible material weakness	• Inquiry of management • Internal control reports
Are there any significant deficiencies that have been communicated to management that remain uncorrected after a reasonable time?	• Identify significant deficiency and possible material weakness	• Inquiry of management • Internal control reports
Has fraud by senior management or key agency personnel been previously reported?	• Identify significant deficiency and possible material weakness	• Inquiry of Office of Inspector General • Congressional Record

Notes

1. This presumption is not explicitly stated in any of the rules, regulations, or professional standards relating to internal control reporting. However, one would have to question the value of an assessment in which the detection of such deficiencies and weaknesses was not reasonably assured.

2. The auditing literature provides guidance to auditors on the qualitative factors that should be considered when assessing materiality. This guidance is provided by an auditing interpretation, which has been codified in the AICPA *Professional Standards,* AU Sec. 9312.15.

3. Christopher Fox and Paul A. Zonneveld, *IT Control Objectives for Sarbanes-Oxley* (Information Technology Governance Institute and the Information Systems Audit and Control Association, 2003), 9, Rolling Meadows, IL.

Chapter 4

Identifying Significant Control Objectives

Chapter Summary

Describe entity-level control objectives that typically are significant:

- Corporate culture
- Personnel policies
- General computer controls
- Alignment between entity objectives and control structures
- Risk identification
- Top-level financial reporting processes
- System-wide monitoring

Provide guidance on identifying significant activity-level control objectives.

INTRODUCTION

The *Framework* of the Committee of Sponsoring Organizations of the Treadway Commission (COSO) recognizes that within the context of an internal control structure (taken as a whole), some controls are more significant than others. When assessing the effectiveness of internal control, an assessment should be sure to encompass these significant controls and will often be limited to testing these controls only.

Controls vary between entities. Moreover, the way in which individual controls combine to create an overall internal control structure will also vary. Different entities may achieve the same control objective by different controls or combinations of controls. For example, suppose that both Department A and Department B have several operating components or divisions, each of which reports financial results that must be consolidated at the departmental level. Both departments have the same control objective: to make sure that the results reported by the department component are accurate, complete, and prepared in a way that facilitates the consolidation. Each department may take a different approach to achieving this same objective. For example, suppose that:

- Department A's operating divisions are all performing similar activities (e.g., research) and the department relies on standardized financial reporting procedures to collect information. Preparers at each operating division or component have different levels of accounting expertise, but all are highly trained on how to execute the standard reporting procedures properly. Third parties not involved in the financial reporting process or outside contractors periodically review each operating division to ensure that existing processes for reporting financial information are reliable. At the departmental level, the operating divisions' financial reports are analytically reviewed, and any unusual relationships are identified and investigated. In this system, the more significant controls involve:

- The design of the standard financial reporting procedures
- The effectiveness of related training addressing the required procedures
- The monitoring of the process executed by third parties

The reviews performed at the departmental level, although important, are somewhat secondary.

- Each of Department B's operating divisions is performing substantially different activities in order to carry out the department's various goals and programs. Assume further that several of these activities require the application of highly specialized accounting standards. To ensure the proper application of these standards, the department requires that all operating division financial directors have extensive experience in the division's unique accounting requirements and practices. The department does not have standardized reporting procedures to support the departmental level consolidation but, instead, requires the operating divisions to provide trial balances and other disclosures to facilitate the preparation of the consolidated financial statements. This information is the subject of an independent review at the operating division level (say agreed-upon procedures performed by the Office of the Inspector General [OIG] or independent auditors). At the departmental level, individual accountants closely review the information submitted by the operating divisions together with the agreed-upon procedures or similar independent third-party reports. For Department B, the more significant controls are:

  - The personnel policies setting forth academic and experience requirements for operating division financial directors
  - The review and monitoring performed by the department level accounting staff
  - The results of agreed-on procedures reports or similar independent third-party reports

To recognize that different controls and combinations of controls can achieve the same objective, this chapter focuses on identifying significant control *objectives*. The guidance provided in this chapter assumes that:

- Certain entity-wide control objectives should be presumed significant for most entities.
- Some activity-level control objectives will be more significant than others, and therefore, guidance is needed to identify these significant activity-level objectives.

The guidance contained in this chapter is built on the COSO *Framework* introduced in Chapter 2; however, it does not follow the COSO *Framework* exactly. Some of the control components and ideas described in the *Framework* have been reorganized in this chapter to facilitate their explanation and the subsequent documentation and testing provided in Chapters 5, 6, and 7.

ENTITY-LEVEL CONTROL OBJECTIVES PRESUMED TO BE SIGNIFICANT

The Public Company Accounting Oversight Board (PCAOB) *Auditing Standard No. 2* provides guidance which federal agencies should find very useful in the identification of significant controls. This guidance emphasizes "relevant assertions" and not "significant controls" as the standard that should govern the evaluation, identification, and testing of internal controls, and it is clear that specific control objectives will vary among federal agencies. However, as also noted in *Auditing Standard No. 2*, entity-level control objectives have a pervasive effect on the design and operating effectiveness of activity-level controls, and some of these control objectives are likely to be significant for most entities.

Organizational Culture

Scholars define culture in many different ways (see Exhibit 4.1). Most of these definitions describe a culture as a system of beliefs and values that are shared among members of a group. More often than not, this process of sharing is informal and is communicated indirectly through symbols and symbolic activities. For example, in a work environment, the physical space where one works is a symbol of that person's status within the organization. A corner office means something; a cubicle in an interior "bullpen" means something else.

Members of a group must become socialized to the culture of the group. This socialization process seeks to make the individual a functioning member of the group. The process teaches individuals what is acceptable and unacceptable within that particular culture. For example, an individual starting work at a new job will quickly learn the acceptable style of dress. In some organizations, a business suit may make the individual seem overly formal, aloof, and unapproachable. In another organization, blue jeans and a collarless shirt may be viewed as too informal and reflective of careless, undisciplined work habits.

The socialization process teaches individuals within the group:

- *Values.* These are the guidelines for behavior accepted by members of the organization. For example, the organization may value informal relationships and communications styles.

- *Norms.* These are the specific ways that organizational values are expressed in behavior. For example, members of the organization may dress in a casual style.

- *Shared beliefs.* These are the ways that the organization expects individuals to behave in particular situations. For example, if someone has a question to ask the person in the office next to him or her, the accepted method of communication might be to ask the person directly or possibly through instant messaging but not through writing a formal memo or e-mail.

In these discussions and definitions of culture, there is a direct link between culture and behavior. An organization's culture—its values, norms, and beliefs—drives the behavior of its members. It is this link between culture and behavior that led to the conclusion in the COSO report that the effectiveness of an entity's internal control cannot rise above its ethical values. Therefore, ethical values are essential elements of internal control because they affect the design, administration, and monitoring of other control components.

Based on the COSO *Framework,* the minimum control objectives related to an organization's culture should include:

- Definition and communication of ethical and behavioral norms. Note that formal, documented statements about values often paint only a partial (or even inaccurate) picture of the agency's values. "Accidental values" can arise spontaneously without being formally defined, and these values can take hold in the entity over time.[1]

- Removal or reduction of incentives and temptations that could motivate people to act outside of the organization's defined ethical norms.

- Reinforcement of stated ethical values and norms through observable behavior of the entity's leaders.

- Appropriateness of remedial action taken in response to departures from approved policies and procedures or violations of the entity's code of conduct.

- Attitudes and actions related to the intervention or override of established control procedures.

Exhibit 4.1   Some Definitions of Culture

Culture is . . .

- Behavior, cultivated through social learning.
- The behaviors, beliefs, values, and symbols accepted by a group, generally without thinking about them, and communicated and imitated among its members.
- Symbolic communication whose meanings are learned and deliberately perpetuated.
- Patterns of and for behavior that are communicated by symbols. On the one hand, culture may be considered as a product of actions taken by individuals; on the other hand, as conditioning influences upon further action.
- The sum total of the learned behavior of a group of people.

Source: Adapted from a list prepared by Gee Ekachai, Associate Professor, Department of Speech Communications at Southern Illinois University at Carbondale, for his course "Communications across Cultures."

Personnel Policies

Internal control is a people-dependent process. That is, the effectiveness of an entity's internal control ultimately depends on how effectively its personnel perform their control-related responsibilities.

Each person in an organization brings a unique background and ability to his/her assignments. People have different needs and priorities. They do not always understand, communicate, or perform consistently. Thus, at the entity-level, the organization must institute a set of policies and procedures aimed at improving the effectiveness with which its people perform their control-related tasks.

Personnel-related controls generally can be grouped into three levels.

1. *Understanding and awareness of the individual's control-related responsibilities.* Before individuals can effectively contribute to an entity's internal control, they must know what is expected of them (see Exhibit 4.2 for an example).

2. *Appropriate organizational structure.* The way an organization is structured can greatly improve the effectiveness of individual performance. By way of analogy, consider a basketball team. The coach of a team must make certain strategic decisions about offense, defense, substitution patterns, and the like in order to help the team win. Players with certain skills will perform better in some systems than others. For example, a player who is quick and athletic, but relatively small, will be more effective playing in a system that takes advantage of those skills than he/she would be in another system that features big, strong, but somewhat slower players.

Exhibit 4.2   What People Must Know to Be Effective

The effectiveness of any internal control system rests primarily on how effectively entity personnel perform their control-related responsibilities. *All* personnel play a role in internal control. As a starting point for improving performance, they need to be aware of the elements of their jobs that contribute to the agency's internal control structure. For example, employees should be able to answer the following questions:

- What is the level of authority and the authority of those around you?
- What behaviors are expected or acceptable, and what is unacceptable?
- What policies and procedures should you follow in your job?
- How do you avoid conflicts of interest?
- How do you appropriately protect the agency's data?
- If you see something you think is wrong, dishonest, or detrimental to the agency, what should you do about it?
- What is proprietary, confidential, and secret in your agency?
- What is your role in protecting agency assets?

Source: This list was prepared by Mike Lambert and Marsha Carter and was printed in "The Missing Link in Implementing Effective Internal Controls," *Compliance Week,* April 24, 2003, *www.complianceweek.com.*

Similarly, in a work environment, an organization should create a structure that allows its personnel to be most effective. Consideration should be given to:

- Formal and informal job descriptions or other means of defining tasks that comprise particular jobs.
- Hiring policies, which serve as a critical starting point for creating an environment in which people can succeed. The entity should have a process for identifying the skills and knowledge needed in the entity, identifying qualified candidates, and hiring new employees who possess the necessary qualities.
- The delegation of responsibility, authority, and accountability. Clear delegation involves establishing well-defined boundaries.
- The establishment of clear reporting relationships.
- Monitoring activities that are commensurate with the significance of the duties delegated and the competence of the personnel.

3. *Provide the necessary resources.* In order to be effective, people must have the necessary resources made available to them. These include:

- Ongoing training
- Performance appraisal and feedback
- Compensation policies that are aligned with entity-wide objectives

Understanding and Awareness of Control Responsibilities.   Every individual in an organization has an internal control role, and these roles and responsibilities will vary. The COSO report provides guidance on the responsibilities of those in the organization who contribute most significantly to the effectiveness of internal control. Exhibit 4.3 summarizes this guidance. Although clearly designed for the private sector, the exhibit is relevant to federal financial management. With the exception of the Board of Directors (where Congress does not quite play a similar role), all other individuals/positions will likely have a counterpart in the federal environment. Even when no audit committee is present, a truly independent OIG function can, for the most part, execute the responsibilities of an audit committee.

Evaluating the Audit Committee.   Although some agencies have audit committees, the practice is not widespread in the federal government. Despite some support for such committees, it is not clear that audit committees will become commonplace in the future. If an audit committee is present, the following should be considered in evaluating its effectiveness:

- Independence of audit committee members from management
- Clarity with which the audit committee's responsibilities are articulated and how well the audit committee and management understand those responsibilities
- Level of involvement and interaction with the independent auditor
- Level of involvement and interaction with the OIG
- Whether the committee includes one or more financial experts

Exhibit 4.3　Control Responsibilities of Entity Personnel Summary of COSO Guidance

Individual	Control-Related Responsibility
Chief Executive Officer	• Ultimate responsibility for internal control system; ensures that all components of internal control are in place • Sets the overall "tone at the top" • Establishes a management philosophy and operating style • Influences selection of the board of directors • Provides leadership and direction to senior management that shapes the corporate culture • Meets with senior managers to review control-related responsibilities and gains knowledge of controls and their effectiveness
Management	• Establishes more specific internal control procedures • Monitors and reports on effectiveness of controls • May perform some control procedures themselves
Finance officers	• Primary responsibility for the design, implementation, and monitoring of the entity's financial reporting system • Provide input to the establishment of entity-wide objectives and risk assessment
Board of Directors	• Provides guidance and oversight to management • Through selection of management, helps define expectations for integrity and ethical values • High-level objectives setting and strategic planning • Investigates any issues they deem important
Audit committee	• Investigates how top management is carrying out its financial reporting responsibilities • Requires corrective action for internal control and financial reporting deficiencies • Identifies and takes action when top management overrides internal controls or otherwise seeks to misrepresent reported financial results
Internal auditors	• Directly examine internal controls and recommend improvements
Other entity personnel	• Perform with due care control-related activities • Communicate to a higher organizational level problems in operations, noncompliance with the code of conduct, or other violations of policy or illegal actions

- Amount of time that the audit committee devotes to control issues, as well as the amount of time that audit committee members are able to devote to committee activity

General Computer Controls

General computer controls are entity-wide controls that apply to many if not all application systems and help ensure their continued, proper operation. For example, the effectiveness of an entity's controls relating to the access of its database will determine whether it will be successful in maintaining the integrity of that data, which may be used in a number of different applications. General computer controls have a pervasive effect on the entity's IT system, and therefore, the related control objectives usually are considered significant to the entity's overall internal control structure. If inadequate general controls exist, it may not be possible to depend on computer controls at the application-level, which rely on the system itself functioning properly. The Control Objectives for Information and Related Technology (COBIT) framework (summarized in Chapter 2) describes general computer control objectives in four distinct domains:

1. *Planning and organization.* This domain covers strategy and tactics and is concerned with the identification of the way IT can best contribute to the achievement of agency and program objectives. Furthermore, the realization of the strategic vision and agency mission needs to be planned, communicated, and managed. Finally, a proper organization and technological infrastructure must be put in place.

2. *Acquisition and implementation.* To realize the IT strategy, IT solutions need to be identified, developed, or acquired, as well as implemented and integrated into the agency's business processes. In addition, this domain includes changes in and maintenance of existing systems.

3. *Delivery and support.* This domain is concerned with the actual delivery of required services, which range from traditional operations over security and continuity aspects to training. In order to deliver services, the necessary support processes must be implemented. Included in this domain are controls related to data center operations and access security, which COSO describes as examples of general computer controls.

4. *Monitoring.* All IT processes need to be regularly assessed over time for quality and compliance with control requirements.

With the exception of planning and organization, all the COBIT domains are encompassed in the COSO *Framework*, although they are organized somewhat differently.

Significant general computer control objectives typically include the following:

- IT systems manage the quality and integrity of information.
- The entity maintains access controls over IT systems and related applications.
- Computer applications include an authorization process.

- Information is provided on a timely basis and is available when needed.
- Confidentiality of sensitive information is maintained.
- Continued reporting is supported by recoverability controls.

Chapter 6 provides more detailed guidance to help with understanding and evaluating IT general controls.

Alignment between Entity Objectives and Control Structures

As described in Chapter 2, internal controls have no intrinsic value. Organizations do not adopt control policies and procedures because they are "good" and not to have them would be "bad." Internal controls are driven by an entity's desire to achieve certain mission or business objectives. Clearly, defined mission/business objectives are a prerequisite for effectively designed controls. Exhibit 4.4 shows this relationship. At the top of the diagram are the entity's mission/business objectives. These should be defined in a way that is broad enough to provide guidance on what the entity desires to achieve in a number of areas, yet at the same time specific enough to relate directly to the entity. The broad mission/business objectives drive strategy, which in turn dictates certain activities that are necessary to implement the strategy.

Exhibit 4.4   Alignment of Objectives and Controls

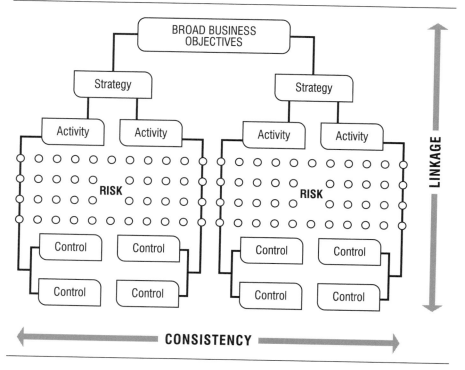

In defining these activity-level objectives, it is important that all levels of management be involved in the objective-setting process and that they identify those objectives that are most important to the achievement of entity-wide objectives.

Reading further down the diagram, risks exist that could prevent the agency from successfully achieving its objectives, and controls are designed to manage these risks. To be effective, these controls should be aligned with the agency's stated business objectives and its operating structure. As indicated in Exhibit 4.4, alignment is achieved when the following occur:

- *Linkage*. Control activities are *linked* directly to the agency's strategies and objectives, as indicated along the vertical axis.
- *Consistency*. Looking horizontally across the diagram, control activities for each of the various activities should be consistent with each other.

Exhibit 4.5 describes a situation in which the entity lacks linkage. The entity has described certain activities for which there are no controls (the right side of the diagram), and it performs some activities that are unrelated to the achievement of any specific objective (the left side of the diagram). When an entity's control objectives are not directly linked to its business objectives, the effectiveness of the

Exhibit 4.5   Lack of Linkage between Controls and Activities

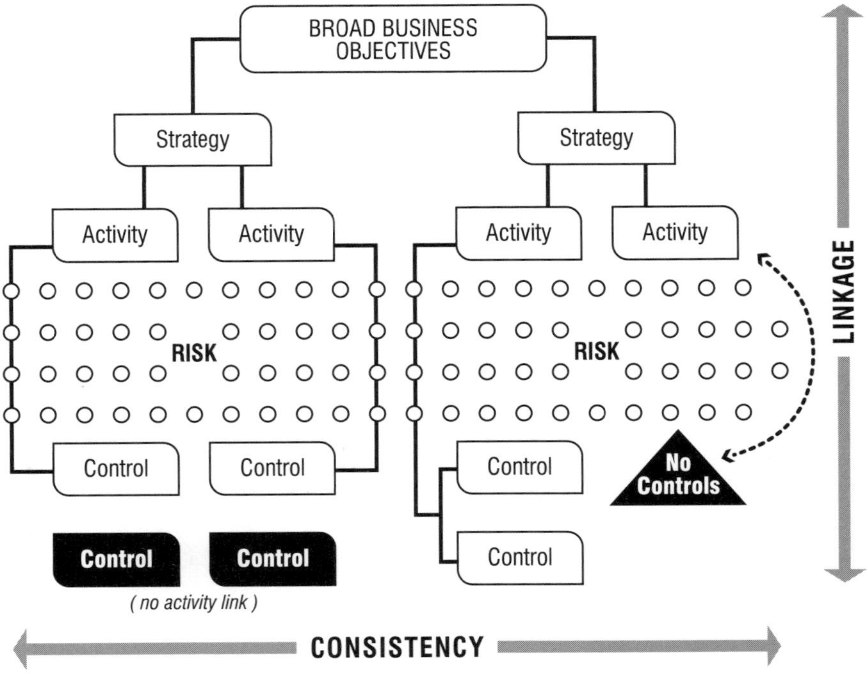

Exhibit 4.6   Lack of Consistency Among Controls

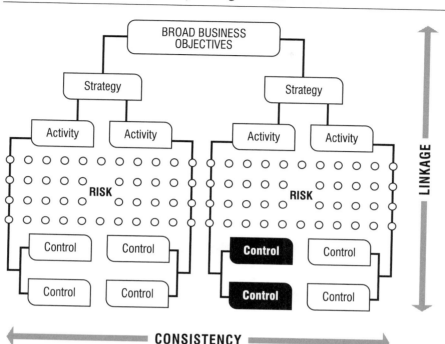

internal control system may be diminished. In Exhibit 4.5, the entity has an entire class of activities that are uncontrolled.

Exhibit 4.6 shows a situation in which control activities are not consistent with each other. Most of the activities have control procedures that are similar (indicated in white), but one activity has adopted controls that are at another end of the spectrum (black). The lack of consistency among control objectives raises questions about the effectiveness of the overall system. Assuming that there is consistency at the strategy level, why would the entity choose one approach to controls for one activity and a different approach for another activity? Are the two activities so dissimilar that they require different control objectives? It may be that the answer to that question is "yes," but if the two activities are similar, then one would have to consider how greater effectiveness is achieved by having dissimilar sets of control objectives.

Risk Identification

As described in Chapter 2, COSO includes an entity's risk assessment process as one of its five components of internal control. The first step in that process is the identification of the risks the entity faces in achieving its objectives. These risks can come from both internal and external sources, and the report provides a list of several factors to consider that may contribute to increased risks. Other than this list of factors, COSO does not provide any additional guidance on how management can most effectively identify risk. The following guidance has been adapted from the article "Predictable Surprises: The Disasters You Should Have Seen Coming," by Michael D. Watkins and Max H. Bazerman.[2]

Entities face risks from many different sources. Some of these risks cannot be foreseen, but the entity should be able to anticipate and identify many of them. Management fails to identify these risks when it remains oblivious to emerging threats or problems. In general, the reasons for failing to identify risks that should have been anticipated can be broken down into three categories.

1. *Management psychology.* As human beings, we all have cognitive biases, and some of these can lead us to ignore or underestimate identifiable risks. These biases include:

   o A tendency to believe that conditions are better than they really are

   o An overemphasis on information that supports an optimistic vision of the future and an underemphasis on information that contradicts that vision

   o Overlooking threats posed from external sources

   o A tendency to procrastinate; to choose *not* to take action now that would mitigate future risks

   o Inability to treat as "real" risks that have not been experienced personally

2. *Organizational vulnerabilities.* It is common for agencies to be organized into "silos." As a result, the information provided to management is often fragmented, and management may not always be successful in synthesizing this information to identify risks. Additionally, risks may be ignored because people assume, incorrectly, that someone else in another business unit will address the issue.

3. *Value imbalance.* Senior management may overvalue the interests of one group while undervaluing other, equally important groups. This imbalance can create management blind spots.

Because of the severity of the consequences of *not* identifying risks, the control objectives related to this activity on the entity-level are usually significant to the overall effectiveness of internal control.

Antifraud Programs and Controls

The COSO *Framework* does not include a discussion related to the prevention and detection of fraud. An established set of criteria for evaluating the effectiveness of fraud-related controls does not exist. Within the auditing literature, the most definitive guidance on fraud-related controls is provided in the document *Management Anti-Fraud Programs and Controls,* which was published as an Exhibit to SAS No. 99, *Consideration of Fraud in a Financial Statement Audit.*[3]

The guidance in the document is based on the presumption that entity management has both the responsibility and the means to take action to reduce the occurrence of fraud at the entity. To fulfill this responsibility, management should:

- Create and maintain a culture of honesty and high ethics.
- Evaluate the risks of fraud and implement the processes, procedures, and controls needed to mitigate the risks and reduce opportunities for fraud.
- Develop an appropriate oversight process.

In many ways, the guidance offered in *Management Anti-Fraud Programs and Controls* echoes the concepts and detailed guidance contained in the COSO report. The primary difference is that *Management Anti-Fraud Programs and Controls* reminds management that it must be aware of and design the entity's internal control to specifically address material misstatements caused by fraud and *not* limit their efforts in the detection and prevention of unintentional errors. The requirements above are discussed further in a later section of this chapter.

The Securities and Exchange Commission (SEC) and the PCAOB also provide guidance on fraud. SEC final rules relating to management's reports on internal control include an extensive commentary on the background of the rules and insight on how the rules should be interpreted and implemented. That commentary includes the following guidance:

> The assessment of a company's [agency's] internal control over financial reporting must be based on procedures sufficient both to evaluate its design and to test its operating effectiveness. Controls subject to such assessment include, but are not limited to: . . . *controls related to the prevention and detection of fraud* [emphasis added].

The PCAOB, in its proposed auditing standard, has highlighted anti-fraud programs and controls as an important element of internal control.

Office of Management and Budget (OMB) Circular A-123 recognizes the need for controls that address fraud risk directly. The related Implementation Guide addresses the need to document, identify, test, and evaluate controls designed to prevent fraud. In addition, the guide states that in evaluating controls at the entity-level, the assessment team should consider the "five standards of internal control that can have a pervasive effect on the risk of error or fraud" (control environment, risk assessment, information and communication control activities, and monitoring). Finally, the guide highlights the consideration of fraud in its suggested "account risk analysis form."

A Culture of Honesty and Ethics.   A culture of honesty and ethics includes the following elements:

- A value system founded on integrity
- A positive work environment that encourages positive employee feelings about the entity
- Human resource policies that minimize the chance of hiring or promoting individuals with low levels of honesty, especially for positions requiring trust

- Training—both at the time of hire and on an ongoing basis—on the entity's values and its code of conduct
- Confirmation from employees that they understand and have complied with the entity's code of conduct and that they are not aware of any violations of the code
- Appropriate investigation and response to incidents of alleged or suspected fraud

Evaluating Antifraud Programs and Controls.   The entity's risk assessment process (as described in Chapter 2) should include a consideration of fraud risk. With the aim of reducing fraud opportunities, the entity should take steps to:

- Identify and measure fraud risk.
- Mitigate fraud risk by making changes to the entity's activities and procedures.
- Implement and monitor an appropriate system of internal control.

Developing an Appropriate Oversight Process.   A key consideration is that procedures be in effect to ensure an appropriate antifraud culture, the identification of fraud risks, and the related implementation of antifraud measures.

Because of the fiduciary nature of federal operations, most federal agencies will already have an effective oversight process. Although in industry this process is typically associated with the audit committee and the board of directors (although it is not always present), this role has traditionally been performed by congressional oversight committees, the Government Accountability Office (GAO), the OMB, and the OIG, among others. In addition, most, if not all agencies provide a mechanism for communicating fraud or suspected fraud to appropriate levels/functions within the agency.

Top-Level Financial Reporting Processes

Top-Level versus Routine, Systematic Processes.   An entity's financial reporting processes can be separated into two general types:

1. *Routine, systematic transaction processing.* These processes are often distributed across the organization and include all levels of entity personnel. The processing of purchase transactions or the payment of payables are two examples of this type of routine processing.
2. *Top-level financial reporting procedures.* These procedures address financial reporting events, rather than routine transactions with external parties. The recognition of an asset impairment loss, the posting of general ledger adjustments, and the preparation of accounting estimates are some examples of top-level financial reporting procedures. Unlike routine, systematic transactions, these top-level processes are usually centralized and performed by senior financial executives within the organization.

The nature of the controls and their relative significance is different for the two types of activities. For example, routine transaction processing is built around a processing "stream" that captures and then manipulates data, changing it from raw data into accounting information (e.g., debits and credits). Typical steps in this processing stream include:

- Initiation of the transaction, including the capture of relevant information
- Processing of information, usually through multiple steps, with controls designed to ensure the integrity of the data processed
- Creation of debits and credits, which are then posted to the general ledger and other accounting records

The Nature of Top-Level Processes.   Top-level financial reporting activities are characterized by an information-gathering, analysis, and decision-making process, rather than data manipulation. Key control objectives in this process include the following:

- *Awareness and understanding.* Management is aware of and understands the need for top-level activity. For example, management is aware of the need to assess the recoverability of long-lived assets periodically to determine whether an impairment loss should be recognized.
- *Gathering of relevant and reliable information.* A process exists to identify and communicate information that is relevant for decision-making purposes. For example, management monitors internal and external information sources to identify events or changes in circumstances that indicate an asset may be impaired.
- *Analysis and decision making.* Using the information gathered, management analyzes the situation and develops an appropriate response. For example, if an impairment loss should be recognized, management would estimate the amount of the loss.
- *Review and approval.* Top-level adjustments and entries to the accounting records should be communicated to, reviewed by, and approved by an appropriate level of authority within the organization. In some instances, that level of authority may be the board of directors or audit committee.

The Need to Consider Top-Level Processes.   Many reports of financial reporting failures cite weaknesses in top-level financial reporting processes as the main cause of the failure. Fraudulent financial reporting schemes are frequently perpetrated through an abuse of these processes. For those reasons, it is important to identify the entity's top-level financial reporting practices and consider whether the control objectives related to these practices are significant to the entity's internal control.

Processes that should be considered include those relating to:

- Recording nonroutine, nonsystematic entries or other post-closing adjustments such as consolidating adjustments or reclassifications
- Preparation of significant accounting estimates
- Consideration of asset valuation issues

- Recognition of obligations that meet the criteria for liability recognition, including contingent liabilities and off-balance-sheet financing
- Recording journal entries to the general ledger
- Recording recurring and nonrecurring adjustments to the financial statements, for example, consolidating adjustments, report combinations, and reclassifications

The Selection and Application of Accounting Principles.   The selection and application of accounting principles may have a significant effect on an entity's reported financial results and on the design of its internal control. For example, suppose that Agency A employs highly technical scientific personnel and negotiates advantageous contracts as a result of in-house technical know-how and bulk purchasing. Because of these factors, Agency A is assigned the responsibility of acquiring specialized research and testing equipment on behalf of other agencies involved in health-related research. Assume the following additional facts surrounding the acquisition and delivery of Agency A's products:

- In executing its mission, Agency A negotiates agreements with "buying" agencies calling for the purchase/production and delivery of specialized equipment.
- Each agreement usually provides for the sale and delivery of several units of different types of equipment.
- Agency A also provides the "buying agency" with options on different "training packages" regarding the operation of the specialized equipment.
- Delivery dates for both equipment and related training are scattered and typically encompass two or more fiscal years.
- Each agreement is funded through the use of reimbursable agreements, and the reimbursable agreement quotes one single cost to the "buying" agency covering the "bundle" of equipment and training services.
- Agency A is responsible for covering all costs including an estimate for overhead costs but is not allowed to realize a "profit" from the transaction. This estimate of direct costs plus overhead constitutes the "price" or cost of the reimbursable agreement.
- The buying agency funds the entire amount of the reimbursable agreement up front, with Agency A's Balances with Treasury account being credited for the entire value of the reimbursable agreement shortly after the signing/approval of the reimbursable agreement (e.g., through the Intra-Governmental Payment and Collection [IPAC] system).

In the selection and application of accounting principles, Agency A's management must make several important decisions, including:

- The proper identification of total costs (including overhead and method of allocating/estimating overhead) to be assigned to the reimbursable agreement
- How reimbursable agreement revenue and related costs should be recognized when equipment and training are delivered over multiple reporting periods and fiscal years

- The proper reporting of deferred income (since the contract was funded up front), recognizing Agency A's future liability (for yet-unfulfilled deliveries of equipment and training)

- The proper capitalization of work in process costs, including overhead (e.g., for equipment that is in the process of being acquired/produced but is either not completed or not yet delivered)

- Recognizing that deferred income represents an intraagency transaction with the buying agency (which should show this amount as an asset) and the need to report this information to Treasury (and if applicable confirming the balance with the buying agency)

These decisions may have a significant effect on how much cost and offsetting reimbursable agreement revenue Agency A will recognize in any given year. In addition, once the decisions are made, the agency will need to implement control policies and procedures to ensure that the accounting policy is applied appropriately. For example, if management determines that reimbursable revenue should be recognized when the equipment is shipped, then the agency should have procedures in place to capture the information necessary to determine what products were shipped when. Similarly, the agency should have procedures in place to capture training that may be in process or completed.

By way of illustration, during the early years of implementation of the Chief Financial Officers Act, it was not uncommon for auditors to find that in the example above, Agency A would have recognized as reimbursable agreement revenue the entire amount funded up front without considering the likelihood that all costs had not been incurred and that the entire reimbursable agreement had not been "earned."

For these reasons, the consideration of an entity's financial reporting processes should include an assessment of the controls over management's selection and application of accounting principles. Although practices have improved considerably since the initial implementation stages of the Chief Financial Officers Act, it is advisable to consider carefully the agency's selection of accounting principles and the mechanism in place to enforce compliance.

The entity's financial statements should be *presented fairly . . .* in accordance with [generally accepted accounting principles] (GAAP)." The overriding requirement is "presented fairly." The phrase "in accordance with GAAP," is *subordinate* to the requirement for a fair presentation. The reason for the subordination is that fair presentation also implies the selection of "fair" or appropriate GAAP. Ultimately, an entity's accounting principles must be appropriate under the circumstances, and they must report transactions and events in accordance with their substance.

The auditing literature provides guidance on the meaning of "presented fairly." In part, the guidance states that a "fair presentation" means:

- The accounting principles selected and applied are generally accepted.

- The accounting principles are appropriate under the circumstances.

- The financial statements, including the related notes, are informative of matters that may affect their use, understanding, and interpretation.

- The information presented in the financial statements is classified and summarized in a reasonable manner, that is, neither too detailed nor too condensed.

- The financial statements reflect the underlying transactions and events in a manner that presents the financial position and results of operations (including financing and budgetary data) within an acceptable range, that is, limits that are reasonable and practicable to attain in financial statements.

When no established principles exist for reporting a specific transaction or event, it might be possible to report the event or transaction on the basis of its substance by selecting an accounting principle that appears appropriate when applied in a manner similar to the application of an established principle to an analogous transaction or event.[4]

No definitive guidelines exist on the controls that should be in place to ensure the appropriate selection and application of accounting policies. However, when considering an entity's process(es), it is important to consider whether the following objectives have been met:

- Management identifies events and transactions for which accounting policy choices should be made or existing policies reconsidered.

- The accounting policies chosen by management are generally accepted and result in a fair presentation of the financial statement information.

- Information processing and internal control policies and procedures are designed to apply the accounting principles selected appropriately.

System-wide Monitoring

Chapter 2 describes the characteristics of the monitoring component of internal control. Under revised OMB Circular A-123 guidance and SEC rules relating to the evaluation of and reporting on internal control, the monitoring component of the COSO *Framework* takes on increased importance.

There are two reasons why monitoring is now so important and may be considered a significant control objective.

1. Under both federal and SEC guidance, management is required to report on all material weaknesses in internal control and any material changes to internal control. To comply with this requirement, it is vital that the entity's monitoring of its internal control be functioning effectively.

2. Most entities will perform a substantial portion of their tests on the operating effectiveness of internal control at various points in time that may be well in advance of the report date. In order to draw a valid conclusion about the continued effectiveness of those controls at the report date, the entity must be able to rely on the monitoring component of its internal control. Without an effective mechanism for monitoring the continued effectiveness of internal control, entities would have to perform all their testwork close to their reporting date.

IDENTIFYING SIGNIFICANT ACTIVITY-LEVEL CONTROL OBJECTIVES

The scope of the project should include those control objectives that relate to the relevant assertions related to all significant financial statement accounts and disclosures. To determine which activity-level control objectives are significant, it is typical to begin with a reading and analysis of the entity's financial statements. In performing this analysis, one would typically consider:

- The magnitude of the account balance and how this compares with financial statement materiality. PCAOB *Auditing Standard No. 2* states that "an account is significant if there is more than a remote likelihood that the account could contain misstatements that individually, or when aggregated with others, could have a material effect on the financial statements." The definition also emphasizes that the standard is equally applicable to understatements and overstatements of balances.

- Qualitative considerations of materiality and the accounts and classes of transactions that have the greatest impact on these qualitative assessments.

- The inherent risk associated with the account balance, which is defined as the risk of material misstatement irrespective of internal controls. Inherent risk is affected by factors such as the complexity of the related accounting standards or the degree of judgment required in the recognition or measurement of the item.

- The critical accounting policies of the entity (e.g., those accounting policies that most directly impact the agency's financial position and operating results).

Auditing Standard No. 2 also provides guidance to auditors regarding the following:

- In some cases, separate components of an account may need to be considered significant accounts because of the agency's organizational structure.

- An account may also be considered significant owing to exposure to unrecognized obligations represented by the account.

The advantages to basing a definition of significant activity-level control objectives on a financial statement analysis include:

- The relatively objective nature of the process
- The familiarity one probably has in performing such an analysis

However, as discussed in Chapter 2, the COSO model defines *activities* not in terms of financial statement accounts but rather as the entity's business process activities. The drawback to a purely financial statement–based approach is that one can become too narrow in the definition of the activity. For example, a federal agency, because of the nature of its operations, or to take full advantage of vendor discounts (or both), pays its accounts payable as quickly as possible, exceeding even the requirements of the Prompt Payment Act. This practice could result in a relatively small balance in accounts payable. As a result, a simple financial statement analysis may not identify payables as a significant financial statement account. However, if, as suggested by COSO, a business process approach was used in conjunction with financial analysis, the assessment would also consider the procurement process. Thus, the assessment team would then analyze the significance of the procurement activity and, if such activity was significant, would conclude that notwithstanding the relatively small balance, accounts payable is a significant account that should be subject to rigorous internal control evaluation and assessment.

Thus, in determining which activity-level control objectives are significant, a blended approach that combines both a financial statement and a business process/ activity analysis should be considered. The classical definition of a business process is provided by Michael Hammer and James Champy, in *Reengineering the Corporation: A Manifesto for Business Revolution:*

> . . . a collection of activities that takes one or more kinds of input and creates an output that is of value to the customer.[5]

The use of the business process concept (e.g., budget formulation, procurement, technology development, human resources management) combined with a financial statement analysis can be very useful in the identification of significant accounts and the related evaluation of risk. However, the use of business processes is not the only alternative. The use of the more traditional accounting cycle should work just as well. In fact, the proposed Chief Financial Officers Council's *Implementation Guide for OMB Circular A-123 Appendix A,* dated May 2005, proposes such an approach.

Exhibit 4.7 shows examples of how business processes/activities or, alternatively, accounting cycles, can be related to accounts.

Subsequent Reconsideration of Significant Activity-Level Controls

As described later in Chapter 6, an evaluation of internal control typically begins with the evaluation of entity-level controls. The results of that evaluation may lead to a reconsideration of the definition of significant activity-level control objectives. If weaknesses exist in entity-level controls, the entity may effectively compensate for this weakness through strong activity-level controls. For example, suppose that a federal bonus plan is in effect for selected personnel based on the achievement of certain performance goals. Depending on how aggressive these goals are, the presence of such a plan could motivate employees to manipulate performance data. This may be considered a control weakness. However, if the entity has strong activity-level controls over performance data, it may successfully mitigate this weakness and allow for the conclusion that, overall, internal control operates effectively.

Example Activity-Level Control Objectives

Appendix 4B provides a list of example control objectives, including activity-level control objectives. Chapter 7 provides additional examples of control objectives and related control procedures.

Exhibit 4.7 Relating Processes/Activities and Accounting Cycles to Financial Statement Accounts

Processes/Activities and Financial Statement Accounts

Process/Activity	Related Financial Statement Account
Budget formulation	Unexpended appropriations
	Balances with Treasury
Human resource management	Employee benefits
	Payroll and other compensation
	Employee benefits
	Pension/retirement liabilities
Procurement	Balances with Treasury
	Accounts payable
	Fixed assets
	Contract expense

Accounting Cycles and Financial Statement Accounts

Line Items or Accounts	Transaction-Related Accounting Cycles				
	Billing	Cash Receipts	Purchasing	Cash Disbursements	Payroll
Cash or Fund Balances with Treasury		X		X	X
Accounts Receivable	X	X			
Inventory	X		X		
Property			X		
Liabilities			X	X	
Revenue	X				
Expenses			X		X
Obligations			X	X	

Source: Adapted from proposed Chief Financial Officers Council's *Implementation Guide for OMB Circular A-123 Appendix A,* May 2005.

COORDINATING WITH THE INDEPENDENT AUDITORS

Once the significant control objectives that will be the focus of testing and evaluation have been identified, it is important to communicate with the external auditors to reach consensus on the following matters:

- The process used to identify significant control objectives, including the criteria used to distinguish significant from less significant objectives
- The list of control objectives determined to be significant

As noted in Chapter 1, proper coordination with the independent auditors and the OIG is a key ingredient in the successful implementation of the revised OMB Circular A-123 requirements. Possibly due to the newness of Sarbanes-Oxley, and in spite of the significant guidance provided by PCAOB on auditor/auditee coordination, many auditors took the extreme position that assisting management in any way would jeopardize their independence. This is an extreme position which is not warranted by the requirements set forth by either PCAOB or the SEC, and which prompted PCAOB to issue additional guidance on this matter.

In this respect, there are important lessons to be learned from the private industry's early experiences with Sarbanes-Oxley implementations. For those interested in this aspect of Sarbanes-Oxley, Appendix 4E discusses the PCAOB guidance and how auditors may assist their clients.

Appendix 4A

Action Plan: Identifying Significant Control Objectives

The following action plan is intended to help in the implementation of the suggestions contained in this chapter for identifying significant control objectives.

1. Entity-Level Control Objectives

Based on the understanding of the entity, the control criteria used to evaluate effectiveness and the expectations of the independent auditors determine significant entity-level control objectives. For example:

- Consider the following entity-level control objectives described in this chapter as significant:
  - Corporate culture
  - Personnel policies
  - General computer controls
  - Alignment between entity objectives and control structures
  - Risk identification

- ○ Antifraud programs and controls
- ○ Top-level financial reporting processes
- ○ System-wide monitoring
- Consider the relevant auditing standards for internal control reporting that will be followed by the independent auditors in their assessment (e.g., PCAOB *Auditing Standard No. 2*). Determine that all controls that independent auditors deem significant have been considered significant for the purposes of the assessment.
- Consider the following to determine whether the list of significant entity-level control objectives is complete:
  - ○ The business activities of the entity and the industry in which it operates
  - ○ The most significant financial reporting risks facing the entity
  - ○ The overall design of the entity's internal control

2. Activity-Level Control Objectives

Based on an understanding of the entity's financial statements and business activities, determine significant activity-level control objectives. For example:

- Review the entity's financial statements and identify the relevant assertions for the most significant:
  - ○ Account balances
  - ○ Classes of transactions
  - ○ Disclosures
- To make this determination, consider:
  - ○ The magnitude of the accounts
  - ○ Qualitative factors that affect materiality
  - ○ Inherent risk
  - ○ The entity's critical accounting policies
- Consider the entity's most significant value-chain activities to assess whether the list of significant activity-level control objectives is complete.

3. Coordinate with Independent Auditors

Reach a consensus with the independent auditors regarding key decisions about significant control objectives. For example:

- Communicate and reach agreement with the auditors on matters such as:
  - ○ The process used to identify significant control objectives
  - ○ The list of control objectives determined to be significant

---

Appendix 4B
Example Significant Control Objectives

Corporate Culture

Establish a culture and a "tone at the top" that fosters integrity, shared values, and teamwork in pursuit of the entity's objectives.

- Articulate and communicate codes of conduct and other policies regarding acceptable business practice, conflicts of interest, or expected standards of ethical and moral behavior.

- Reduce incentives and temptations that can motivate employees to act in a manner that is unethical, opposed to the entity's objectives, or both.

- Reinforce written policies about ethical behavior through action and leadership by example.

Personnel Policies

The entity's personnel have been provided with the information, resources, and support necessary to carry out their responsibilities effectively.

- Identify, articulate, and communicate to entity personnel the information and skills needed to perform their jobs effectively.

- Provide entity personnel with the resources needed to perform their jobs effectively.

- Supervise and monitor individuals with internal control responsibilities.

- Delegate authority and responsibility to appropriate individuals within the organization.

General Computer Controls

The entity's IT governance structure and policies create an environment in which computer application programs and controls can operate effectively.

- Develop, communicate, and plan an overall IT strategy that allows the achievement of entity-wide controls.

- Provide the resources and organizational infrastructure necessary to implement the IT strategy.

- Identify, acquire, and integrate IT applications and solutions that are necessary for implementing the IT strategy.

- Monitor IT processes to ensure their continued effectiveness.

Alignment between Objectives and Organizational and Control Structures

The entity's business objectives, organizational structure, and internal control structures are linked to and consistent with each other.

- Articulate and communicate entity-wide objectives and related business strategies.
- Design and periodically review activity-level objectives and resources to ensure they are linked to and consistent with each other and the entity-wide objectives.

Risk Identification

Implement a process that effectively identifies and responds to conditions that can significantly affect the entity's ability to achieve its objectives.

- Develop mechanisms to anticipate, identify, and react to:
  - Routine events or activities that affect the entity or activity-level objectives.
  - Unusual, significant events that can have a more dramatic and pervasive effect on the entity

Antifraud Programs and Controls

Reduce the incidence of fraud.

- Create a culture of honesty and high ethics.
- Evaluate antifraud processes and controls.
- Develop an effective antifraud oversight process.

Top-Level Financial Reporting Processes

Nonroutine, nonsystematic financial reporting adjustments are appropriately identified and approved.

- Management is aware of and understands the need for certain financial reporting adjustments.
- Information required for decision-making purposes is
  - Identified, gathered, and communicated.
  - Relevant and reliable.
- Management analyzes the information and responds appropriately.
- Management's response is reviewed and approved.
- Selection and application of accounting principles result in financial statements that are "fairly presented."
- Management identifies events and transactions for which accounting policy choices should be made or existing policies reconsidered.

- The accounting policies chosen by management have general acceptance and result in a fair presentation of financial statement information.
- Information processing and internal control policies and procedures are designed to apply the accounting principles selected appropriately.

System-wide Monitoring

Identify material weaknesses and changes in internal control that require disclosure.

- Reach a common understanding of internal control deficiencies and changes that are considered "material" and require disclosure.
- Identify material weaknesses in internal control on a timely basis.
- Identify material changes in internal control on a timely basis.

Activity-Level Control Objectives

Adequately control the initiation, processing, and disclosure of transactions.

- Identify, analyze, and manage risks that may cause material misstatement of the financial statements.
- Design and implement an information system to record, process, summarize, and report transactions accurately.
- Design and implement control activities, including policies and procedures applied in the processing of transactions that flow through the accounting system in order to prevent or detect material misstatements promptly.
- Monitor the design and operating effectiveness of activity-level internal controls to determine whether they are operating as intended and, if not, to take corrective action.

Appendix 4C
Map to the COSO *Framework*

Chapter 2 described the COSO *Internal Control—Integrated Framework* as consisting of five separate components. This chapter describes a process for identifying significant control objectives within the overall COSO *Framework*. The information presented in this chapter does not follow the exact organization of the COSO report but rather has been interpreted and organized in a way that will facilitate the identification of significant controls and their documentation and testing. Exhibit 4.8 links the five components of internal control described in the COSO *Framework* to the main topics presented in this chapter.

Exhibit 4.8 Internal Control in the COSO *Framework*

COSO Control Components	Chapter 4 Reference								
	Culture	People	Computer Controls	Alignment	Risk Identification	Anti-fraud	Top-Level Processes	System-wide Monitoring	Activity-Level Controls
Control Environment									
Integrity and ethical values	X								
Commitment to competence		X							
Senior management		X							
Management philosophy	X								
Organizational structure				X					
Assign authority and responsibility		X							
Human resources policies and practices		X							
Risk Assessment									
Objectives and linkage				X					
Entity-level risk assessment					X				
Activity-level risk assessment									
Managing change					X				X
Control Activities									
Computer general controls			X						
Computer application controls									X
Information and Communications									
Information									X
Communication									X
Monitoring									
Ongoing monitoring activities			X		X			X	X

Appendix 4D
Map to the Auditing Literature

PCAOB *Auditing Standard No. 2* for the independent auditor's audit of internal control requires the auditor to evaluate management's process for assessing internal control. The proposed standard also provides management with guidance on the execution and documentation of its evaluation of internal control. Exhibit 4.9 links controls that the independent auditors will probably expect management to test to the main topics presented in this chapter.

Appendix 4E
Working with the Independent Auditors: Lessons Learned from the Initial Implementation of Sarbanes-Oxley

During the first-year implementation of Sarbanes-Oxley, several firms (or rather, individual Partners at firms) generally refused to look at anything the auditee did until the auditee completed its Sarbanes-Oxley compliance activities and issued an assertion. These auditors took the position that if the client did something (for example, showed the auditors an example of some documentation or a testing plan), and sought the auditors' advice, then the auditors would be effectively "functioning in the capacity of management"; thus their independence would be impaired.

Even though there was early guidance from PCAOB regarding coordination between the auditee and the independent auditors, it has taken time for auditors and management to reach a common sense approach to collaboration on areas such as permissible sharing of audit documentation and proffering of audit advice. Federal agencies should be able to profit from these early lessons learned by industry, as discussed further in this appendix.

Working with the Independent Auditors

To render an opinion on either the financial statements or the effectiveness of internal control, an entity's independent auditors are required to maintain their independence, in accordance with applicable SEC rules. These rules are guided by certain underlying principles, which include:

- The audit firm must not be in a position where it audits its own work.
- The auditor must not act as management or as an employee of the client.

PCAOB *Auditing Standard No. 2* incorporates SEC's principles and then expands on these principles in important ways. Although maintaining independence is primarily the responsibility of the auditors, several of the independence requirements

Exhibit 4.9 Auditing Standard Requirements

	Culture	People	Computer Controls	Alignment	Risk Identification	Anti-fraud	Top-Level Processes	System-wide Monitoring	Activity-Level Controls
Initiation, recording, processing, and reporting of significant accounts and disclosures									X
Selection of accounting principles							X		
Antifraud programs									
Controls on which other controls depend	X	X	X	X	X		X	X	
Nonroutine and nonsystematic transactions							X		
Period-end financial reporting process							X		

of the auditing standard impose certain responsibilities on management and the audit committee. These requirements (taken from *Auditing Standard No. 2,* paragraphs 32 through 35) include:

- *Preapproval by the audit committee.* Each internal control-related service to be provided by the auditor must be preapproved by the audit committee. In its introduction to the standard, PCAOB clarifies that "the audit committee cannot preapprove internal control-related services as a category, but must approve each service."

- For proxy or other disclosure purposes, the entity may designate some auditor services as "audit" or "nonaudit" services. The requirement to preapprove internal control services applies to any internal control-related service, regardless of how it may be designated.

- *Active involvement of management.* Management must be "actively involved" in a "substantive and extensive" way in all internal control services that the auditor provides. Management cannot delegate these responsibilities, nor can it satisfy the requirement to be actively involved by merely accepting responsibility for documentation and testing performed by the auditors.

- *Independence in fact and appearance.* The entity's audit committee and external auditors must be diligent to ensure that independence, both in fact and appearance, is maintained. As articulated in paragraph 35 of *Auditing Standard No. 2:*

  > The test for independence in fact is whether the activities would impede the ability of anyone on the engagement team or in a position to influence the engagement team from exercising objective judgment in the audits of the financial statements or internal control over financial reporting. The test for independence in appearance is whether a reasonable investor, knowing all relevant facts and circumstances, would perceive an auditor as having interests which could jeopardize the exercise of objective and impartial judgments on all issues encompassed within the auditor's engagement.

Determining How the Auditors May Assist Management

No matter how detailed the independence rules may become, they cannot possibly address every possible interaction between the entity and its auditors. During the initial implementation of Sarbanes-Oxley, many situations arose that called into question whether the auditor could interact with the entity in a particular way and still maintain its independence.

For example, if the entity was unsure of whether its documentation of internal control would be acceptable, could it approach its auditors for advice? If the auditors made recommendations on how to improve the documentation and the entity then incorporated those recommendations, wouldn't that put the audit firm in the position of auditing its own work when it reviewed that documentation? The form and content of an entity's documentation of its internal control is the responsibility of management. If the auditor becomes significantly involved in that decision, doesn't that imply that they are acting in the capacity of management?

In the initial implementation of Sarbanes-Oxley, it became common for auditors to provide as little advice as possible to their clients on internal control matters. Due to concerns over possible violations of the independence rules, auditors chose to largely remove themselves from their clients' efforts.

As a practical matter, both the SEC and the PCAOB understood that public interest is not well-served if the independent auditors are completely detached from the entity's efforts to understand and assess its internal control. There must be some sharing of information between the entity and its auditors, and the auditors must be able to provide assistance and advice on some matters.

In June of 2004, the SEC and PCAOB issued guidance in this area. That guidance essentially allows the auditor to provide "limited assistance to management in documenting internal controls and making recommendations for changes to internal controls. However, management has the ultimate responsibility for the assessment, documentation and testing of the entity's internal control."

PCAOB provided more extensive guidance on how entity management may solicit advice from and share advice with their auditors on internal control matters. The guidance was in response to a question directed specifically to an auditor's review of the entity's draft financial statements or their providing advice on the adoption of a new accounting principle or emerging issue—services that historically have been considered a routine part of a high quality audit. The PCAOB staff had the following observation, which is taken from "PCAOB's Staff Questions and Answers Auditing Internal Control Over Financial Reporting June 23, 2004 (Revised July 27, 2004) Answer No. 7."

The inclusion of this circumstance in Auditing Standard No. 2 as a significant deficiency and a strong indicator of a material weakness emphasizes that a company must have effective internal control over financial reporting on its own. More specifically, the results of auditing procedures cannot be considered when evaluating whether the company's internal control provides reasonable assurance that the company's financial statements will be presented fairly in accordance with generally accepted accounting principles. There are a variety of ways that a company can emphasize that it, rather than the auditor, is responsible for the financial statements and that the company has effective controls surrounding the preparation of financial statements.

Modifying the traditional audit process such that the company provides the auditor with only a single draft of the financial statements to audit when the company believes that all its controls over the preparation of the financial statements have fully operated is one way to demonstrate management's responsibility and to be clear that all the company's controls have operated. However, this process is not necessarily what was expected to result from the implementation of Auditing Standard No. 2. Such a process might make it difficult for some companies to meet the accelerated filing deadlines for their annual reports. More importantly, such a process, combined with the accelerated filing deadlines, might put the auditor under significant pressure to complete the audit of the financial statements in too short a time period thereby impairing, rather than improving, audit quality. Therefore, some type of information-sharing on a timely basis between management and the auditor is necessary.

A company may share interim drafts of the financial statements with the auditor. The company can minimize the risk that the auditor would determine that his or her involvement in this process might represent a significant deficiency or material weakness through clear communications (either written or oral) with the auditor about the following:

- State of completion of the financial statements;
- Extent of controls that had operated or not operated at the time; and
- Purpose for which the company was giving the draft financial statements to the auditor.

For example, a company might give the auditor draft financial statements to audit that lack two notes required by generally accepted accounting principles. Absent any communication from the company to clearly indicate that the company recognizes that two specific required notes are lacking, the auditor might determine that the lack of those notes constitutes a material misstatement of the financial statements that represents a significant deficiency and is a strong indicator of a material weakness. On the other hand, if the company makes it clear when it provides the draft financial statements to the auditor that two specific required notes are lacking and that those completed notes will be provided at a later time, the auditor would not consider their omission at that time a material misstatement of the financial statements.

As another example, a company might release a partially completed note to the auditor and make clear that the company's process for preparing the numerical information included in a related table is complete and, therefore, that the company considers the numerical information to be fairly stated even though the company has not yet completed the text of the note. At the same time, the company might indicate that the auditor should not yet subject the entire note to audit, but only the table. In this case, the auditor would evaluate only the numerical information in the table and the company's process to complete the table. However, if the auditor identifies a misstatement of the information in the table, he or she should consider that circumstance a misstatement of the financial statements. If the auditor determines that the misstatement is material, a significant deficiency as well as a strong indicator of a material weakness would exist.

This type of analysis, focusing on the company's responsibility for internal control, may be extended to other types of auditor involvement. For example, many audit firms prepare accounting disclosure checklists to assist both companies and auditors in evaluating whether financial statements include all the required disclosures under GAAP. Obtaining a blank accounting disclosure checklist from the company's auditor and independently completing the checklist as part of the procedures to prepare the financial statements is not, by itself, an indication of a weakness in the company's controls over the period-end financial reporting process. As another example, if the company obtains the blank accounting disclosure checklist from its auditor, requests the auditor to complete the checklist, and the auditor determines that a material required disclosure is missing, that situation would represent a significant deficiency and a strong indicator of a material weakness.

These evaluations, focusing on the company's responsibility for internal control over financial reporting, will necessarily involve judgment on the part of the auditor. A discussion with management about an emerging accounting issue that the auditor has recently become aware of, or the application of a complex and highly technical accounting pronouncement in the company's particular circumstances, are all types of timely auditor involvement that should not necessarily be indications of weaknesses in a company's internal control over financial reporting. However, as described above, clear communication between management and the auditor about the purpose for which the auditor is being involved is important. Although the auditor should not determine that the implications of Auditing Standard No. 2 force the auditor to become so far removed from the financial reporting process on a timely basis that audit quality is impaired, some aspects of the traditional audit process may need to be carefully structured as a result of this increased focus on the effectiveness of the company's internal control over financial reporting.

Thus, "some type of information-sharing on a timely basis between management and the auditor is necessary." However, when management seeks the assistance of the entity's auditors to help with its internal control assessment, it should make it clear that management retains the ultimate responsibility for internal control. The PCAOB places the burden on management to clearly communicate with the auditors the nature of the advice they are seeking and the purpose for which the auditor is being involved.

Notes

1. The term *accidental values* is described by Patrick Lencioni in his article, "Make Your Values Mean Something," *Harvard Business Review,* July (2002).
2. This article originally appeared in the *Harvard Business Review,* March (2003).
3. This document may be downloaded free of charge from the American Institute of Certified Public Accountants (AICPA) website at www.aicpa.org/antifraud/homepage.htm. From the "select a topic" menu, choose "Prevent Fraud" and you will be linked to a new page. Select "Instituting Antifraud Programs and Controls" to link to the documents.
4. See AICPA *Professional Standards,* vol. 1, sec. 411.04, 411.09, 411.14, and 411.15.
5. Michael Hammer and James Champy, *Reengineering the Corporation: A Manifesto for Business Revolution* (New York: Harper Business, 1993), 35.

Chapter 5

Documentation of Significant Controls

Chapter Summary

- Describe the importance of adequate documentation of internal control.
- Describe the importance of considering all significant control objectives.
- Summarize contents of anticipated key documents for significant entity-level control objectives.
- Describe documentation requirements for activity-level controls.
- Provide an example flowcharting method for documenting activity-level controls.
- Describe the necessary design features and key implementation issues related to automated documentation tools.

DOCUMENTATION: WHAT IT IS AND IS *NOT*

The Importance of Documentation

Adequate documentation of internal control is important for the following reasons:

- *Improved reliability of internal control.* As described in Chapter 6, documentation of internal control policies and procedures improves the effectiveness and reliability of internal control. Without adequate documentation, the performance of the system depends exclusively on the skills and competence of the individual(s) responsible for performing the control procedure. As such, performance can vary greatly between individuals or over time. Adequate documentation reduces this variability by facilitating the consistent dissemination of critical information, namely, the policy or procedure to be performed, by whom, when, and for what purpose. Additionally, by clearly stating the parameters within which a control procedure should be performed, it becomes easier to identify deviations from the policy or procedure—that is, material weaknesses can be identified.

- *Enabling of effective monitoring.* As described in Chapter 1, management is required to report material changes in internal control periodically. Thus, one of the most important features of the monitoring component of the entity's internal control system is its ability to identify change. Documentation facilitates this monitoring element. Documentation is *not* internal control any more than a reflection of yourself in the mirror is actually you. However, like the image in a mirror, internal control documentation should be a highly accurate representation of the actual system. Changes in the documentation should represent changes to internal control itself. By monitoring these changes to the documentation, you effectively monitor changes to internal control.

At too many federal agencies, the year-end closing depends not on a process, but on ad hoc (even heroic) efforts undertaken by financial managers to prepare auditable financial statements. Adequate documentation will go a long way in solving this problem. In addition to enhancing the overall effectiveness of internal control, documentation will also facilitate management's assessment of effectiveness by providing a basis for:

- Evaluating design effectiveness
- Planning tests of operating effectiveness

Finally, both the auditing standards of the Public Company Accounting Oversight Board (PCAOB) and the guidance provided by Circular A-123 of the Office of Management and Budget (OMB) would consider inadequate documentation to be a deficiency in internal control that may rise to the level of material weakness.

What Documentation Is Not

As the analogy of the reflection in the mirror suggests, the documentation of internal control should never be confused with internal control itself. In a similar vein, the mere documentation of a control policy or procedure provides *no evidence* to support the operating effectiveness of the control. For example, the documentation of an entity's values and its commitment to integrity and ethical values gives one a starting point for determining whether its "corporate" culture is conducive to effective controls. Based on reading this statement of values, one may determine that the intent of the policies is consistent with a strong control environment; however, this documentation, by itself, will not allow conclusions to be drawn about whether the policy is operating as designed. To support a conclusion about operations, it is necessary to gather evidence by performing testwork. An entity that automates certain control-related business processes is not relieved of this obligation to test control performance.

The Objective of This Phase of the Assessment Project

In almost every entity there is a difference between the way a system is *supposed to work* and the reality of how it *actually works*. Sometimes these differences are minor, and sometimes they are not. At this phase of the project the goal is to gather and analyze documentation about how the system *is supposed to work*. In the next phase of the project the goal will be to gather evidence to determine how the system actually functions in practice.

A lack of documentation does not mean that a control does not exist. In many instances, it may only mean that the existing control (which may have been developed informally) has not been documented. In some instances, one may need to expand the scope of the project to include the documentation of controls when adequate documentation does not exist. To avoid misunderstandings with the "owner" of the business process being documented, it is usually best to perform the documentation phase of the engagement in two steps:

1. Assess the adequacy of documentation.
2. Create additional documentation as required.

Automated Documentation Tools

Often, entities will use a computer-based tool to aid in the accumulation, creation, and storage of internal control documentation. The guidance provided in this chapter is applicable to *all* forms of documentation, whether facilitated by a computerized system or not. Appendix 5B provides guidance on evaluating the design and implementation of automated documentation tools.

ASSESSING THE ADEQUACY OF EXISTING DOCUMENTATION

As described in Chapter 1, at each phase of the assessment project, one should begin by assessing the efforts already taken by management to determine whether these efforts have been sufficient to meet the stated objective. For this phase of the effort, it is important to identify the agency's existing documentation of controls and assess whether it provides adequate support for management's assertion about whether controls have been suitably designed. In assessing the adequacy of documentation, one should determine whether:

- *All significant control objectives have been considered.* Control policies and procedures should be documented for *all* significant control objectives. If control policies have *not* been documented for certain identified significant control objectives, then one must determine whether:
  - Controls do not exist to achieve the stated control objective; in which case, the entity must design, implement, and document new control procedures.
  - Controls exist to achieve the control objective but are informal, communicated verbally, or otherwise not documented. In this case, suitable documentation must be developed to facilitate an evaluation of the effectiveness of the design of the control.
- *Documentation is sufficient.* To be sufficient, documentation should allow management and the independent auditor to:
  - Determine whether the policy or procedure is adequately designed to:
    - Create an environment that allows the effective functioning of activity-level controls.
    - Prevent or detect material financial statement misstatements in a timely manner by people performing their assigned functions.

    ○ Design and perform procedures to test the operating effectiveness of the controls.

Exhibit 5.1 describes this process for evaluating the adequacy of existing documentation. The steps in the process in black represent step 1 in the process, which is an assessment of the adequacy of documentation. Steps in white represent step 2 in the process, which is the creation of existing documentation.

What Should Be Documented

Documentation of controls should contain the following elements:

- A link between the control objective and the control policy or procedure
- A description of the control policy or procedure that achieves the control objective

Appendix 5C includes example control policies and procedures, organized by significant control objective and giving:

- Information about:
  - ○ How transactions are initiated, recorded, processed, and reported

Exhibit 5.1   Assessing the Adequacy of Existing Client Documentation

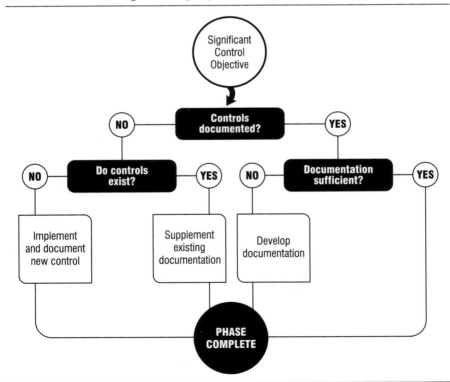

- The flow of transactions to identify where material misstatements owing to error or fraud could occur
- A description of:
  - How the control procedure is to be applied
  - Who is responsible for performing the procedure
  - How frequently the procedure is performed

DOCUMENTATION OF ENTITY-LEVEL CONTROL POLICIES AND PROCEDURES

Corporate Governance Documents

Several of the entity-level control objectives described in Chapter 4 fall under the general topic of "corporate" governance. In practice, corporate governance is often associated with private entities. A popular definition of corporate governance is the following:

> Corporate governance is the system by which business corporations are directed and controlled. The corporate governance structure specifies the distribution of rights and responsibilities among different participants in the corporation, such as the board, managers, shareholders and other stakeholders, and spells out the rules and procedures for making decisions on corporate affairs. By doing this, it also provides the structure through which the company objectives are set, and the means of attaining those objectives and monitoring performance.[1]

The above definition can be easily adapted to the federal government by, for example, substituting "agency" for "corporation," "Congress" for the "board," and "taxpayers" for "shareholders." Regardless of the chosen definition, in the federal government, "corporate governance" is defined by laws, rules, and regulations enacted by Congress or an appropriate oversight agency such as the OMB, the Government Accountability Office (GAO), or the Department of Treasury. These rules result in the federal government usually having relatively formal, well-documented policies that describe entity-level controls related to the following broad control areas:

- "Corporate" culture
- Alignment between objectives and controls
- Risk identification
- Disclosure controls and procedures
- Top-level financial reporting processes

To evaluate the adequacy of documentation related to the agency's corporate governance policies, it is a good idea to compare the agency's documentation with that of other agencies.

The following is a brief description of relevant corporate governance documentation that may address these entity-wide control objectives.

Documentation of Agency Mission.   There are several sources of information in this area including the original law creating the department or agency. One should consider budgetary submissions to the President and Congress and formal descriptions of the agency's "vision" and related mission usually developed in connection with the requirements of the Government Performance and Results Act of 1993. A review of this documentation is essential to understanding an agency's internal control environment and its goals, including performance goals and critical programs.

Code of Conduct.   A written code of conduct can help the entity achieve certain significant control objectives in a variety of ways, including:

- Increased awareness of and sensitivity to ethical issues among its personnel
- Clear guidance on permissible and impermissible behavior

As described in Chapter 4, a "corporate" culture is a socialization process that involves the establishment of values, norms, and shared beliefs. A written code of conduct will aid greatly in this process. Within the federal government, the Office of Government Ethics (OGE) is responsible for issuing "Standards of Ethical Conduct for Employees of the Executive Branch." The OGE was established by the Ethics in Government Act of 1978 and became an individual agency on October 1, 1989, pursuant to the Office of Government Ethics Reauthorization Act of 1988. One of the agency's goals is to prevent conflicts of interest on the part of government employees and to resolve those conflicts of interest should they occur. Federal agencies designate an official to work with the OGE in the development of the agency's own ethics program. In addition, the OGE holds an annual conference to keep federal officials abreast of developments in this area. Within the guidelines set by the OGE, agencies generally adopt a formal code of conduct. This code of conduct will typically include:

- A statement of the agency's values
- A statement of the people or group of people who are affected by the agency (i.e., taxpayers, stakeholders, Congress, employees)
- A discussion of the types of ethical problems that agency personnel are likely to encounter and guidance on how these situations should be resolved
- The identification of key behaviors that are acceptable and unacceptable in the workplace
- Recommendations on how to identify and resolve conflicts of interest
- Recommendations on how to report violations of the code and to whom
- Consequences of violating the code
- How reported violations will generally be investigated

Human Resource Policies and Personnel Handbook.   The Office of Personnel Management (OPM) is responsible for developing guidance governing the development of human resource policy by federal agencies. Following this guidance, agencies will typically document their human resource policies and communicate these policies to their employees through a personnel manual or handbook. Human resource policies may address dozens of issues, which can include everything from guidelines on attendance and cell phone use to vacation plans and workplace diversity. For the purpose of evaluating internal controls, documentation should focus on those policies most directly related to:

- Demonstrating the entity's commitment to competence
- Communicating messages to employees regarding expected levels of integrity, ethical behavior, and competence

Both of these elements of the entity's control environment were discussed in Chapter 2.

Personnel policies that typically have significant internal control implications include those related to:

- Recruiting potential employees, including screening and background checks
- Hiring new employees
- New employee orientation, including senior management hired from outside the agency or the federal government
- Ongoing training
- Compensation and benefits
- Promotion
- Performance appraisal and feedback
- Disciplinary measures
- Employee termination procedures

Issues such as conflicts of interest and use of agency property may or may not be included in the personnel handbook. To provide a comprehensive discussion, these policies are included in this discussion of the entity's code of conduct.

Accounting Manuals. The agency's accounting manual should provide information relating to the procedures used to capture and process accounting information, the documents required in the processing, and the related control procedures. Typically, this information is most useful for documenting activity-level controls. However, the accounting manual may provide some documentation that is relevant for entity-wide controls, particularly those related to top-level financial reporting control objectives.

For this purpose, when reviewing the entity's accounting manual, look for documentation related to:

- Procedures and related controls for closing the books at the end of the accounting period
- The process used to identify nonroutine, nonsystematic journal entries and the approvals required before these are recorded

- Reclassifications and other adjustments required to combine the financial information of various component units or otherwise prepare the financial statements
- The process used to prepare significant accounting estimates

DOCUMENTING ACTIVITY-LEVEL CONTROLS

The processing of accounting transactions is relatively linear, as indicated in Exhibit 5.2.

Reading from left to right, the entity enters into a transaction, for example, the purchase of goods or materials. That transaction generates data, some of which are significant for accounting purposes, and some of which are not. In this example, the description of the items purchased, the amount paid, and when the goods were received are all significant factors in the recognition, measurement, presentations, or disclosure of the transaction in the financial statements. The vendor's invoice number is also included as part of the transaction data, but this information has no relevance for accounting purposes.[2]

Raw transaction data must be transformed into information that can be processed by the accounting system, that is, information that will eventually result in a debit and credit to the general ledger. Once the accounting information has been prepared, the transaction enters the accounting system to be recognized and measured for financial reporting purposes. As indicated in Exhibit 5.2, several discrete processing steps may be required before the information is ultimately posted in the general ledger and other accounting records.

This entire process, which begins with the capture of raw transactional data and ends with posting to the general ledger, is the activity-level processing stream. Through this journey, raw data is changed; it is combined with other data, added, multiplied, subtracted, and divided, or otherwise manipulated to create new information. Controls are needed to ensure that, throughout this multistep transformation process, the information retains its original integrity. It must remain complete and accurate. The processing stream itself must also retain its integrity, accepting all valid transactions and preventing unauthorized ones from entering the stream.

When one is evaluating the effectiveness of significant activity-level controls, it is important to assess the internal controls of the processing stream taken as a whole. Thus, when one is documenting activity-level controls, the control structure for the entire stream should be considered, starting with the transaction data, all the way through to the posting of debits and credits.

Documentation Requirements

Earlier in this chapter, the elements that should be included in the documentation of controls were discussed. Essentially, how the control procedure is related to the control objective should be addressed, and a description of the control that is sufficient to gauge the effectiveness of design should be provided. The discussions that follow address controls to be documented and the possible forms documentation may take.

Exhibit 5.2   Processing Accounting Transactions

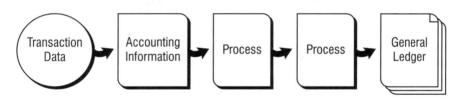

Determine the Controls to be Documented.   This book describes a risk-based, top-down overall approach to assessing control effectiveness. This approach recognizes that *not all* of an entity's controls should be documented and tested. Before beginning the documentation of activity-level controls, it is important to have a thorough understanding of:

- The entity's overall business objectives
- The significant classes of transactions that the entity routinely enters into to achieve those objectives
- The financial reporting risks associated with those transactions
- The control objectives related to those risks

Understanding these items will allow for the focusing of efforts on documenting only the controls that matter. Redundant controls and controls related to insignificant financial reporting risks need not be documented or tested.

If the assessment process begins with the assumption that documentation of all of the entity's control procedures is required, then the entity is destined to perform excess work that is not required to comply with OMB Circular A-123 requirements (or Sarbanes-Oxley requirements, for that matter).

How to Design Internal Control Documentation.   The way in which the entity's routine transactions are documented is entirely up to the entity. The major requirement is that the documentation of controls is sufficiently detailed and clear to allow:

- Those affected by the procedure to understand it and either perform the procedure or monitor its performance
- The Project Team to assess design effectiveness and design tests of operating effectiveness

In addition, PCAOB *Auditing Standard No. 2* provides guidance which, although not specifically required by A-123 guidance, can be very useful in ensuring the completeness of documentation. Documentation, though not one of the COSO components, is an integral part of the internal control structure. High quality documentation enables the effective communication of prescribed control procedures across the organization and over time. Documentation allows for the consistent performance and monitoring of controls, which allows internal control to be institutionalized, become part of a *system,* and become less reliant on the competency and diligence of individual employees. As control documentation is designed, it is important to consider whether it is capable of achieving these broader objectives.

There are three basic documentation techniques:

- Flowcharts
- Narratives
- Matrices

Each technique has its relative strengths and weaknesses. Typically, a combination of two or all three techniques is used to document a given transaction or business process. Occasionally, to document one of the entity's less significant transactions, for example, one technique may suffice.

The process followed to design internal control documentation typically involves the following steps:

1. Decide on objective(s) for the documentation. For example, is the documentation being prepared solely for the Project Team to comply with the requirements of the internal control assessment? Or will the documentation be distributed widely at the entity to communicate control procedures and responsibilities?

2. Determine the content necessary to achieve entity objectives.

3. Decide which documentation techniques are best suited to communicate entity needs.

4. Design individual documents and overall document architecture. Regardless of which documentation technique is used, it is important to design individual documents or set basic guidelines for their creation. The entity should also determine how the individual documents relate to each other—that is, the overall documentation architecture. This design of individual documents and overall architecture is a fluid process in which the design of one will affect the design of the other.

Functional Considerations in Structuring a Documentation Architecture.
When designing the entity's documentation of internal control, consider the following functional features that should be included:

- *Maintainability.* Documentation should be able to facilitate easy updating and maintenance as business processes and controls change over time.

- *Ease of Review.* The documentation of internal control should be designed in a user-friendly fashion. For compliance purposes, the Project Team and the external auditors are the primary users, so the documentation should allow these individuals to:

  o Easily assess the effectiveness of the design of internal control.

  o Facilitate the design of tests of controls.

- *Information Gathering.* The creation of new or update of existing documentation will require people to gather information about the entity's business processes and controls. The entity's documentation methods should recognize this need and, to the extent possible, make it easy to gather and input the information required to create appropriate documentation.

- *Scalability.* Documentation techniques should be equally adept at handling processes with many control points and those with only a few.

- *Clarity.* Whether your documentation allows individual employees to easily understand their responsibilities and to facilitate the communication of business processed and controls and roles and responsibilities throughout the organization.

Documentation Content Considerations. Paragraph 42 of PCAOB *Auditing Standard No. 2* imposes certain information requirements to be included in the documentation of routine transactions. As noted earlier, although this guidance does not apply to federal agencies, the assessment Project Team will likely find the following documentation requirements useful:

- The design of controls over all relevant assertions related to all significant accounts and disclosures in the financial statements. The documentation should include the five components of internal control over financial reporting.

- Information about how significant transactions are initiated, authorized, recorded, processed, and reported.

- Sufficient information about the flow of transactions to identify the points at which material misstatements due to error or fraud could occur.

- Controls designed to prevent or detect fraud, including who performs the controls and the related segregation of duties.

In addition to the Sarbanes-Oxley required content elements, the entity may find that documenting the following information will also help improve the overall effectiveness of the internal control documentation architecture:

- *Labels for control procedures, control objectives, or other information.* Assigning a unique label to information (for example, one control procedure may be labeled "C-1," another "C-2," etc.) allows for the easy linking or cross-referencing between individual documents.

- *Links to tests of operating effectiveness.* When evaluating the results of tests of controls, the control objective that the control procedure was designed to achieve should be considered. Providing that link in the documentation of internal control will facilitate the effective review of test results.

- *Links to overall conclusion on design effectiveness.* This evaluation typically is performed for the transaction or business process as a whole and not for individual control procedures.

- *Date prepared or modified, date reviewed, and by whom.* This information will help assess the currency or continued accuracy of the documentation.

FLOWCHARTING

Flowcharting allows for the graphic description of the overall information processing stream for a transaction or group of transactions. Markers on the flowchart may then be used to indicate the point in the stream where control procedures are performed and to reference a description of the control procedure itself. Flowcharts may be embedded within a narrative to provide the reader with a high-level, more general depiction of the details described in the narrative.

Strengths and Weaknesses

Strengths of Flowcharting as a Documentation Method for Routine Activity-Level Controls

- Easy to recognize the point in the processing stream at which errors could be introduced and control procedures should be located. This information aids in evaluating design effectiveness and determining which controls should be tested.
- Highly effective at capturing the overall flow of information.
- For visual learners, flowcharts are the most effective means of communicating information about information processes and controls.
- Scalable and highly flexible format.

Weaknesses of Flowcharting as a Documentation Method for Routine Activity-Level Controls

- By itself, not capable of capturing all required documentation elements or the necessary detailed description of control procedures
- Must be supplemented with other types of documentation

Tips for Flowcharting

Follow the Flow of Information.   Accounting manuals and other traditional means of documenting accounting processes frequently focus on the flow of documents through the system. For example, if a four-part receiving form is completed to document the receipt of goods or materials, one approach to documentation would be to track the processing and eventual disposition of each of the four copies of the form. For the purpose of understanding activity-level controls, it is usually more effective to track the flow of *information* rather than the flow of documents. By tracking the flow of information, it is easier to identify the processes that change that information. Whenever information is changed, the risk of error enters the system, and that risk must be controlled.

To focus on the flow of information, one should consider working *backward,* beginning with the posting to the general ledger. Obtain answers to a series of questions that seek to determine what *information* is created throughout the process and *how it is processed*. For example:

- What is posted as a debit to equipment and a credit to accounts payable?
  Monthly purchases.

- How is this information created?
  It is an accumulation of individual transactions throughout the month.

- How is the information related to individual transactions created?
  Invoices are matched with receiving reports and purchase orders and entered into the system on a real-time basis.

In this short example, how information is created and processed from initiation through posting was determined. The fact that one copy of the purchase order is sent to the vendor or that program managers receive updates on raw material receipts is not considered.

Exhibit 5.3 describes this process. To highlight this method of working *backward,* the flowchart has been reoriented vertically, rather than the horizontal process depicted in Exhibit 5.2. In this depiction, the general ledger accounts are at the top of the flowchart, and then work *downward* to eventually identify the documents that captured the original transaction data.

Define the Boundaries of the System. Accounting systems have limits, and it is important to define them clearly. The entity's control procedures start at the perimeter of its accounting system.

For example, an entity's purchase of goods or materials may begin when the entity places the orders. The process continues through the vendor's selection, packing, and shipment of the product. Ultimately, the entity receives the goods/materials it ordered. In this scenario, the entity's controls begin when it receives the goods. It would be unreasonable to extend the control system any further upstream, for example, to the vendor's procedures for selecting and packing the materials.

In this instance, the boundary of the activity-level accounting system is defined as the point at which the transaction information is approved and authorized and is in a format that is usable for accounting purposes (i.e., allows for the posting of debits and credits). This definition of the accounting system boundary has several important implications. As a "gatekeeper" to the system, the system boundary must include control policies and procedures to ensure that:

- Only valid, authorized transactions are allowed to enter the processing stream.
- All valid, authorized transactions are captured for processing.
- The accounting information that is captured accurately reflects the terms of the transaction.

Documentation of activity-level controls should include a description of the control policies and procedures that meet these boundary control objectives.

Exhibit 5.4 describes how the control boundary functions. Note that invalid, unau-thorized transactions may attempt to enter the system at any point in the process-ing. Thus, the control boundary is depicted as a perimeter that encompasses the entire processing stream. For example, controls should exist to ensure that unauthorized journal entries are prevented from being posted directly to the general ledger account,

Exhibit 5.3   Capturing Information Flow

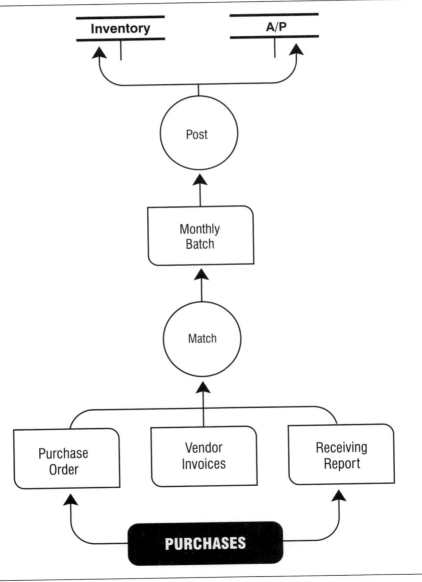

thereby bypassing the processing stream and the controls built into that stream. Note that the boundary is established after the determination that a valid transaction exists, at the point at which the information is presented in a form that contains accounting information. In this example, this occurs after entity personnel match the receiving reports and purchase order with the vendor invoice.

Transactions versus Events. Accounting information can be generated from either transactions or events. So far, the control implications related to business transactions, for example, the purchase of goods or materials, have been discussed. However, what about the recording of depreciation expense? The process of calculating and posting depreciation expense is initiated not from a transaction with an external party, but rather with an event, namely, the passage of time.

Exhibit 5.4   Control Boundary

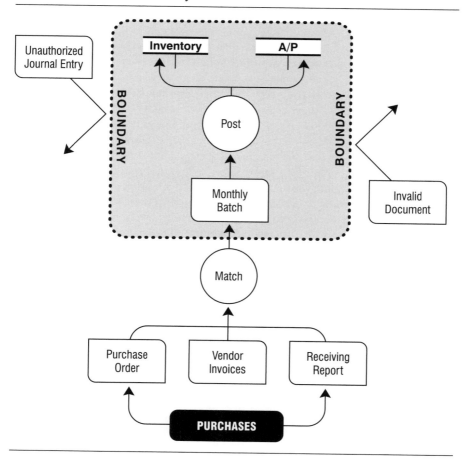

Like transactions, events occur at the perimeter of the accounting system. The "gatekeeper" control objectives relating to events are the same as those relating to transactions; however, the way those objectives are achieved usually varies.

At the boundary, *transactions* usually are controlled in real time, on a transaction-by-transaction basis. Proper authorization of each transaction is critical. *Events* can be triggered merely by the passage of time. For example, the recording of depreciation expense is initiated by the arrival of the end of the month, and so authorization of each individual event is not as critical. The processing of the event may be initiated by the system itself. The control procedures are usually performed after the fact, not at the time the event is processed. For example, the agency's accountants may scan the general ledger to ensure that depreciation expense was recorded only once.

Preventive versus Detective Controls.   Controls can be designed:

- Either to identify errors as they occur and prevent them from further processing
- Or to detect and correct errors that have already entered the system

There are trade-offs for each approach. *Preventive* controls are more timely and help ensure that errors are never recorded in the accounting records to begin with. However, to design and perform preventive controls at each step in the processing stream may be costly, whereas *detective* controls may be cheaper to design and perform. For example, performing a reconciliation once a month between the general ledger and a subsidiary ledger may be more efficient than performing preventive controls on each transaction at each step in the process. However, the drawback to detective controls is that they are performed after the fact, sometimes well after the fact. The lack of timely performance of a detective control could mean that errors remain in the accounting records for extended periods. Most systems rely on a combination of preventive and detective controls, and it is common to build some redundancy into the system, by which more than one control meets the same objective.

Preventive and detective controls have one important thing in common: both types of controls contain both an error detection and a correction component. The fact that a control procedure can identify an error does not make the control effective. It is the process of communicating identified errors to individuals who can make corrections that makes the control complete.

Information Storage and Retrieval.   It is common for systems to capture data, store it, and then retrieve it for later use. For example, an entity may maintain a database of approved vendors. This database is updated regularly as vendors are added or removed. When the time comes to authorize a payment, the control procedure requires someone to access the database and determine whether the vendor has been approved. If the vendor is in the database, then payment is authorized; if not, then the matter is brought to someone of appropriate authority to take follow-up action.

Databases and other types of information storage repositories should be considered part of the activity-level processing stream and therefore "protected" by the control boundary. All the control boundary objectives should be addressed for gaining

access to the information storage repository. In this example, controls should exist
to ensure:

- All approved vendors are in the database.
- No unapproved vendors are in the database.
- Only authorized users have the ability to access and modify the information maintained in the database.

Computer Application Controls.   Many control procedures are programmed
into the entity's computer system. For example, the process of matching a vendor
to a database of preapproved vendors may be completely computerized. A user submits an invoice for payment, the computer performs the match, and, if the vendor
is on the list, processing is allowed to continue. The user is informed only when the
computer detects an error, namely, that the vendor has not been preapproved. It is
then the user's responsibility to take the appropriate follow-up action. Again, the
follow-up of the identified errors is a critical component of the control.

Ultimately, the effectiveness of computer application controls will depend on
the effectiveness of computer general controls, including:

- *Systems development.* The application was properly developed and tested to make
  sure that the control functions as designed.
- *Access.* Access to the program is monitored to ensure that unauthorized changes
  to the program cannot be made.

The control objectives for computer application controls are the same as the objectives for manual controls—information must remain complete and accurate at all
phases, from initiation (data input) through processing.

NARRATIVES

A narrative is simply a description of the information processing steps and related
controls. Typically, this information is presented as a linear text, although it is possible to include nontext elements (for example, multimedia files) or to construct an
overall documentation architecture that is nonlinear.

Strengths and Weaknesses

Strengths of Narratives as a Documentation Method for Routine Activity-Level Controls

- On one hand, narratives can be the most flexible of the primary documentation
  methods. The overall structure of the narrative can serve a variety of primary
  objectives. For example, it can be organized to trace the flow of transactions or
  track the relationship of risks to control objectives.
- For textual learners, narratives are a highly effective method of communicating
  information about processing streams and controls.

- Well-written narratives on how information is processed and controlled will provide a natural lead-in to a discussion of the assessment of the overall design effectiveness of the system.

Weaknesses of Narratives as a Documentation Method for Routine Activity-Level Controls

- On the other hand, narratives can be relatively *inflexible* and rigid. Once the organizational scheme of a narrative is set, it is difficult to reengineer that scheme to achieve a different purpose. For example, a narrative written to help the external auditors evaluate control design effectiveness may not be useful for employees who need to know what procedures they are responsible for performing unless the narrative is completely rewritten.

- Due to the static nature of the medium, narratives may be difficult to maintain and update as processes and controls change.

- It is easy for narratives to become bloated, which reduces their effectiveness. Narratives can be used to capture any and all information, but with too much information the text loses focus and becomes confusing.

- Narratives are an effective way to communicate information, but the form does not readily lend itself to capturing information from operational personnel about information processes and controls.

Tips for Preparing Narratives

There are two basic ways that narratives can be used in the documentation of internal control—as the primary documentation means, supplemented by flowcharts, matrices, or both, or as a supplement to other forms of documentation.

Narratives as the Primary Documentation Means.   The best way to prepare effective and efficient narrative documentation of internal controls is to develop one general format for the narrative and use it repeatedly to document all significant transactions. This consistency will benefit:

- Documentation preparers, who will become more adept at documenting internal control if they are required to master only one general narrative structure

- Project Team members and external auditors who review internal control documentation and who will quickly appreciate reviewing a consistent format and approach

- Operations personnel who provide the information on processes and controls necessary to create good documentation

Additionally, with one standard narrative format, the entity will be better able to ensure that all documentation contains each of the elements required by PCAOB *Auditing Standard No. 2,* and they will be able to more quickly modify documentation as changes to processes or controls occur.

In developing a standard narrative structure, the main requirements are that the narrative structure includes all required documentation elements and that the narration is logically organized and easy to follow. The following is an example outline that achieves the above objectives.

Example Outline

Narrative Documentation of Internal Controls

I. Overview
    A. Description of transaction being described
    B. General ledger accounts affected and relevant assertions
    C. Business process owner and groups involved in the process
    D. Subledger and subsidiary accounting records involved in the process
    E. Information Technology (IT) systems and electronic files involved in the process

II. Transaction Initiation
    A. The process for initiating the transaction
    B. Whether, and if so how, the process is documented
    C. The financial reporting-related risks inherent in the process (that is, "what could go wrong?")
    D. Description of the controls in place to address the issues raised in C
        i.   Who performs the control procedure
        ii.   How frequently and when the procedure is performed
        iii. Whether, and if so how, the control procedure is documented
        iv.   Whether the control is computerized, manual, or a combination of both
        v.   If applicable, an indication of which control(s) are the "key" controls most responsible for ensuring that the financial reporting objectives related to the transaction are met

III. Transaction Authorization
    A. The policies and procedures followed for authorizing the transaction
    B. Whether, and if so how, the performance of the authorization procedures is documented
    C. The financial reporting-related risks inherent in the process (that is, "what could go wrong?")
    D. Description of the controls in place to address the issues raised in C
        i.   Who performs the control procedure
        ii.   How frequently and when the procedure is performed
        iii. Whether, and if so how, the control procedure is documented
        iv.   Whether the control is computerized, manual, or a combination of both
        v.   If applicable, an indication of which control(s) are "key" controls most responsible for ensuring that the financial reporting objectives related to the transaction are met

IV. Recording the Transaction
    A. The process for initially recording the transaction

    B. Whether, and if so how, the recording of the transaction is documented
    C. The financial reporting-related risks inherent in the initial recording of the transaction (that is, "what could go wrong?")
    D. Description of the controls in place to address the issues raised in C
      i. Who performs the control procedure
      ii. How frequently and when the procedure is performed
      iii. Whether, and if so how, the control procedure is documented
      iv. Whether the control is computerized, manual, or a combination of both
      v. If applicable, an indication of which control(s) are "key" controls most responsible for ensuring that the financial reporting objectives related to the transaction are met

V. Transaction Processing
    A. Once recorded, the information processing steps required to eventually post the transaction to the general ledger and any related subsidiary ledgers
    B. Whether, and if so how, each step of the information processing is documented
    C. The financial reporting-related risks inherent in each step of the information processing (that is, "what could go wrong?")
    D. Description of the controls in place at each step to address the issues raised in C
      i. Who performs the control procedure
      ii. How frequently and when the procedure is performed
      iii. Whether, and if so how, the control procedure is documented
      iv. Whether the control is computerized, manual, or a combination of both
      v. If applicable, an indication of which control(s) are "key" controls most responsible for ensuring that the financial reporting objectives related to the transaction are met.

In reviewing the outline, note that:

- After a brief overview of the transaction, the overarching structure follows the basic information processing stream and includes four of the five required elements of internal control documentation described in paragraph 42 of PCAOB *Auditing Standard No. 2*. This processing stream begins with the initiation of the transaction and ends with its posting to the general ledger. (The fifth required element, how the transaction is reported in the financial statements, is documented as part of the entity's period-end financial reporting process.) This linear structure is logical and easy to follow.

- Within each section is the same information, organized in the same fashion. The organizational scheme described in the outline tracks the COSO *Framework*, which is echoed in PCAOB *Auditing Standard No. 2*. After describing how the information is processed, the financial reporting-related risks ("what could go wrong") and how the control procedures are designed to mitigate those risks are discussed.

- The documentation of the other information listed in the outline includes suggestions that will help in planning the tests of operating effectiveness.

To prepare a narrative consider the following:

- Distinguish between information *processes* and *controls*. A *process* changes or manipulates the data, for example, by performing a mathematical or logical operation. Extending an invoice by multiplying the number of items shipped by their sales price is a process. When data is processed, errors can occur.

  A *control* is a procedure to prevent or detect the errors that can be introduced in the processing of data. Recalculating the extended invoice or otherwise is an example of a control.

  A narrative will be much clearer and easier to understand if the entity clearly distinguishes between the information processing steps and the control procedures related to those steps.

- When considering "what could go wrong," be sure to cover all relevant assertions for the affected account(s). Financial reporting-related risks are directly related to financial statement assertions. For example, there is a risk that not all authorized transactions will be recorded (completeness assertion) or that fictitious transactions will be processed (existence assertion). To ensure that all possible risks have been considered, review the relevant assertions and verify that each one has been addressed.

- When describing controls, check to make sure that at least one control has been identified to address each of the identified risks.

- When writing the narrative, use subheadings and bullet points to make the document more readable.

Narratives as a Supplement to Other Forms of Documentation. Narratives can be used to supplement other forms of documentation such as a matrix or a flowchart. The most common ways to use narratives in this fashion include the following:

- Add analysis or higher level understanding to a matrix. A matrix presents information at a high level of detail, and it is sometimes difficult for a user to absorb and understand its meaning. A narrative can be attached to a matrix to provide this type of analysis. For example, the narrative can provide an "executive summary" of conclusions about design effectiveness or an approach to testing control effectiveness. The matrix itself would then support the detail that justifies the entity's conclusions.

- Add detail and "walk the reader through" a flowchart. A flowchart presents highly summarized information. Narratives frequently are attached to flowcharts as a way to add details about the processing steps or related control procedures. In addition, some readers may find flowcharts vague or confusing ("Should they be read left to right? Top to bottom? Bottom to top?"). A narrative can be added as a way to walk the reader through the sequencing of the processing steps to ensure there are no misunderstandings.

MATRICES

A matrix is a spreadsheet of rows and columns. It is a two-dimensional worksheet that links a set of independent variables with a set of dependent variables. Typically, the control procedures comprise the independent variables, while the dependent variables are made up of the various data about the control procedures that are required to be documented.

Strengths and Weaknesses

Strengths of Matrices as a Documentation Method for Routine Activity-Level Controls

- Highly effective at showing relationships or links between elements, for example, the link between the control procedure and the related financial statement assertion
- Effective way to structure the capture and communication of information about information processes and controls
- Capable of capturing and relating a great deal of information
- Relatively easy to maintain and update
- Scalable and flexible

Weaknesses of Matrices as a Documentation Method for Routine Activity-Level Controls

- Difficult to "see" overall transaction flow and evaluate the effectiveness of control design
- Easy to document too much detail, making the matrix cumbersome to work with and confusing

Tips for Preparing Matrices

When preparing a matrix, the main problem that the entity should guard against is creating a matrix that tries to do *everything,* capturing or summarizing every conceivable detail about a control procedure. The result is an overload of information that is difficult to understand. It is better to create a series of worksheets, each with just a few columns, rather than a worksheet with 30 columns.

A matrix is a simple database, and it helps to think of preparing a matrix in the same way that you would work with a database. Each row in the matrix is like an input form in a database. The row is used to gather all the relevant information about a subject, for example, the control objective or control procedure. A database separates the information *gathering* function from the information *communication* function. A database has a report writer function that allows the user to choose selected data and present it in a concise, easily understandable format for the reader.

When preparing a matrix to document transactions and controls, it is important to consider a similar approach. Create a matrix to help capture the required elements and other information. From that master matrix, create a series of derivative tables, each of which is designed to achieve one objective.

Example Matrices

GAO's *Financial Auditing Manual* and the CFO Council's *Implementation Guide* include numerous examples of the use of matrices to assist in the evaluation of internal controls. This section includes additional examples of individual matrices to consider. If a database program is used to warehouse control descriptions, then these matrices describe the reports that can be written from this database. If a spreadsheet program is used to create these matrices, then common information between individual spreadsheets may be linked.

Information Gathering Matrix

Purpose.   The purpose of this matrix is to facilitate the easy gathering of information about each control procedure. If the entity is working with a database, then this is the information that should be captured in the form to be stored in the database.

Creating the Matrix.   The independent variable is the control number. The dependent variables are all of the relevant pieces that will be needed later to evaluate control design and track the testing of design and operating effectiveness. The following is a highly summarized example of the matrix—space constraints prevent showing all the details. A more detailed description of each dependent variable follows.

Financial Statement Information	Control Information	Control Number	Control Testing Information
		001	
		002	
		003	

Information to Capture.   The following are some suggestions on what information should be captured about each control, that is, the titles for each column in the matrix.

Financial Statement Information

- *Description of the transaction.* Examples of information that would be entered in this column are "sales," "cash disbursements," or "payroll."
- *IT system.* This column would capture the name of the IT system involved in processing the transaction. This information is helpful when planning IT-related tests, such as testing IT general or application controls or reviewing a Statement on Auditing Standards (SAS) 70 report.
- *Electronic files.* This column should be used to capture the name(s) of the electronic file(s) involved in processing. Again, this information will be useful when planning IT-related tests.

- *General ledger/accounts.* List the general ledger accounts that are affected as a result of this transaction, for example, property purchases which affect "Property, Plant & Equipment" and "Accounts Payable."
- *Relevant assertions.* Describe the relevant assertions for the general ledger accounts affected by the transaction. "Completeness" is an example of a relevant assertion for property purchase transactions.

Control Information

- *Processing stage.* A proper evaluation of internal control requires documentation of each of the following stages of transaction processing (incidentally, this is also a PCAOB requirement):
  - Initiation
  - Authorization
  - Recording
  - Processing

  Capturing this information will help to evaluate design effectiveness.
- *Control objective.* Control objectives are related to the financial statement assertions and stage of processing. For example, "To ensure that all valid, property purchase transactions are captured at initiation" is an objective related to the completeness assertion at the initiation of the transaction.
- *Control description.* This is where the entity should document its description of the control procedure. In addition to describing the procedure performed, the following should also be captured:
  - The name of the responsible person or department
  - If or how the performance of the control procedure is documented
  - Whether the control procedure is manual or automated
  - How frequently the control procedure is performed
  - Whether the control procedure is considered a "key control" for achieving the stated control objective. This determination should be made only after evaluating the design effectiveness over the group of controls for a given transaction.

Control Number

- Assign a unique control number to each control procedure.

Testing Information

- *Design effectiveness.* Use this column to track the conclusion as to whether the control procedure is designed effectively.
- *Operating effectiveness test procedure.* Describe, summarize, or cross reference to the planned test(s) of operating effectiveness of the control.
- *Date test performed.* Track the date as of which the tests of operating effectiveness were performed. This information will help to determine whether and how tests will be updated at year-end.

- *Operating effectiveness conclusion.* Indicate the conclusion as to whether the control is operating effectively.

Evaluate Control Design by Processing Stage

Evaluating the control design by processing stage facilitates the identification of key points within a cycle or process which may be particularly susceptible to fraud or misstatement. Thus, this approach allows for the assessment of the design effectiveness of the controls over a given transaction. The matrix depicted below will help to make this assessment.

How to Prepare the Matrix.   Prepare a separate matrix for each significant transaction. If a spreadsheet is being used, sort the main information gathering spreadsheet first by transaction type and then by processing stage.

Example Matrix

Transaction: Property, Plant & Equipment Purchase					
Processing Stage	Assertion	Control Number	Control Description	Key Control Y	N
Initiation	Complete	002	Describe	❑	❑
		014	Describe	❑	❑
	Exist	005	Describe	❑	❑
		016	Describe	❑	❑
		017	Describe	❑	❑
	Accurate	004	Describe	❑	❑
		010	Describe	❑	❑
Authorization	Complete	002	Describe	❑	❑
Etc.					

How to Use the Matrix. For each transaction, be sure that controls exist for each relevant assertion for each of the four processing stages: initiation, authorization, recording, and processing. If no controls for an assertion or for a processing stage are present, then a flaw exists in the design of the controls for this transaction. Next, review the description of each control procedure to determine whether it would effectively address the stated assertion. Look at the group of controls aimed at the same assertion and determine which ones are "key controls" that should be tested.

Evaluate Control Design by Assertion

In addition to requiring that the entity evaluate internal control by processing stage, Paragraph 42 of PCAOB *Auditing Standard No. 2* also requires the entity to document "controls over all relevant assertions." Again, there is no equivalent requirement for federal agencies; however, this approach will allow for the assessment of the design effectiveness of the controls over the transaction.

How to Prepare the Matrix. Prepare a separate matrix for each significant transaction. If a spreadsheet is being used, sort the main information gathering spreadsheet by transaction type and then by control number.

Example Matrix

Transaction: Property, Plant & Equipment Purchase								
Ctrl. No.	Control Description	Asssertions						
		Key	Complete	Exist	Val	Auth	Rights	Disclose
001	Describe	Y	X	X		X		
002	Describe	Y			X			X
003	Describe	N				X		
004	Describe	Y	X	X	X	X		
005	Describe	Y			X			
Etc.								

How to Use the Matrix. Review each control and determine which assertion the control relates to. When all controls for the transaction have been evaluated, review each column of assertions. A preponderance of controls for one assertion indicates that there is probably some control redundancy. Chances are that some of these controls are more significant than others, and these should be the entity's key controls. Reevaluate planned tests of controls to ensure the testing plan focuses on these key controls. It may not be necessary to test the others.

Conversely, however, if the analysis reveals a scarcity of controls for a given assertion, that may indicate that a control deficiency exists because there are not controls to cover the assertion.

Finally, this matrix can help in evaluating the significance of control deficiencies. A deficient control related to an assertion for which redundant controls exist may not be considered significant if the redundant controls operate effectively. On the other hand, a deficiency in a control which is the only control for a given assertion probably will be, at least, a significant deficiency.

Summarize IT Related Controls to Plan Scope of Tests

Purpose. Coordinating the tests of IT controls can be challenging. One of the most important considerations in testing IT controls is ensuring that the scope of the IT testwork is adequate—that it includes all of the IT general and application controls that are relevant to internal control over financial reporting. This matrix can be used to help communicate with an IT specialist about the controls that should be included within the scope of his/her work.

How to Prepare the Matrix. If a spreadsheet is being used, sort the main information gathering spreadsheet by transaction IT system and then by general ledger account.

Example Matrix

IT System	G/L Account	Transaction Type	Control Number	Control Description
Procurement & Disbursements	PP&E	Purchases	001	Description
			002	Description
			005	Description
	Accts. Pay.	Purchases	001	Description
			002	Description
			005	Description
			023	Description
			024	Description
Etc.				

How to Use the Matrix.   Use this matrix to communicate to the IT specialist important information about the scope of his/her work. From this matrix, the IT specialist will know which IT systems need to be included within the scope of the engagement and, for each system, which specific controls should be tested.

COORDINATING WITH THE INDEPENDENT AUDITORS

Early in this phase of the assessment, efforts should be coordinated with the agency's independent auditors and the Office of Inspector General (OIG). Before proceeding too far, consensus should be reached on significant matters such as:

- Criteria to be used to determine whether documentation is sufficient

- In general, what the documentation will contain

- The process to be followed for gathering and assessing documentation

- Plans for addressing documentation deficiencies

The form and content of an entity's documentation of internal control can vary greatly. For that reason, it is important to work with the independent auditors to develop a process that allows them to review documentation periodically, to determine whether it is adequate. For example, one may wish to "pilot test" the documentation of significant activity-level processes and controls and provide this to the auditors as soon as it becomes available. Providing them with examples of actual documentation will help accelerate the process of reaching a consensus on what should be documented.

Appendix 5A
Action Plan: Documentation

The following action plan is intended to help you implement the suggestions contained in this chapter for evaluating an entity's documentation of its internal control. It is important that before extending procedures anticipated at the outset of the project, the assessment team consider whether the extra effort was understood to be part of the project. If it was not, then the assessment team should consult with the appropriate level of management (e.g., the Senior Management Council) before proceeding. In any event, the Senior Management Council and the Senior Assessment Team (if the assessment is being executed by a group designated by the Senior Assessment Team) should be kept abreast of developments throughout the projects, particularly when the assessment team encounters less than optimal conditions.

1. Assess Existing Documentation

Determine whether existing documentation is sufficient to evaluate the design and plan tests of operating effectiveness. For example:

- Determine that documentation exists for all significant control objectives:
  - If documentation does not exist, then determine whether: (a) controls do not exist, or (b) ad hoc, informal controls exist but have not been documented
  - If controls do not exist, design, document, and implement new control procedures
  - If controls exist but are not documented, document existing controls.
- Determine that documentation contains the following elements:
  - A link between the control objective and the control policy or procedure.
  - A description of the control policy or procedure that achieves the control objective. Appendix 5C includes example control policies and procedures, organized by significant control objective.
- Information about:
  - How transactions are initiated, recorded, processed, and reported
  - The flow of transactions to identify where material misstatements owing to error or fraud could occur
  - A description of:
    - How the control procedure is to be applied
    - Who is responsible for performing the procedure
    - How frequently the procedure is performed

2. Evaluate Automated Documentation Tool

Assess the adequacy of the documentation warehouse of the entity's automated compliance tool. For example:

- Determine that users have an adequate understanding of the entity's operations, internal control concepts, and financial reporting processes.
- Information integrity is maintained through the use of:
  - Logical access controls
  - Controls over the systematic updating of documentation
- Changes to documentation are captured and monitored for possible disclosure.

3. Entity-Level Controls

Assess the adequacy of the documentation of significant entity-level controls. Take corrective action as necessary. For example, consider key documents such as:

- Mission statements
- Human resource policies and the personnel handbook
- Accounting policies manual

4. Activity-Level Controls

Assess the adequacy of the documentation of significant activity-level controls. Take corrective action as necessary. For example, determine whether the documentation includes:

- The flow of information from initiation through posting to the general ledger
- Clear delineation of processing stream boundaries
- Consideration of both transactions and events
- Maintenance of the integrity of information stored by the system for later use (e.g., the approved vendor master file)

5. Coordinate with Independent Auditors

Reach a consensus with the independent auditors regarding key decisions about the documentation of internal control. For example, communicate and reach agreement with the auditors on matters such as:

- The criteria you will use to determine whether documentation is sufficient
- In general, what the documentation will contain
- The process you will follow for gathering and assessing documentation
- Plans for addressing documentation deficiencies

Appendix 5B

Evaluating the Design and Implementation
of Automated Compliance Tools

INTRODUCTION

Since the passage of the Sarbanes-Oxley Act, many entities with a wide variety of expertise have developed computer software products that aid in complying with the internal control provisions of the Act. With the issuance of a revised A-123 and the increasing demands being placed on federal managers in the areas of internal controls, it is anticipated that many federal agencies will either buy or develop such software tools (or revise/replace tools already in existence).

These software tools typically center on helping entities automate the documentation of internal control policies and procedures, although some products automate other processes as well. In general, automated compliance tools are designed to facilitate one or more of the following:

- *Warehouse internal control documentation.* The program provides a repository for all of the entity's documentation relating to the design of internal control. In those instances in which the documentation of the control or the control itself either does not exist or is otherwise deficient, the software allows the company to either document existing policies or design and document new ones efficiently.

- *Automate business processes.* Many software programs are designed to automate business processes. This automation can occur on two different levels:

   o *Testing and evaluation of internal controls.* To support its assessment of internal control, management must test both its design and operating effectiveness. Software tools can help manage this process, for example, by tracking the progress of testwork or accumulating the conclusions reached about the achievement of significant control objectives.

   o *Implementation of internal control policies and procedures.* Software tools can automate or make systematic the performance of a wide variety of business tasks, including the performance of control procedures. For example, the software tool automatically may send an e-mail to an employee to remind him or her to prepare the monthly bank reconciliation. The software may then facilitate the actual performance of this control procedure, including its subsequent review by a supervisor. Within this context, the software can help monitor the performance of control procedures, for example, by providing summaries for supervisors on which control tasks have been completed.

Note that these two functions are not mutually exclusive but rather closely aligned. It is the design of the internal control procedures, as maintained in the internal control documentation warehouse, that drives any automation of business processes. That is, without a well-defined control system, there would be no business process to automate. The design of internal control policies and procedures must precede the automation of either their implementation or tests of effectiveness.

Implementation Is Critical

The installation of an automated Sarbanes-Oxley/A-123 software tool is analogous to the installation of an accounting software package. The installation of a new general ledger system does *not* ensure reliable financial statements prepared in accordance with generally accepted accounting principles (GAAP); the installation of a Sarbanes-Oxley/A-123 compliance tool does *not* guarantee compliance with the guidance.

Ultimately, the effectiveness of any automated tool will depend on how well the entity identifies and addresses critical implementation issues. Even the most well-designed tool can be rendered ineffective if it is deployed improperly. The following discussion highlights several of the most important design and implementation issues that should be considered.

Assessing the Control Warehouse Function

The warehouse function of an automated Sarbanes-Oxley/A-123 tool serves as a central repository for the description of the entity's internal control policies and procedures. In assessing this function, you should consider the following.

What to Document

As indicated in Chapter 5, the documentation of controls should be adequate in that:

- *All control objectives have been considered.* Control policies and procedures have been documented for *all* significant control objectives.
- *Documentation is sufficient.* To be sufficient, the documentation should allow management and the independent auditor to:
  - Evaluate the effectiveness of design.
  - Design and perform procedures to test the operating effectiveness of the controls.

The documentation of individual control policies and procedures should contain:

- A link between the control objective and the control policy or procedure
- A description of the control policy or procedure that achieves the control objective
- Information about:
  - How transactions are initiated, recorded, processed, and reported
  - The flow of transactions to identify where material misstatements owing to error or fraud could occur
- A description of:
  - How the control procedure is to be applied
  - Who is responsible for performing the procedure
  - How frequently the procedure is performed

Documentation Process

Automated documentation tools typically use a combination of the following methods for creating and accumulating internal control documentation:

- *Reference existing documentation.* In many instances, the documentation of a policy or procedure already exists, for example, the company's code of conduct. When that is the case, the automated tool should simply allow this existing documentation to be reviewed by the user. To allow for this sharing of existing information, the automated tool may have to:

○ Interface with existing systems

○ Import existing data.

The ease and accuracy with which the tool accomplishes this task will greatly affect its utility.

- *Menu-driven responses.* To create documentation for a new or existing control procedure, the automated tool may provide users with choices from a pull-down menu. For example, in order to describe a control objective, the user may be presented with a choice of: "ensure proper authorization of transactions," "verify accuracy," "ensure the capture of all valid transactions," and so on.

- *Free responses.* Instead of choosing from a predetermined list of possibilities, users may enter their own response into a text box. Regardless of the method used to document new or existing controls, the goal remains the same—to describe the entity's control policies and procedures accurately, as they currently exist. Whether that goal is achieved depends primarily on the qualifications, knowledge, and training of the user. To document the entity's control policies and procedures effectively, the user should have an in-depth understanding of all of the following:

○ The entity's operations and existing control policies and procedures

○ Internal control concepts, as described in the COSO *Framework* (or other framework, if the entity does not use COSO)

○ The financial reporting process

○ The assertions that are represented in the financial statements (see Chapter 7 for a discussion of financial statement assertions)

Note that a new control policy or procedure does not end with the creation of the documentation. If a control is found to be missing and a new one must be created, then the new policy or procedure must be communicated to all affected parties and placed in operation.

Review Features

One of the objectives of documentation is to facilitate the review of internal control design and to allow for the planning of tests of control effectiveness. To enable these objectives, the automated tool must allow for the effective review of the documentation stored in the warehouse.

Different reviewers will have different objectives, and the tool should accommodate multiple perspectives. At a minimum, controls should be able to be reviewed from the following perspectives:

- *By control objective.* This perspective will allow the user to review the control policies and procedures for each significant control objective.

- *By business process.* This perspective is one way for the user to evaluate significant activity-level control objectives.
- *By general ledger account.* This perspective is the other way for a reviewer to assess activity-level controls, and it provides a direct link between the financial statements and internal control.

Maintaining Information Integrity

If the documentation exercise is successful, then ultimately, the documentation maintained in the warehouse will be a true and accurate reflection of what *actually should be occurring* in the day-to-day operations of the entity. Once that state is achieved, it must be maintained. Reviewers must be able to rely on the accuracy of the documentation.

To maintain the integrity of the information kept in the warehouse, the automated tool should have the following features.

- *Logical access controls.* The ability to modify documentation should be tightly controlled in the same way that access to all of an entity's sensitive information and computer applications is controlled. Individual users should be granted access privileges only to those areas of documentation that pertain to their assigned responsibilities. Once they have documented the controls in their area and the documentation has been reviewed, the access privileges should be revoked until the documentation needs to be updated. Someone on your Project Team should assume the responsibility for administering logical access controls over the documentation warehouse.
- *Standardized updating procedures.* The agency's internal control will change over time. Additionally, testing of control effectiveness may reveal that the documentation is not an accurate reflection of what actually occurs in the entity, and the documentation will need to be changed. Changes to documentation should be controlled. When required changes are identified, the affected control objectives, business process, and general ledger accounts should also be identified immediately, allowing users to know that the documentation in these areas is subject to change and they cannot rely on it. Modifications to the documentation should be done in an orderly fashion ensuring that *all* required changes are made. Once the changes have been made, they should be reviewed.

Monitoring Documentation Changes

Once the documentation warehouse becomes established as an accurate reflection of internal control, and standardized updating procedures are in place, then any changes to the documentation should represent actual changes to internal control. This feature enables management to report material changes in internal control. The automated documentation tool should have a means for identifying changes since the last reporting date. To help reviewers evaluate their significance, these changes should be able to be grouped in a variety of ways, including business process, control objective, and financial statement account grouping.

AUTOMATED TESTING OF CONTROLS

Management must support its assessment of the effectiveness of internal control by testing significant control objectives. Once these objectives and the related control policies and procedures have been documented and stored in the warehouse, it would be natural for the automated compliance tool to link to the documentation and help manage the testing process. In this capacity, the automated tool *neither:*

- Performs test work *nor*
- Draws conclusions about effectiveness

Instead, the function of the system is to assist in the coordination of the testing and evaluation of controls by allowing the effective flow of information. To achieve this objective, the automated tool should include the following features:

- *Project administration.* All the information necessary to manage the assessment and coordinate and direct team members should be accumulated, stored, and made available to the team. For example, this information might include the overall work plan, identification and contact information for Project Team members, due dates, project status summary, and so on.

- *Work programs.* The system should allow work programs to be created, or stored, or both. These programs should link automatically to the controls as documented in the warehouse. Changes to the documentation should be flagged to facilitate review and update of work programs as necessary.

- *Monitoring of testing status and results.* As work program steps are completed and conclusions reached about whether control objectives have been met, the progress of the assessment team should be captured and made available for review.

- *Communication and collaboration.* Individual participants in the project do not work in a vacuum. They are part of a team. Timely, effective communication and collaboration among all stakeholders is required for the assessment team to function at its highest level. As described in Chapter 1, stakeholders in your project include both internal team members and external parties such as the entity's independent auditors, the OIG, and the agency's legal counsel, among others. E-mail lists are a common method for facilitating this communication. However, a chat room type of feature may be more effective at creating a more collaborative environment in which different perspectives can be exchanged and considered by all participants and a consensus reached more quickly.

- *Resource library.* During the performance of the assessment, questions will arise constantly. A self-help resource library can provide Project Team members with the information necessary to research issues related to the testing, evaluation, and reporting of internal control. With this research, individuals can either resolve the issue themselves or form an opinion that can be vetted among the group members to reach a consensus. The resource library should be dynamic, allowing for the easy posting of relevant, helpful guidance as it becomes available.

AUTOMATED CONTROL PROCEDURES

Once a control procedure has been defined, that process can be automated. For example, the entity may define a process for the review, approval, and payment of vendor invoices or the identification, preparation, and review of a significant accounting estimate.

The compliance tool can be used to automate many elements of the control procedures, for example, by:

- Providing required information on a timely basis to the person responsible for performing the procedure
- Routing the work product (e.g., a check request or an accounting estimate) to the person responsible for initiating the next phase in the process
- Tracking the progress and results of the procedure to allow for monitoring of control performance at a supervisory level
- Initiating follow-up action in those instances in which control procedures have not been performed in a timely manner

The overall objective of automating control procedures is to enhance their effectiveness and efficiency. To achieve this objective, the system should include the following features:

- *Interface with existing systems.* The compliance tool should "sit on top of" and interface with the entity's existing systems. It should do so in a way that is minimally invasive and has a relatively benign effect on the existing system. This ability to interface with other systems is necessary if the tool is to extract the information needed to perform the control procedure successfully.
- *Ease of use.* The software should be easy to use and intuitive. Little training should be required for users to employ the system effectively.
- *Flexibility.* The software must be easily configurable to accommodate a virtually limitless number of control processes.
- *Handling of exceptions and special circumstances.* It is inevitable that unusual transactions or events will arise. To enable the effective functioning of internal control, the system should:
  - ○ Identify the existence of those unusual transactions or events
  - ○ Provide guidance or a structured escalation procedure to the individual who processes and controls the activity.
- *Resource library.* Individuals may have questions about company policies, techniques for performing certain procedures, or other matters that affect the performance of their tasks. Guidance on these matters should be provided in a reference library to allow for the effective and efficient resolution of issues as they arise.
- *Monitoring.* The progress and results of the performance of the control procedure should be captured to allow for the monitoring required at a supervisory level.

THE VALUE OF AN AUTOMATED COMPLIANCE TOOL

We anticipate that in the long run, many agencies will adopt an automated tool to assist in the documentation, testing, and evaluation of internal control. At first, the necessity of adopting such a tool will probably be driven by a need for efficiency. The sheer magnitude of the task will require the entity to automate certain aspects. As entities begin to deploy the tool, they will quickly realize significant additional benefits. Formal documentation of policies and control procedures will enhance the reliability of internal control. Entities that use a software tool to automate business processes will need to make decisions about how the tool should be configured and deployed. Making these decisions will require management to consider carefully the processes they put in place, the information resources people need to perform their assigned task, and how controls are monitored and exceptions handled. All these considerations will add further definition to the entity's internal control and improve its effectiveness.

Appendix 5C

Linkage of Significant Control Objectives to Example Control Policies and Procedures

---

The following table (Exhibit 5.5) summarizes the significant control objectives described in Appendix 4B and links these objectives to example control activities. Note that Appendix 6D provides example control activities related to significant general computer control objectives.

Exhibit 5.5   Linkage of Significant Control Objectives to Example Control Policies and Procedures

Control Objective	Example Control Policy or Procedure
Corporate Culture	
Articulate and communicate codes of conduct and other policies regarding acceptable business practice, conflicts of interest, or expected standards of ethical and moral behavior	• Comprehensive codes of conduct are developed and maintained and are periodically acknowledged by all employees. • Procedures are established that allow employees to take appropriate action to report unacceptable behavior they observe. • Senior management evaluates corporate culture and "tone at the top." • The entity's code of conduct and ethical standards are communicated to outside parties such as vendors and stakeholders.

(continues)

Exhibit 5.5   Linkage of Significant Control Objectives to Example
Control Policies and Procedures *(Continued)*

Control Objective	Example Control Policy or Procedure
Corporate Culture (cont'd)	• Feedback mechanisms with outside parties exist that allow them to report concerns about corporate culture and ethical behavior.
Reduce incentives and temptations that can motivate employees to act in a manner that is unethical, opposed to the entity's objectives, or both.	• Management identifies compensation policies and other incentives that can motivate unethical behavior. • Management monitors identified incentives and motivations (including compensation) to identify unintended consequences (e.g., possible violation of codes of conduct).
Reinforce written policies about ethical behavior through action and leadership by example.	• Management takes appropriate remedial or disciplinary actions in response to violations of acceptable behavior. • Actions in response to unacceptable behavior are communicated to employees as a means of providing an effective deterrent. • Management takes appropriate action on all complaints, suggestions, and feedback about ethical behavior and possible control weaknesses, including that received from outside parties.
Personnel Policies Identify, articulate, and communicate to entity personnel the information and skills needed to perform their jobs effectively.	• Responsibilities and expectations are communicated clearly to individuals, especially those in supervisory positions and new personnel. • Job descriptions are developed and maintained. • Job descriptions contain specific references to control-related responsibilities. • Management determines the information needs of personnel. • Information is provided to the right people in sufficient detail and on time to enable them to carry out their responsibilities efficiently and effectively.
Provide entity personnel with the resources needed to perform their jobs effectively.	• Organizational structure is designed to facilitate the flow of information upstream, downstream, and across all business activities. • Senior management is comprised of individuals from several functional areas, not just a few.

Exhibit 5.5   Linkage of Significant Control Objectives to Example
Control Policies and Procedures *(Continued)*

Control Objective	Example Control Policy or Procedure
Personnel Policies (cont'd)	
	• Recruiting and hiring policies ensure that only competent individuals are hired. • Training needs are evaluated and appropriate training provided to all entity personnel (including senior management). • Management evaluates the adequacy of the workforce—both in numbers and experience—necessary to carry out entity objectives.
Supervise and monitor individuals with internal control responsibilities.	• Senior management has frequent interaction with operating management, particularly those operating from geographically remote locations. • Supervisory personnel provide performance evaluation feedback and suggestions for improvement to subordinates. • Promotion, retention, and compensation criteria consider the individual's adherence to behavioral standards and standards of performance.
Delegate authority and responsibility to appropriate individuals within the organization.	• Authority, responsibility, and accountability are linked and delegated together. • Boundaries of authority are established and communicated. • The delegation of responsibilities considers the need to segregate incompatible activities. • Management periodically evaluates the entity's organizational structure to assess its continued effectiveness.
General Computer Controls	
Develop, communicate, and plan an overall IT strategy that enables the achievement of entity-wide controls.	• Management identifies and analyzes external reporting requirements for their IT impact and takes appropriate action to comply. • Management actively identifies, assesses, and responds to IT-related risks. • Planning, implementation, and maintenance of IT system appropriately considers user needs.
Provide resources and organizational infrastructure necessary to implement the IT strategy.	• Management budgets for the continued funding of IT systems development. • A structured approach exists to address training, service, and user documentation.

(continues)

Exhibit 5.5   Linkage of Significant Control Objectives to Example
Control Policies and Procedures *(Continued)*

Control Objective	Example Control Policy or Procedure
General Computer Controls (cont'd)	

Identify, acquire, and integrate IT applications and solutions that are necessary for implementing the IT strategy.	• Specific functional and operational requirements are developed.
	• The entity has policies such as the following to ensure that appropriate hardware and software are acquired and implemented:
	  – Entity-wide standardized hardware and software standards
	  – Regular assessment of hardware and software performance.
	• The entity has a formal migration, conversion, and acceptance plan for new systems and systems modifications.
	• Input and processing controls ensure that data remains complete, accurate, and valid during its input, processing, and storage.

Personnel Policies	• Logical access controls restrict access to systems, data, and programs.
	• The entity's IT operating policies and procedures include the:
	  – Development and testing of a continuity plan
	  – Installation of suitable environmental and physical controls.

Monitor IT processes to ensure their continued effectiveness.	• Management has defined relevant performance indicators, which are reported and reviewed on a timely basis.
Alignment between Objectives and Organizational and Control Structures	
Articulate and communicate entity-wide objectives and related operating strategies.	• Management develops and periodically updates the entity's strategic plan. • The entity's strategic plan is communicated to all employees and reviewed and approved by senior management. • Management obtains feedback from key managers, other employees, and stakeholders on the entity's strategic plan.
Design and periodically review activity-level objectives and resources to ensure they are linked to and consistent with each other and the entity-wide objectives.	• Activity-level objectives are established for all value-chain activities. • Managers participate in establishing activity objectives for which they are responsible.

Exhibit 5.5   Linkage of Significant Control Objectives to Example
Control Policies and Procedures *(Continued)*

Control Objective	Example Control Policy or Procedure
Alignment between Objectives and Organizational and Control Structures (cont'd)	• The process for establishing activity-level objectives includes the consideration of past practices and performances or industry examples. • Activity-level objectives include the resources required for achievement, a definition of critical success factors, and measurement criteria for monitoring.
Risk Identification	
Develop mechanisms to anticipate, identify, and react to routine events or activities that affect the entity or activity-level objectives.	• Management identifies risks arising from both external and internal sources. • Risks are identified and addressed at sufficiently high levels in the organization so their full implications are identified and appropriate action plans considered. • Risk identification is included in the entity's strategic planning process. • Senior management oversees and monitors the risk identification and assessment process.
Develop mechanisms to anticipate, identify, and react to unusual, significant events that can have a more dramatic and pervasive effect on the entity.	• Risks related to significant change are identified, including those relating to: – Changed operating environment – New personnel – New or redesigned information systems – Rapid growth – New technology – New lines, activities, and acquisitions – Restructuring – Changes in accounting principles.
Antifraud Programs and Controls	
Create a culture of honesty and high ethics.	• Management is made aware that they are expected to set a high ethical standard within the entity. • Create policies that contribute to a positive workplace environment. • Personnel policies minimize the chance of hiring or promoting individuals with low levels of honesty. • Employees are trained about the entity's values and code of conduct.

(continues)

Exhibit 5.5   Linkage of Significant Control Objectives to Example
                   Control Policies and Procedures *(Continued)*

Control Objective	Example Control Policy or Procedure
Antifraud Programs and Controls (cont'd)	• Alleged incidents of fraud are appropriately investigated and disciplinary action is taken.
Evaluate antifraud processes and controls.	• Management actively identifies and assesses fraud risk. • Management makes changes to the entity's activities and business processes to mitigate identified fraud risks. • Internal control policies and procedures are designed to specifically address identified fraud risks.

Develop an effective antifraud oversight process.	• The OIG provides an appropriate level of oversight with regard to:
	  – Management's identification of fraud risks
	  – The implementation of antifraud measures
	  – The creation of an appropriate culture and "tone at the top"

Top-Level Financial Reporting Processes Management is aware of and understands the need for certain financial reporting adjustments.	• Senior management, key personnel, and the OIG include individuals with appropriate levels of financial expertise. • Senior management, key personnel, and the OIG stay current on financial accounting and reporting matters. • When the entity is structuring nonsystematic, nonroutine transactions, accounting personnel are consulted early in the process.

Relevant and reliable information required for decision-making purposes is identified, gathered, and communicated.	• Management considers information from both external and internal sources that may affect:
	  – The assumptions underlying significant accounting estimates
	  – The valuation of assets
	  – The recognition of liabilities.
	• Information used to make estimates and consider the recognition and measurement of assets and liabilities is consistent with industry conditions, entity plans, budgets, and its past performance.
	• Information gathering and communication processes are reviewed and updated to reflect changed accounting and reporting needs.

Exhibit 5.5   Linkage of Significant Control Objectives to Example
Control Policies and Procedures *(Continued)*

Control Objective	Example Control Policy or Procedure
Top-Level Financial Reporting Processes (cont'd)	• Support is provided for nonroutine, nonsystematic journal entries.
Management analyzes the information and responds appropriately.	• Management develops and maintains a process for closing the books and preparing financial statements at the end of an accounting reporting period. • Nonroutine, nonsystematic journal entries are identified. • Management seeks advice from independent auditors on significant accounting issues.
Management's response is reviewed and approved.	• Management reviews significant accounting estimates and support for significant unusual transactions and nonroutine, nonsystematic journal entries. • Senior management assesses the quality of the entity's accounting principles.
Management identifies events and transactions for which accounting policy choices should be made or existing policies reconsidered.	• Management regularly reviews its significant accounting policies and considers: – Accounting principles applied by the entity for which acceptable alternative principles are available – Judgments and estimates that affect the financial statements – Evolving business and accounting issues and choices that affect financial reporting – The accounting for unusual arrangements.
The accounting policies chosen by management have general acceptance and result in a fair presentation of statement information.	• Management assesses the clarity and transparency of the entity's financial statements and disclosures. • Management considers input from auditors, regulators, and others when choosing or reconsidering its existing choice of accounting principles. Based on this input, it takes appropriate action. • When considering new or reevaluating existing accounting policies, management obtains input from financial accounting experts. • Other matters, such as the accounting policies of other entities that report the same or similar events or transactions, are considered. • The choice of accounting principles is reviewed and approved by senior management and the OIG.

Exhibit 5.5   Linkage of Significant Control Objectives to Example Control Policies and Procedures *(Continued)*

Control Objective	Example Control Policy or Procedure
Top-Level Financial Reporting Processes (cont'd) Information processing and internal control policies and procedures are designed to appropriately apply the accounting principles selected.	• Entity accounting policies are documented and communicated to all those that may affect their proper implementation. • Changes to accounting policies are communicated on a timely basis. • Training in the proper application of entity accounting policies is provided as necessary.
System-wide Monitoring Reach a common understanding of internal control deficiencies and changes that are considered "material" and require disclosure.	• Management describes internal control weaknesses and changes that are required for disclosure after considering input from the entity's independent auditors. • Policies related to the disclosure of internal control deficiencies and changes are documented and communicated to senior management and, when applicable, the disclosure committee and the audit committee.
Identify material weaknesses in internal control on a timely basis.	• Management identifies significant controls that should be closely monitored and evaluated for deficiencies. • Management identifies individuals related to each significant control who are best able to identify potential material weaknesses that should be disclosed. • Management establishes policies for the timely communication of material weaknesses to senior management and, when applicable, the disclosure committee and the audit committee, and the Agency Director and CFO. • The disclosure committee, audit committee, and senior management review all material weaknesses identified by the independent auditors, and they take appropriate action.
Identify material changes to internal control on a timely basis.	• Changes to internal control documentation are captured and communicated to management. • Changes to internal control that may *not* have been reflected in the documentation are captured and communicated to management. • Management reviews all changes to internal control and discloses these changes when appropriate.

Notes

1. From the Organization for Economic Co-operation and Development (OECD), April 1999. This definition was reported by the *Encyclopedia about Corporate Governance,* www.encycogov.com.

2. For the purpose of tracking or controlling the transaction, the entity may wish to capture the invoice number anyway, but this is purely optional. However, capturing the amount of the purchase is *not* an option.

Testing and Evaluating Entity-Level Controls

Chapter Summary

- Define an internal control reliability model for evaluating effectiveness.
- Using the reliability model, describe testing strategies and techniques for evaluating the effectiveness of significant entity-level controls.
- Provide practice aids for testing and evaluation of entity-level controls.

INTRODUCTION

Two Dimensions of Effectiveness

The overall objective of an internal control project is to provide management with a basis for making an assertion about the effectiveness of the entity's internal control. Consider the following statement about effectiveness:

Sue is the most effective point guard in basketball.

This statement seems straightforward, but on further consideration, it is likely that two important questions will be raised:

1. *Effective compared with whom?* In this example, the person making this statement would probably be comparing Sue with her peers—others who play her same position, at the same level of competition.

2. *Effective measured how?* Basketball, like most other sports, has a variety of statistical and nonstatistical measures of a player's effectiveness. The person making a claim about Sue could point to measures such as the average number of assists or turnovers per game or to a variety of measures related to scoring points as a way to measure effectiveness.

Similarly, assertions about the effectiveness of internal control must be supported along two dimensions:

3. *Effective compared with what?* Typically, the entity's internal control will be compared with that of the Committee of Sponsoring Organizations of the Treadway Commission (COSO) as one means of assessing effectiveness. Chapter 2 provides a detailed discussion of the COSO integrated model for internal control.

Exhibit 6.1   Two-Dimensional Process for Evaluating Internal Control
Effectiveness

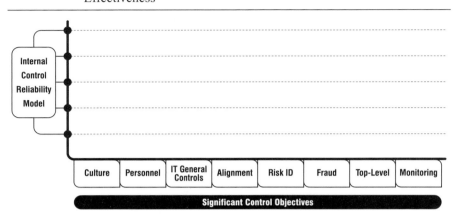

4. *Effective measured how?* COSO provides an overall framework of the five
   integrated components of internal control but provides little guidance on how
   to measure relative effectiveness. There are no commonly accepted measurement
   techniques for internal control (as there are for basketball players). For example,
   COSO identifies integrity and ethical values as being an important piece of the
   entity's control environment, and the report makes a compelling argument for
   why this is so. However, the report does not describe how to measure or otherwise evaluate whether an ethical climate is "effective." This chapter introduces an
   "internal control reliability model" that can be used as a tool for making such an
   evaluation.

   Exhibit 6.1 describes this two-dimensional process for evaluating internal control
effectiveness. Across the horizontal axis are the entity's significant control objectives,
which mirror the COSO *Internal Control-Integrated Framework (Framework)*. (Appendix 4C maps how these control objectives relate to the COSO *Framework*.) The vertical axis depicts the internal control reliability model. As indicated, this model has
five different levels of effectiveness, which will be described later in this chapter.

   Exhibit 6.2 provides an example of a matrix that has been completed at the
conclusion of a hypothetical test of effectiveness. The controls for each significant
control objective have been evaluated and "scored" for effectiveness based on the
reliability model. The result is a visual interpretation of the effectiveness of the entity-
level controls *taken as a whole*.

The Relationship between Testing and Evaluation

While it is possible to evaluate the design of a system of internal control without
performing related tests of operating compliance, as noted in Chapter 1, no assertions
on internal controls can be made unless the operational effectiveness of internal

Exhibit 6.2   Visual Interpretation of the Effectiveness of the Entity-Level
Controls

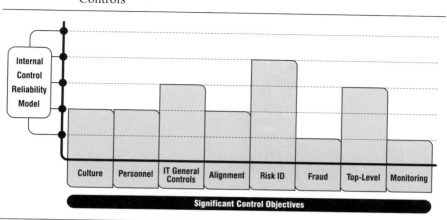

control is tested. Thus, evaluation, as used in this chapter, refers to the final evaluation of internal control based on testing results.

The way an evaluation of internal control effectiveness is planned ultimately
drives the design of the engagement tests. Using the model summarized in Exhibit
6.1, tests should be planned to include each of the significant control objectives identified across the horizontal axis. Additionally, the nature and scope of these tests
should be sufficient to allow evaluation of the control reliability level, as indicated
by the vertical axis.

This chapter provides guidance on the testing and evaluation of internal control.
In practice, one will test first and then evaluate. However, because the design of
tests is so dependent on how effectiveness will be evaluated, this chapter will present guidance on evaluating test results *before* providing guidance on the design and
performance of the tests themselves.

Chapter 2 provides a discussion of the COSO *Framework,* that is, the horizontal
axis. A discussion of the second dimension of assessing effectiveness, the internal
control reliability model, follows.

INTERNAL CONTROL RELIABILITY MODEL[1]

Five Levels of Reliability

Over time, as businesses expand and change, internal controls evolve. What starts
out as a relatively informal process can mature and become more well-defined and
reliable. Exhibit 6.3 summarizes this development process. It identifies five distinct
levels of internal control reliability, and describes what entities must do in order to
for their systems to evolve from one level to the next.

Exhibit 6.3   Internal Control Reliability Model

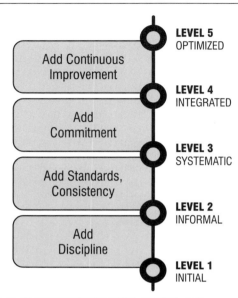

Reliability Level 1: Initial.   Control objectives are not well defined or consistently understood throughout the organization. Policies and procedures are ad hoc and generally undocumented. As a result, control policies and procedures generally are not linked to objectives or are inconsistent with each other. The effectiveness of an initial system depends almost exclusively on the skills, competence, and ethical values of the individual. Because of this dependence on the individual rather than the organization, the reliability of this system can vary greatly over short periods or among business units.

Reliability Level 2: Informal.   Common, intuitive control practices begin to emerge, but documentation is sporadic and inconsistent. Informal communication of information about internal control matters exists, but the lack of formal communication methods, together with a lack of training, prevents much of this information from reaching below managerial and supervisory levels. Management is aware of the need for controls but still views internal control as separate from, not integral to, the operation of the business. However, the emergence of repeatable processes and improved communication and dissemination of information improves the reliability of the system and reduces risk.

Reliability Level 3: Systematic.   Management understands that internal control is an integral part of the company's business and that maintaining an effective system is one of its primary responsibilities. Management begins to devote substantial resources in a coordinated effort to develop and maintain more reliable internal controls. Individual control components combine into a cohesive whole. Documentation

Exhibit 6.4 Summary of Internal Control Reliability Model

Reliability Level	Documentation	Awareness and Understanding	Attitude	Control Procedures	Monitoring
Initial	Very limited	Basic awareness	Unformed	Ad hoc, unlinked	
Informal	Sporadic, inconsistent	Understanding not communicated beyond management	Controls are separate from business operations	Intuitive, repeatable	
Systematic	Comprehensive and consistent	Formal communication and some training	Controls integral to operations	Formal, standardized	
Integrated	Comprehensive and consistent	Comprehensive training on control-related matters	Control processes considered as part of strategy	Formal, standardized	Periodic monitoring begins
Optimized	Comprehensive and consistent	Comprehensive training on control-related matters	Commitment to continuous improvement	Formal, standardized	Real-time monitoring

of control policies and procedures is comprehensive and consistent; some training exists on control-related matters. With more formal, standardized controls in place, the system is more reliable as its overall effectiveness depends more on the organization and less on the capabilities of the individual.

Reliability Level 4: Integrated. Management understands the full requirements for maintaining an effective system of internal control. Control implications and issues are routinely considered as business decisions are evaluated and made. Controls are fully integrated into the strategic and operational aspects of the business. Comprehensive training exists. The company begins a formal process for the regular monitoring of the effectiveness of internal control.

Reliability Level 5: Optimized. Management commits to a process of continuous improvement of controls. The entity uses automation and sophisticated tools and techniques to monitor controls on a real-time basis and make changes as needed.

Exhibit 6.4 summarizes the Internal Control Reliability Model along five different characteristics used to gauge system reliability.

What the Model Can and Cannot Do

The internal control reliability model provides you with a framework for:

- Designing tests of control effectiveness
- Evaluating the effectiveness of controls
- Presenting and discussing findings with management

Recognize that the boundaries between the various levels are hazy and that the levels of reliability themselves may not be discrete. In reality, components of an entity's internal control may exhibit qualities of more than one of the identified levels. The purpose of the model is not to determine the proper way to categorize an entity's controls, but rather to have a basis for analyzing control effectiveness to determine whether controls are capable of achieving their ultimate aim—to reduce to an acceptable level the risk that material misstatements to the financial statements will go undetected.

The testing of internal control is required to support management's assertion about its effectiveness. When applicable (i.e., if an opinion on internal controls is forthcoming), the independent auditors will rely, in part, on this testwork to reach their conclusions about management's assertion. To be effective, the tests should have:

- Clearly stated objectives
- A design that is appropriate to achieve those objectives
- A scope that is comprehensive enough to draw a reliable conclusion

Relationship between Entity-Level and Application-Level Controls

As described in Chapter 2, the COSO *Framework* describes controls as existing at two different levels, the general, entity-wide level, and the specific, application-level. To plan and perform tests of entity-level controls, it is important to remember how these controls are fundamentally different from activity-level controls. Consider the following analogy.

Suppose that the citizens of Anytown wish to build a new school. The objective of building the new school is to educate the children of the community. To achieve that objective, certain elements must be in place. Good teachers must be hired, books, computers, and other resources must be acquired, and so on. All these elements will have a direct effect on the quality of the child's education. At the end of his/her school years, a child will look back and say "my fifth grade social studies teacher made all the difference for me," or "that book I read in tenth grade will stay with me for the rest of my life."

In order for the teacher to be hired, for the book to be purchased, and for the student to even have the physical space to receive and complete assignments, an important prerequisite must be satisfied. The people of Anytown must raise sufficient funds to build the school, hire the teachers, buy the books, and so on. It is the funding that allows all the other elements to operate effectively. On graduation day no one ever says, "I'd like to thank the taxpayers for their continued support of our school," but without sufficient funding, the chances for success are greatly reduced. The school simply does not have the resources to hire enough teachers or buy the books or provide other resources.

Similarly, internal controls operate on two different levels: application-level and entity-level.

Application-level controls are analogous to the teachers and the books. They have a direct effect on the financial statements in that weaknesses in these controls can lead directly to financial statement misstatements. The objective of an application-level control is relatively straightforward—to provide reasonable assurance that material misstatements are prevented or detected in a timely manner. For example, tests of controls related to expense recognition would be designed to determine whether a material misstatement of operating expenses could somehow slip undetected through the accounting system and be presented in the financial statements.

In contrast, entity-level controls have an *indirect* effect on the financial statements. They are similar to the school district funding in our analogy. A weakness in an entity-level control does not necessarily lead to a financial statement misstatement. Entity-level controls *allow* the effective functioning of activity-level controls. Within this context, the objective of an entity-level control is to provide an overall environment in which activity-level controls can operate effectively. In other words, if an activity-level control has been designed properly but in operation performs poorly, the underlying cause of the poor performance is most likely a weakness in entity-level controls.

For example, Agency A requires monthly reconciliations of all Fund Balance with Treasury accounts. However, at year-end, the agency discovers that reconciliations have not been performed for the last several months on many of its accounts. Additionally, those accounts that have had reconciliations performed have been conducted poorly. When investigating the cause of this poor performance, the agency discovers that:

- The performance of reconciliations was considered a low priority by accounting personnel.

- The accounting supervisor was overworked and did not have the time to supervise employees.

- Because of a general lack of supervision, the employees responsible for performing the reconciliations received little feedback on how to perform them properly.

In the above example, the control procedure was properly designed. The failure of the control was performance related. The reasons for the performance failure all had to do with ineffective entity-level controls. The environment in which the control was performed was *not* conducive to effective performance.

Design Effectiveness versus Operational Effectiveness

The literature on internal controls typically distinguishes between the design of internal control and its operating effectiveness. Ultimately, management must make an assertion of the *operating effectiveness* of the entity's internal control, not its design. That is, an effective internal control design is irrelevant if the system of internal control is not operating as designed.

When testing controls, information and evidence related to operational effectiveness are frequently obtained when one is gathering information related to the design of a control. Distinguishing between the two—"does this relate to design or performance?"— is usually an academic exercise since the assertion about controls relates only to operation. For that reason, these materials do *not* draw a distinction between tests of design and tests of operational effectiveness. The testing approach and techniques described here are designed to provide support about an assertion of operational effectiveness.

TESTING TECHNIQUES

This chapter provides a comprehensive, integrated approach to testing and evaluating entity-level controls. Exhibit 6.5 summarizes the various testing techniques suggested and how these are used to gather evidence to support an assertion for each significant entity-level control objective.

The Nature of the Available Evidence

The effect that entity-wide controls have on the financial statements is indirect. It is nonlinear, subjective, and not easily quantified. Supporting an assertion on the effectiveness of entity-wide controls is challenging because the assertion cannot be verified by confirmation, inspection, and observation—that is, the types of tests normally considered by auditors to be the most reliable. Entity-wide controls are *not* transaction oriented, so it is not possible to test their effectiveness by performing transaction-based tests. The techniques described here are the most effective way to gather evidence to support an assertion about entity-wide controls.

Exhibit 6.5 Entity-Level Controls Testing Techniques

	Testing Technique			
Control Objective	Employee Survey	Management Inquiry	Computer General Controls	Document Review
Corporate Culture	X	X		X
Entity Personnel	X	X		X
General Computer Controls		X	X	X
Alignment—Objectives and Controls		X		X
Risk Identification		X		X
Antifraud Programs		X		X
Top-Level Financial Reporting		X		X
System-wide Monitoring		X		X

Exhibit 6.6   Common Problems with Surveys

The following are the most common problems with surveys, which will reduce their reliability.

- Questionnaire is too long or hard to read.
- Questions are difficult to answer because:
  - Language is unclear.
  - More than one question is being asked.
  - Respondents do not have information available to answer question.
- Choices in a multiple-choice question are incomplete, hard to interpret, or not mutually exclusive.
- Directions or transitions between sections of the survey are hard to follow.

Survey and Inquiries of Employees

Surveys are an effective way of collecting information that should come directly from people, not documents. In particular, surveys are essential to the evaluation of whether an entity's culture and personnel policies create an environment that allows the effective functioning of activity-level controls. In other words, a company's written code of conduct or personnel policies, by themselves, will not be sufficient to support an assertion about these entity-level controls. To determine whether the policies are operating effectively, feedback from employees is necessary. For most entities, that information will be gathered most efficiently through a survey (see Exhibit 6.6 for common problems with surveys).

Included in Appendix 6B is an example survey for gathering and evaluating information from employees regarding the entity's culture and personnel policies.

Who and How Many to Survey.   The reliability and validity of survey results are directly related to who was surveyed and how many responses were received. It is often impractical, if not downright impossible, to apply statistical techniques to obtain a quantified precision in support of an assertion about the effectiveness of entity-wide controls. Nonstatistical sampling methods and qualitative analysis of the results should suffice. However, in order to ensure the most reliable and valid results, the survey should be designed in a way that incorporates the main concepts underlying statistical sampling methods, including:

- *The more respondents, the more reliable the results.* Within reason and the resources made available to the project, sample as many employees as possible. However, as in statistical sampling, the additional value of the information obtained decreases as the sample approaches 100% of the universe. Team members experienced in evaluating controls and judgmental sampling should be involved in this decision.
- *Stratified samples yield better results.* If the agency has several components or locations, make sure that the survey includes employees from each. It is also

important to try to obtain results from all the different levels of employee within
the organization, from top management on down.

- *To be valid, any sample must be representative of the population.* A simple
  random sample in which every employee has an equal chance of being selected
  for the survey is one technique that can produce a representative sample of
  the population. In contrast, a block sampling technique (e.g., surveying only
  those employees whose last name begins with the letter "S") will not produce
  a representative sample.

- *Think twice before knowingly excluding a group from the population.* An
  engagement is limited to testing the effectiveness of internal control over financial reporting. However, it would be a mistake to limit a survey about corporate
  culture and personnel policies to only those individuals directly involved in
  the financial reporting process. Operational and administrative personnel can
  provide valuable insights into the operating effectiveness of several components
  of the entity's internal control.

Determining whether enough responses to the survey were received to draw a
valid conclusion is a matter of judgment. To help in that decision, consider the information gathered from other tests. Does it diverge from the results of the survey or
does it tend to corroborate the survey findings? One should also consider addressing the issue with the Office of the Inspector General (OIG) and the independent
auditors. How many responses would they consider to be sufficient for supporting
an assertion about entity-level controls?

When and How Often.   Most tests will have to address the issue of timing. If
the tests are performed too far in advance of the entity's reporting date, they may
need to be updated or reperformed at a later time. If the tests are performed too close
to the reporting date, there will be little or no time to take corrective action if the
results identify a weakness (or to develop a reasonable correction plan to include
in the Performance and Accountability Report [PAR] and other reports, including
the ability to report that the material weakness had been corrected when using a June
30 reporting date).

Surveys can take a long time. Individuals need time to respond, and if they don't,
it will be necessary to follow up and obtain more responses. The evaluation of survey
results, especially if they include open-ended, nonnumeric responses, can also be
time consuming.

Additionally, the nature of the subject matter of the survey should be considered,
which is the entity's culture and the effectiveness of its personnel policies. Both of
these typically change slowly over time. Thus, in most instances, the biggest risk would
be performing tests too late to take corrective action, *not* performing them too early
and having them change.

If a survey is performed well in advance of the entity's reporting date, it is important to consider resurveying later in the reporting period if:

- The entity makes significant changes to its policies or takes corrective action
  for identified weaknesses.

- Other significant events occur that could affect the entity's culture or effectiveness of its personnel policies. For example, unanticipated layoffs can alter employees' perceptions about the entity's culture.

- The entity's system-wide monitoring of control effectiveness is weak.

When developing the timing of the test, remember that the report date prescribed by the Office of Management and Budget (OMB) is June 30, unless the agency chooses to obtain an audit opinion on internal controls. In this latter case, the agency is allowed to adopt an "as of" reporting date that coincides with the independent auditor's date.

Pilot Testing.   Consider pilot testing the survey. By pilot testing and making necessary corrections to the survey, response rates will be increased, creating more reliable and valid results. In their book, *How to Conduct Surveys,* Arlene Fink and Jacqueline Kosecoff provide the following suggestions for pilot testing a survey:[2]

- *Pilot test in segments.* For example, one may want to start by testing just the instructions or the wording of a few questions.

- *Test the administrative details.* If the survey is relatively simple, such as a paper-based survey that is filled out and mailed back, this test may not be that crucial. However, if the administration of the survey is more complex, such as an online survey, testing the delivery mechanism in advance will be more important.

- *Informal testing can work just fine.* The whole point of pilot testing is to identify weaknesses either in the survey questions or in the way it is delivered that can affect the reliability of the survey results. That objective may be accomplished in a relatively informal fashion, for example, by showing the questions to several prospective respondents and asking them how they might respond.

- *Focus on the clarity of the questions and the general format of the survey.* The following may indicate that the survey is unreliable or otherwise needs revision:
  - ○ Failure to answer questions
  - ○ Several answers provided to the same question
  - ○ Writing comments in the margin

- If a range of responses are expected from the survey, then be sure that the pilot test includes equal representation from both ends of the range.

Data Analysis and Reporting Results.   When planning the survey, give some thought to how data will be analyzed and interpreted, and report conclusions to management. For example, a report to management on a survey of employees about the company's culture might read as follows:

> We sent a survey to all the agency's 750 employees asking for their feedback on the agency's culture and climate for ethical behavior. Four hundred of those surveys were returned to us. Responses to the questionnaire indicated that approximately 60 percent of those who responded were not aware that the agency has a code of conduct, which is posted on the agency intranet and reproduced in the employee handbook. Answers to the questionnaire also indicated that only 15 percent of respondents had read the code. However, of those who read the code, nearly 80 percent agreed

with the statement: "The agency's code of conduct helps me identify unacceptable business practices."

The response to this survey question, combined with our own reading of the agency's code of conduct, led us to conclude that, as written, the code could contribute toward creating a control environment that is conducive to the effective operation of activity-level controls. However, in order to be effective, the agency should take steps to ensure that more employees are aware of the code's existence and familiar with its contents.

When one is designing a survey and finds that it is difficult or impossible to describe how data will be analyzed and conclusions will be reported, the survey design should be reconsidered.

Writing Survey Questions.   The survey included in Appendix 6B is just an example. This survey should be modified to meet the needs of specific engagements. Fink and Kosecoff offer the following advice for writing survey questions:

- *Each question should be meaningful to respondents.* If questions are introduced that have no obvious purpose (e.g., demographic information) some transitional text will be needed to explain to the respondent why you are asking the question.

- *Use standard English.* Avoid specialized words, such as *entity-level controls,* whose definition is not readily known.

- *Make questions concrete.* Questions should be as close to the respondent's personal experience as possible. For example, the question "Does management conduct itself in an ethical manner?" is abstract. A more concrete question that addresses the same issue would be "Has your supervisor ever asked you to take action that is labeled as unacceptable in the agency's code of conduct?"

- Avoid biased words and phrases.

- *Each question should have just one thought.* For example, a respondent could be confused by the question "Are the activities of the agency's employees and senior management consistent with the agency's ethical values?" What if the respondent believes that the actions of senior managers are consistent with the ethical values but those of other employees are not? How should he or she respond? To avoid confusion, the question should be split into two questions, one that asks specifically about senior management, and a second that asks about other employees.

Inquiries of Management

Purpose of the Inquiries.   The overall purpose of the inquiries is to gather evidence about the effectiveness of entity-level controls. The primary purpose is *not* to gather information about what the policy is—that information can be gathered mostly through reading the relevant documentation (see Chapter 5 for further guidance). The goal is to determine whether the stated policy is working as intended. To accomplish this objective it is important to consider:

- *Whom to ask.* Inquiries should be made of those individuals who are responsible for the design or implementation of the policy. In many instances several people may be involved in this process. Plan on making inquiries of as many as possible. By gaining multiple perspectives, the effectiveness of the procedure will be increased.

- *What to ask.* Ask questions that will allow for the evaluation of the effectiveness of the policy using the Internal Control Reliability Framework. Appendix 6C includes a list of example questions that may be considered. The example control objectives and procedures provided in Appendix 5B can also be used to help in developing additional questions.

- *What to look for.* As an inquiry technique, it is often helpful to ask objective, nonthreatening questions first. For example, one might ask "What process does management follow to . . . ?" Although the literal answer to the question is important (e.g., "first we . . . then we . . ."), the qualitative, subjective aspects of the response need to be evaluated. Use the Internal Control Reliability Model as a guide. For example, based on the way the respondent answers the question "What is the process for . . .?" consider:

  ○ Whether the process seems well defined, as opposed to ad hoc.

  ○ Whether the respondent understands the process at a level that is appropriate given his/her responsibilities for implementing or monitoring the control.

  ○ The person's attitude about or evaluation of the process. Does he or she think it works? Is it valuable or more trouble than it's worth?

Other Tips for Improving Effectiveness.
Inquiries of management regarding entity-level controls are fundamentally the same as the inquiries made on other professional assignments. In assigning team members to this task it is important that the team member has the requisite understanding of the techniques and also the prior experience necessary to have developed the interpersonal skills critical to the success of this task. The previous section highlighted two important considerations when asking management about the effectiveness of entity-level controls.

1. *Ask more than one person.* For inquiries to be a reliable source of evidence about the effectiveness of controls, interviews should be conducted with more than one person. When several different people tell the same story, it is much more likely that the evidence gathered is reliable.

2. *Ask empirical questions first.* This strategy will help:

   ○ Put the respondent at ease. (People are usually more comfortable describing facts than offering an opinion.)

   ○ Establish a factual basis for asking additional questions.

Once the facts have been established, respondents can be probed more deeply to clarify attitudes, opinions, or interpretations of those facts.

Other tips that should be considered include:

- *Start with open-ended questions.* Try to get the respondent talking so he or she will volunteer information.

- *Carefully choose the interviewer.* The interviewer should have the requisite experience, as well as the stature and demeanor necessary to conduct a meaningful interview. The most junior member of the engagement team should *not* interview the chairman of the board.

- *Don't tip your hand.* Before performing the interview, one should have prepared thoroughly, for example, by reading the agency's documents related to the policy. In addition, one or more other people may have already been interviewed about the same subject. It is important to get an unbiased answer from the person being interviewed. Avoid prefacing questions with information that could lead to a predetermined answer, such as "Your code of conduct says . . ." or "Other people I have talked to . . . ."

- *Nonverbal cues matter.* A study by the Institute of Internal Auditors concluded that only 7 percent of a message communicated in an interview is conveyed through *what* is said. Thirty-eight percent of the message is conveyed by word emphasis and tone and 55 percent through nonverbal cues.[3]

- *Debrief with other team members.* Research conducted by the Canadian Institute of Chartered Accountants indicates that the effectiveness of inquiries can be improved when the information about interviews is shared among audit team members. Through the comments and questions received from others, it is easier to identify pertinent information gathered and recognize the importance of things that otherwise might have been overlooked or forgotten.

- *Don't take too many notes.* During the interview, making sure that all the information necessary is gathered should be the focus. Rather than taking extensive notes during the interview, consider making short, abbreviated notes during the conversation and then writing more notes immediately after the interview is over.

General Computer Controls

Information Technology (IT)-related controls consist of two distinct types, both of which must work effectively to achieve a proper level of control. General controls are defined by COSO as those that apply to many, if not all, application systems and help ensure their continued, proper operation. Application controls ensure the proper processing of various types of transactions and include both the computerized steps within the application software and the related manual follow-up procedures (e.g., the investigation and resolution of items identified in a computer-generated exception report). As described in Chapter 2, this book supplements the guidance provided in the COSO *Framework* with the guidance provided in the Control Objectives for Information and Related Technology (COBIT) report, including guidance on what might be considered general controls.

Preliminary Analysis.   Before jumping directly into a detailed assessment of computer general controls, it helps to obtain an understanding of IT-related risks and control objectives at a relatively high-level. Some of the questions that should be answered include:

- Have there been any significant changes to the entity's IT system, including changes to hardware, software, processes, or personnel? If so, what general risks do the changes create? If there have not been any significant changes, what previously existing risks remain? How are risks identified and managed?

- How many different computing platforms or environments exist at the entity? How do multiple systems interface with each other; for example, how are data exchanged and how is this exchange controlled?

- What might impair the reliability of the entity's IT system or otherwise negatively affect the entity's ability to capture, process, and maintain data?

- How could the integrity of the entity's IT system be compromised? What risks exist that might affect the entity's ability to protect its data and systems from unauthorized access, corruption, or loss?

- What risks are posed by the entity's e-commerce activities?

The Computer General Controls Review. Chapter 2 provides a high-level summary of the COBIT report. Salient points of that summary include the following:

- Underlying the COBIT framework is the notion that an understanding of information technology should focus on *information,* not the technology. Thus, in order to obtain a high-level understanding of IT-related risks, start by obtaining a high-level understanding of the information required to run the agency's programs. Chapter 2 provides a summary of the general qualities of information required by management.

- IT processes manage IT resources to produce information that has the necessary qualities. A review of the effectiveness of computer general controls should address the following processes:

  - *Planning and organization,* which covers strategy and tactics directed toward the identification of the way one can best contribute to the achievement of stated agency objectives

  - *Acquisition and implementation,* which includes the identification, acquisition (or in-house development), deployment, and integration of IT solutions

  - *Support,* which includes back-up and disaster recovery plans and maintaining a suitable physical environment

  - *Monitoring,* which is the regular assessment of IT processes to assess their continued effectiveness.

Appendix 6D includes a checklist that can aid in the design of tests of computer general controls.

A general computer controls review may require special expertise, the development of which is beyond the scope of this book. Because of the complexity and size of federal agencies, an IT specialist (either a team member or team consultant) will almost always be required by the team to perform the computer general controls tests and evaluate the test results.

Reading and Assessment of Key Documents

The mere existence of documentation does not provide any evidence as to the effectiveness of the policy documented. To assess effectiveness, it is important to read the document and make a qualitative assessment of the policy. Chapter 5 provides a description of what one would expect to find in the key documents relating to entity-level controls. Appendix 5C provides examples of the control objectives and policies that should be addressed in these documents. When reading the documentation of entity-wide policies, this guidance from Chapter 5 should be considered.

Observation of Processes

For the most part, the functioning of entity-level controls is not observable. However, certain exceptions do exist, and it is important to be alert for opportunities to observe certain entity-level control policies. These opportunities include the observation of meetings of senior management including senior policy-making committees (e.g., risk management, disclosure, human resources, ethics, audit), particularly when any of the following matters are being discussed, reviewed, or approved:

- Financial statements, including meetings with the entity's independent auditors
- Internal controls or financial reporting processes
- Internal audit results
- Strategic planning
- Risk management
- Promotion criteria, bonus compensation, and other personnel policies
- Ethics or other "corporate governance" matters

When one is observing meetings, the primary objective is to evaluate the effectiveness of the process. Use the Internal Control Reliability Model as a guide for making this evaluation and consider questions such as:

- Does the process seem well defined and structured (i.e., have they done this before)?
- Does the group have a relatively well-defined set of criteria for decision making or do the decisions seem ad hoc?
- Are the committee members actively involved in the process? Are they well prepared? Do they have the information necessary to make informed decisions?
- What do the group dynamics reveal about the company's culture?
- When discussing operational matters, does the group consider internal control and financial reporting implications?

To increase the reliability of the evidence gathered from observations, several meetings of the same group should be observed.

As described in Chapter 5, the entity may use an automated tool to aid in the assessment and reporting of internal control effectiveness. This automated tool may include features that monitor the performance of certain control policies and procedures. The design of the documentation tool should allow for the observation of functions of the entity's monitoring process.

The mere reporting on the timely performance of a control procedure does not constitute effective internal control. As described in Chapter 2, the COSO description of internal control defines monitoring as including all of the following:

- Assessing control design

- Assessing its operating effectiveness (which includes both the timeliness of its performance and whether the procedure was performed properly)

- Taking necessary corrective action

When observing the entity's automated monitoring process, it is important to consider whether all the elements described in the COSO *Framework* can be observed. For example, suppose that Employee A is responsible for reconciling the accounts payable detailed trial balance to the general ledger's control account. The agency has an automated process that monitors Employee A's performance of this control procedure and reports to his supervisor on whether it was performed on a timely basis. If Employee A fails to perform the procedure in a timely manner, the system may automatically send him a reminder that his reconciliation is overdue.

The functioning of this automated process is observable. However, this observation alone is not sufficient to draw a conclusion about the effectiveness of monitoring because:

- The timely performance of a procedure is only one element of effectiveness. In addition to being timely, the procedure also must be performed *correctly*. To be properly monitored, the entity should have a policy that requires supervisory review of the procedure performed.

- The control policy should be reviewed periodically to determine whether its design remains adequate.

- Appropriate corrective action should be taken. Sending Employee A a reminder may not be sufficient. If he is chronically late in performing his task, perhaps he has too many responsibilities, and some of his work should be reassigned. If the reconciliation is not being properly performed, then perhaps he needs additional training.

To address these issues, observation of the monitoring feature of the entity's automated compliance tool should be supplemented with personnel inquiries. Appendix 6C provides some example inquiries.

EVALUATING THE EFFECTIVENESS OF ENTITY-LEVEL CONTROLS

Making the Assessment

The evaluation of the effectiveness of entity-level controls is a process that allows for:

- Determining whether entity-level controls create an overall environment that permits the effective operation of activity-level controls

- Identifying weaknesses in entity-level controls that affect the design of activity-level tests

Tests of entity-level controls are directed at specific control objectives, but the evaluation should consider the controls *taken as a whole,* rather than individual control objectives. For example, weaknesses in one control area may be compensated for by the design and operation of strong controls in other areas.

Exhibit 6.2 provided an example of one method used to understand and document an assessment of the overall effectiveness of entity-level controls. The process used to make the evaluation involves:

- Using the Internal Control Reliability Model to rate the effectiveness of each control objective
- Combining the individual control objectives into a complete picture of entity level controls

How reliable do controls need to be before they are considered effective? Do entity-level controls have to reach the highest level of reliability in order to be effective? The answer to these questions is a matter of judgment that should be made by management with input from the OIG and the independent auditors. In making that determination, the chief executive officer (CEO) and chief financial officer (CFO) should consider the following:

- *Taken as a whole.* Ultimately, the effectiveness of internal control is assessed for the system as a whole, not for individual components. In designing its system, the agency may make trade-offs, leaving opportunity for improvement in certain elements of the system and compensating for this decision through stronger controls elsewhere.
- *Reasonable assurance and materiality.* Internal control can provide only reasonable, not absolute, assurance. The effectiveness of internal control is evaluated within the context of the financial statements and whether any errors that internal control fails to detect or prevent are material.

It would seem unlikely that an initial system of internal control would have the reliability and consistency necessary to provide reasonable assurance that material misstatements are identified and corrected before reaching the financial statements. In a similar vein, it would seem that many entities maintain internal control that would be widely acknowledged as "effective" without having all components of that system operating at an "optimized" level of reliability.

How should one make a final assessment of the effectiveness of controls? The Canadian Institute of Chartered Accountants has done some relevant research in this area, and one particular conclusion reached is worth noting.

> Evidence is more than a collection of facts. It is the integration of everything the auditor learns. Evidence does not come in a neatly ordered sequence—it is non-linear. It comes piecemeal and must be managed, sorted and synthesized. Some of it is concrete fact that is objectively verifiable. Much of it, however, is [your] impression of what has been seen, heard, or sensed. It includes the attitudes and intentions of people in the entity and its organizational culture and ethical tone. Knowingly or not, [you] take all these factors into account—[you] use them as evidence—when forming conclusions.[4]

Chapter 8 provides additional guidance on evaluating deficiencies and forming a final conclusion about the effectiveness of internal control as a whole.

Responding to Identified Weaknesses

Testwork may reveal weaknesses in entity-level controls that require one of the following responses:

- Corrective action
- Modifications to planned activity-level controls

Corrective Action. Weaknesses in entity-level controls may be so severe that they require corrective action—to *not* correct the condition would most likely result in a material weakness in the entity's overall internal control.

Exhibit 6.4 summarized the qualities of reliability that are considered in the Internal Control Reliability Model. The nature of the corrective action taken will depend on the source of the control weakness.

- *Documentation.* A lack of documentation can be remedied by creating the necessary documentation. Chapter 5 provides additional guidance on creating documentation.
- *Awareness and understanding.* The awareness and understanding of control-related matters can be improved through comprehensive, formal communications and training programs.
- *Attitude.* Changing attitude is a difficult and time-consuming process. However, some of the actions taken in other areas will change attitude as well as behavior. For example, the introduction of a training program on the company's code of conduct and acceptable behavior will not only help employees understand the code but will also send the message that the company is serious about ethics, which is a change in attitude. The engagement to study the effectiveness of controls can also send a message to employees that changes their attitudes. Improved communication, training, and coaching can also drive changes in attitude.
- *Procedures.* The most effective way to spur the evolution of an entity's control procedures, from ad hoc and inconsistent to formal and standardized, is through documentation, the training of personnel, and timely, consistent supervision.
- *Monitoring.* The engagement and the company's continued compliance with OMB Circular A-123 reporting requirements is the first stage of monitoring, a periodic review. To move to the next level, real-time monitoring will most likely be required.

Planning Tests of Activity-Level Controls. In response to identified possible control weaknesses, the planned testing approach of activity-level controls should be modified by considering the following:

- *The identification and testing of effective compensating controls.* For example, employees with significant control responsibilities for financial reporting must have a working knowledge of their responsibilities if the control procedures are to be effective. Suppose that this level of working knowledge does not exist for all employees. It is possible that this weakness may be compensated for by other controls, such as close supervision or redundant control procedures that address the same control objective.

- *Expanding the scope of application-level control testing.* For example, one may wish to:
  - ○ Test controls over certain business processes or locations that previously were not considered significant.
  - ○ Modify the nature and extent of the testing of the effectiveness of other significant entity-level aspects of application-level controls.

DOCUMENTING TEST RESULTS

It is important to document test procedures performed and the results of those tests. In addition to providing evidence of compliance with OMB guidance, if the agency's internal controls are being audited, this documentation is necessary for the independent auditors to conduct their audit, including their requirements to:

- Evaluate management's process for assessing the effectiveness of the entity's internal control.
- Rely, at least in part, on the tests performed by management as a basis for reducing the scope of their own work.

Currently, the OMB and the Public Company Accounting Oversight Board (PCAOB) provide only broad guidance on what management should include in the documentation of its tests. In general, one should consider including a description of the following:

- Tests performed and the control they were designed to test
- The time period covered by the tests
- The scope of the testwork, including the consideration of multiple locations or business units, and how that scope was determined
- The results of the tests
- All control deficiencies identified as a result of the tests, a conclusion as to the severity of the deficiencies, and how the existence of these deficiencies was communicated to the board, the independent auditors, and others, as necessary
- Any remedial action taken in response to identified deficiencies, including changes to internal control
- An overall conclusion as to the effectiveness of internal control based on the results of the testwork performed

An additional source of guidance is the GAO/PCIE *Financial Audit Manual* (FAM) of the Government Accountability Office (GAO) and the President's Council on Integrity and Efficiency (PCIE). Although the FAM was designed specifically to provide guidance to auditors performing financial statement audits of federal agencies, it can be an excellent reference source of guidance. Paragraph 490 of the FAM provides additional detailed guidance on documenting tests of controls and/or the accounting records.

COORDINATING WITH THE OIG AND
THE INDEPENDENT AUDITORS

If the agency's OIG and/or its independent auditors have developed a framework similar to the Internal Control Reliability Model, this framework should be obtained, understood, and used to help guide the design of tests. Additionally, an ongoing dialogue with the entity's OIG and auditors should be established to gain consensus on matters including:

- The overall approach to testing entity-level controls, whether directly or inductively, through the performance of activity-level control tests

- The nature and extent of planned procedures and whether they are considered sufficient to draw a reliable conclusion

- The circumstances under which the planned nature and extent of the procedures should be modified

- The planned timing of tests and whether this timing will allow for drawing conclusions about the design and operating effectiveness of entity-level controls as of year-end

- The nature and extent of procedures that may be required to update conclusions about effectiveness from the time procedures are performed until June 30 (or year-end if internal controls are subject to audit)

- The results of tests and the tentative and final conclusions reached regarding the effectiveness of entity-level controls

- How the test procedures and results will be documented

- The general type of deviations or conditions that might be considered significant deficiencies or material weaknesses

- The implication that the identification of significant deficiencies or material weaknesses has on other aspects of the assessment

---

Appendix 6A

Action Plan: Testing and Evaluating Entity-Level Controls

The following action plan is intended to help you implement the suggestions contained in this chapter for testing and evaluating entity-level controls.

1. Design Tests

Plan the nature, timing, and extent of tests necessary to draw a conclusion about the operating effectiveness of internal control. For example:

- Consider and describe the framework that will be used to measure effectiveness, for example, the Internal Control Reliability Model or a similar framework used by the OIG and/or the independent auditors.
- Determine whether you will test entity-level controls directly or indirectly through the testing of activity-level controls.
- Determine the combination of testing techniques that will be used to assess the operating effectiveness of each significant entity-level control. Consider:
    - Employee surveys
    - Inquiries
    - Computer general controls review
    - Document review
    - Direct observation

2. Perform and Document Tests

Perform the planned tests. Update as necessary to support a conclusion about operating effectiveness as of year-end. Document the procedures performed and test results.

3. Assess Test Results

Evaluate the effectiveness of entity-level controls based on the results of your test work. For example:

- Determine whether entity-level controls create an overall environment that permits the effective operation of activity-level controls.
- Identify weaknesses in entity-level controls.
- Respond to identified weaknesses in one or both of the following ways:
    - Take corrective action.
    - Modify planned activity-level controls.

4. Coordinate with the OIG and the Independent Auditors

Establish an ongoing dialogue with the OIG and the independent auditors that allows you to reach a consensus on:

- Your overall approach to testing entity-level controls, whether directly or inductively through the performance of activity-level control tests
- The nature and extent of your planned procedures and whether these are considered sufficient to draw a reliable conclusion

- The circumstances under which the planned nature and extent of the procedures should be modified
- The planned timing of your tests and whether this timing will allow you to draw conclusions about the design and operating effectiveness of entity-level controls "as of" June 30 (or year-end)
- The nature and extent of procedures that may be required to update your conclusions about effectiveness from the time your procedures are performed until the reporting date
- The results of your tests and the tentative and final conclusions reached regarding the effectiveness of entity-level controls
- How the test procedures and results will be documented
- The general type of deviations or conditions that might be considered significant deficiencies or material weaknesses
- The implication that the identification of significant deficiencies or material weaknesses has on other aspects of the assessment

---

Appendix 6B
Survey Tools

This appendix contains several tools that will help you in conducting employee surveys related to the operating effectiveness of entity-wide controls. Included are:

- Example Letter to Employees in Advance of Employee Survey
- Example Employee Survey of Corporate Culture and Personnel Policies
- Evaluation of Employee Survey Results.

EXAMPLE LETTER TO EMPLOYEES IN ADVANCE OF EMPLOYEE SURVEY

Dear _____,

To comply with the Office of Management and Budget Circular A-123, we are conducting an annual review on the policies and procedures we use to manage and control our agency. The scope of this review is quite broad and includes evaluating not just the individual tasks you perform in your daily work assignments but also the environment in which you perform those assignments.

To help us perform our review, we are conducting a survey of all employees to obtain their observations about the way in which our Agency is managed. Within the next two weeks you will be receiving this survey. We have tried hard to balance our need for comprehensive feedback with everyone's desire to keep the survey as short as possible. We believe we have reached a suitable compromise.

I urge you to complete this survey and return it as soon as possible to _____. Your prompt attention to this matter is important, not only because it will allow us to comply with certain legal requirements, but also because it will help us to improve our management practices continually. All individual responses to the questionnaire will be kept strictly confidential.

/s/ Chief Executive Officer

Notes

- This letter should be sent out a week or two in advance of sending the actual employee survey. The purpose of the letter is to prepare the employees for its arrival and to encourage them to complete it as soon as possible.
- The letter assumes that *all* employees will be receiving a survey. If that is not the case, then the letter should explain how the individual employee was selected, for example, "We are sending the survey to 50 percent of all our employees and management. Your name has been selected at random."
- To convey a proper sense of urgency and importance to the completion of the survey, the letter should be signed by a member of senior management, for example, the Agency Head or CEO.

EXAMPLE EMPLOYEE SURVEY OF CORPORATE CULTURE AND PERSONNEL POLICIES

Purpose of the Survey

By law, Agency A is required to review and report on the policies and procedures used to manage and control the Agency. The scope of this review is broad and includes an evaluation of the overall environment in which individual employees perform their assigned responsibilities.

The purpose of this survey is to obtain input from all employees on how the agency is managed.

Confidentiality

Individual responses will not be disclosed. All responses will be evaluated as a group and reported to agency management in a summarized fashion.

Instructions

Please respond by indicating the degree to which you agree or disagree with the statements presented. When you are done, please mail your completed questionnaire to _____. A self-addressed, stamped envelope has been provided for your convenience.

	Strongly Disagree	Disagree	Neither Agree nor Disagree	Agree	Strongly Agree
Ethical Values					
1. I have read the agency's code of conduct.	❏	❏	❏	❏	❏
2. The agency's code of conduct helps me identify unacceptable business practices.	❏	❏	❏	❏	❏
3. If I observe unacceptable behavior on the job and report it to a member of the management team, I believe that the matter will be investigated.	❏	❏	❏	❏	❏
4. I believe that people who demonstrate a commitment to high ethical standards of behavior will be rewarded (e.g., through compensation or advancement).	❏	❏	❏	❏	❏
5. I believe that people who act in an unethical manner will be punished (e.g., through diminished compensation, lack of advancement, or termination).	❏	❏	❏	❏	❏
6. At no time in the last three years have I been asked by someone senior to me to take action that would be considered unethical.	❏	❏	❏	❏	❏
7. At no time in the last three years have I heard of someone at the agency who has been asked by someone senior to them to take action that would be considered unacceptable.	❏	❏	❏	❏	❏
8. For the most part, agency employees act in an ethical manner.	❏	❏	❏	❏	❏
9. For the most part, agency management acts in an ethical manner.	❏	❏	❏	❏	❏
Personnel Policies					
10. My job responsibilities have been communicated to me.	❏	❏	❏	❏	❏
11. I understand my job responsibilities.	❏	❏	❏	❏	❏

(continues)

	Strongly Disagree	Disagree	Neither Agree nor Disagree	Agree	Strongly Agree

Personnel Policies (cont'd)

	Strongly Disagree	Disagree	Neither Agree nor Disagree	Agree	Strongly Agree
12. The criteria for assessing my performance have been communicated to me.	❏	❏	❏	❏	❏
13. The feedback I receive on my performance helps me improve.	❏	❏	❏	❏	❏
14. The information I need to perform my job is communicated to me:					
• Accurately	❏	❏	❏	❏	❏
• Timely	❏	❏	❏	❏	❏
• Completely	❏	❏	❏	❏	❏
15. The training I receive helps me do a better job.					
16. I have been delegated the decision-making authority necessary to perform my job effectively.	❏	❏	❏	❏	❏
17. For the most part, I have been provided with the following resources necessary to perform my job effectively:					
• Budget/funding	❏	❏	❏	❏	❏
• Personnel	❏	❏	❏	❏	❏
• Supervisory guidance	❏	❏	❏	❏	❏

Agency Values

18. Please list the behaviors that are most frequently rewarded (see question 4 for example rewards). Example behaviors might include customer service, innovation, team building, cost reduction, and so on.

_____

_____

_____

19. Please comment on any other aspect of the agency's culture or management policies that contributes to or detracts from your job responsibilities effectively. If a family member or friend were considering employment at your agency and asked "What's it like working there?" how would you respond?

_____

_____

_____

Notes

- If an outside consultant has been engaged by the agency to conduct or assist with the survey, consider printing the survey on the consultant's letterhead, as this will probably reinforce the message that responses are confidential and encourage more candid responses.

- All responses should be returned directly to the assessment team.

- Questions 4 through 9 make reference to "high ethical standards" and personal ethics, which may introduce an element of unreliability to the survey because what may be unacceptable to one person may be acceptable to another. Alternatively, the questions may be reworded to refer to the agency's stated ethical policies or values. However, if you choose to refer to agency policies in these questions, you should include these policies as part of the survey. Without easy, immediate access to the agency's stated policies, most individuals will not be able to respond to the statement.

- The example behaviors listed in question 18 have been deliberately worded in a way that makes them all seem positive. If negative behaviors are noted in response to this question, then this could indicate the strong presence of negative elements in the entity's control environment. The question leads the respondent to consider only positive characteristics. If the employee makes note of negative characteristics, it is probably because these characteristics have made a strong impression on the respondent.

EVALUATION OF EMPLOYEE SURVEY RESULTS

The example employee survey focuses on two entity-level control objectives: company culture and personnel policies. It is designed to gather information about the effectiveness of each of these controls in three different categories, which are described in more detail in Chapter 6. These categories are:

- Awareness/understanding
- Action
- Attitude

The form in Exhibit 6.7 can be used to summarize the results of the survey. You should complete the form by:

- Assigning a numeric value to each of the five possible responses. For example, "strongly agree" = 5 and "strongly disagree" = 1
- Calculating an average value of the response for each question.
- Entering that average in the form in the space provided. Note that the form distinguishes the category (awareness, action, attitude) that the question was meant to address.

Further guidance on how to interpret and respond to the summarized results is provided in the following discussion.

Exhibit 6.7   Employee Survey Questionnaire

	Average Response		
Ethical Values	Awareness	Action	Attitude
1. I have read the agency's code of conduct.			
2. The agency's code of conduct helps me identify unacceptable business practices.			
3. If I observe unacceptable behavior on the job and report it to a member of the management team, I believe that the matter will be investigated.			
4. I believe that people who demonstrate a commitment to high ethical standards of behavior will be rewarded (e.g., through compensation or advancement).			
5. I believe that people who act in an unethical manner will be punished (e.g., through lack of advancement or termination).			
6. In the last three years, I have been asked by someone senior to me to take action that would be considered unethical.			
7. I know someone at the agency who, in the last three years, has been asked by someone senior to them to take action that would be considered unacceptable.			
8. For the most part, agency employees act in an ethical manner.			
9. For the most part, agency management acts in an ethical manner.			
	Average Response		
Personnel Policies	Awareness	Action	Attitude
10. My job responsibilities have been communicated to me.			
11. I understand my job responsibilities.			
12. The criteria for assessing my performance have been communicated to me.			
13. The feedback I receive on my performance helps me improve.			
14. The information I need to perform my job is communicated to me: • Accurately • Timely • Completely			
15. The training I receive helps me do a better job.			
16. I have been delegated the decision-making authority necessary to effectively perform my job.			
17. For the most part, I have been provided with the following resources necessary to perform my job effectively: • Budget/funding • Personnel • Supervisory guidance			

Evaluating the Results

For each of the two control objectives, scan the summarized results for each of the three categories.

Awareness/Understanding.   Low scores in this category indicate that employees lack an awareness or understanding of key control policies. At a minimum, employees should be aware of the existence of agency policies and procedures that affect them in the performance of the jobs. Ideally, they would have a working knowledge and detailed understanding of the full implications of those policies.

Corrective Action: A lack of understanding or awareness of important agency policies is a symptom of ineffective communications. The agency should review its communication efforts to identify the ways that awareness or understanding can be improved, for example:

- Increasing the frequency of communication
- Revising existing documentation to make the policies more clear
- Requiring signed acknowledgment from employees that policies have been read and understood

Action.   Studies show that much of the information we receive and process is communicated through action, not through words. The questions that fall into this category gauge the effectiveness of management's actions relating to certain control objectives and whether those actions are consistent with high ethical standards or the company's stated policies and values. Low scores in this area indicate a disconnect between what management says and what it does.

Corrective Action: The entity needs to have its managers act in ways that are consistent with stated policies. If inconsistencies are discovered, then the entity needs to determine whether the problem is caused by the policies or the managers. If the policies are sound, then the behavior of managers needs to be changed.

Additional investigation is required to determine the root cause of the behavior. For example, it may be that managers are simply unaware of how their behavior affects employees, or it could be that they are overburdened with other responsibilities (lack of resources), which causes them to devote less time than is necessary for effective supervision. If the behavior of managers needs to change, the agency should consider one or more of the following:

- Formal training
- Informal coaching or mentoring of managers
- Changes to the way the agency provides incentives to its employees
- Allocation of additional resources

Alternatively, the agency may determine that management behavior is appropriate, in which case the written policies should be revised.

Attitude.   These questions are designed to broadly assess employees' attitudes and perceptions about those elements of their work environment that can affect the performance of application-level controls. Low scores indicate a negative attitude that may adversely affect controls. For example, a widely held perception that management will *not* thoroughly investigate reported instances of wrongdoing may encourage employees in ways that run counter to the agency's objectives.

Corrective Action: Additional information should be gathered to obtain a more complete understanding of employee attitudes and the cause of any negative perceptions. Improving attitudes and perceptions may require actions such as:

- Changes in the behavior that gives rise to the negative perceptions
- Improved communications within the entity, for example, an emphasis on candid, interactive communications between management and employees.

Implications for the Design of Additional Tests.   Low scores in any one area by itself may indicate a material weakness in the system of internal control. For example, employees with significant control responsibilities for financial reporting must have a working knowledge of their responsibilities if the control procedures are to be effective.

However, it is possible that weaknesses identified as a result of the responses to this survey may be compensated for by other controls. For example, close supervision or redundant control procedures that address the same control objective may adequately compensate for a lack of employee understanding of a particular control procedure.

In response to identified possible control weaknesses, you should modify your testing approach by considering:

- The identification and testing of compensating controls for effectiveness
- Expanding the scope of application-level control testing. For example, you may wish to:
  - Test controls over certain business processes or locations that previously were not considered significant
  - Modify the nature and extent of the testing of the effectiveness of other significant entity-level or application-level controls.

Appendix 6C

Example Inquiries of Management Regarding Entity-Level Controls

---

INSTRUCTIONS FOR USE

The form shown in Exhibit 6.8 is designed to be used by an interviewer in face-to-face interviews with members of management. The form consists of example questions, organized according to control objective. At the conclusion of each section you will be asked to document your initial evaluation of the results of the conversation.

Example Questions

Most of the example questions are relatively objective and focus on the actions taken by management. They are intended to introduce the subject matter in a relatively non-threatening way. Follow-up questions should be asked to develop an impression of the respondent's awareness, understanding, and attitude toward the subject. Since these questions will depend primarily on the responses the individual gives to the initial question, the form includes only a limited number of follow-up questions. Appendix 5A includes a list of example control objectives and related control policies. These examples can be helpful in formulating potential follow-up questions.

Exhibit 6.8   Example Questions

Corporate Culture

1. What was the process followed to develop the agency's code of conduct?

2. How often is the code reviewed and updated?

3. What was senior management's main reason for developing the code?

   a. Has that objective been met?

      Yes   How can you tell?

      No   What have been the major barriers to achieving the objective?

4. If management becomes aware of an allegation of unacceptable behavior, what is the process for investigating the matter?

   a. Do you have any specific examples? How was the action of management in this matter perceived by the employees?

5. Has senior management identified policies or incentives that may motivate unethical behavior by employees?

      Yes   What are they? How do you monitor these policies for possible unintended consequences?

      No   What criteria are considered when setting incentive policies and programs?

6. Has management become aware of any control deficiencies in the last three years?

   a. How did you become aware?

   b. What action was taken?

7. Do you receive all the information needed to perform your job effectively?

      Yes   Is it reliable? Timely?

      No   What is missing?

(continues)

Exhibit 6.8　Example Questions *(Continued)*

Corporate Culture (cont'd)

8. Does senior management periodically discuss the agency's culture and "tone at the top" and how these affect the overall effectiveness of controls?

    Yes　What observations has senior management made?

    No　What prevents you from doing so?

    a. Do you believe that the agency has established standards of behavior that create an effective control environment?

ASSESSMENT:

Policies related to corporate culture seem to be (mark the scale)

```
|                              |                              |
```

Initial/　　　　　　　　　　Systematic　　　　　　　　　Integrated/
Informal　　　　　　　　　　　　　　　　　　　　　　　　Optimized

Entity Personnel

1. How did management determine the overall organizational structure for the agency?

    a. When was the last time the structure was reviewed for continued relevance and effectiveness?

    b. How do you determine that the structure is effective?

    c. How are internal control and financial reporting matters considered when evaluating the agency's organizational structure?

2. Is there a formal process used to determine which responsibilities should be delegated to lower levels?

    a. (Yes or No). How do you ensure that responsibility, authority, and accountability are linked and delegated together as a unit?

3. What is the process for determining the resources that are necessary for employees to perform their responsibilities effectively? Resources include:

    - Training
    - Budget/funding
    - Personnel
    - Supervision and feedback

4. Once management decides to pursue a certain strategy, what is the process for determining the human resource needs required to implement the strategy? Consider:

    - Number of people needed
    - Required skills
    - Experience level
    - Training

Exhibit 6.8   Example Questions *(Continued)*

Entity Personnel (cont'd)

ASSESSMENT:

Policies related to personnel seem to be (mark the scale)

| Initial/ | Systematic | Integrated/ |
| Informal | | Optimized |

Alignment between Objective and Controls

1. Describe the agency's strategic planning process.

   a. What is the process for soliciting feedback from key managers?

   b. How is this feedback integrated into developing the plan? In its most recent strategic planning effort, what significant issues were raised by senior management in their review and approval process? How were these issues resolved?

   c. How are internal control and financial reporting implications considered in the process? In its most recent strategic planning effort, what internal control issues did the agency identify? How were these issues resolved?

   d. Does management identify the critical success factors required for the achievement of the strategic plan?

   e. How is progress for the achievement of the plan measured and monitored?

ASSESSMENT:

Policies related to the alignment of strategic objectives with controls seem to be (mark the scale)

| Initial/ | Systematic | Integrated/ |
| Informal | | Optimized |

Risk Identification

1. Describe the process used to identify achievements as well as failures reported in the agency's most recent PAR.

   a. Who is involved in the process?

   b. What criteria are used to determine the risks to report?

2. How does the agency decide how to manage identified risk?

3. As part of the strategic planning process, how are risks identified?

4. How is senior management involved in the risk management process?

   What concerns and issues have they raised recently about the risks facing the entity?

(continues)

Exhibit 6.8   Example Questions *(Continued)*

Risk Identification (cont'd)

5. In the past three years, what new risks has the agency encountered?

    a. Did management anticipate these risks?

    b. How did the agency respond?

ASSESSMENT:

Policies related to risk identification seem to be (mark the scale)

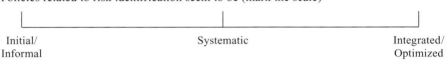

Initial/   Systematic   Integrated/
Informal   Optimized

Antifraud Programs and Controls

1. What steps does management take to instill a culture of honesty and high ethics that mitigates the risk of fraud within the entity? For example, consider:

    a. Hiring and promotion policies

    b. Training

    c. Investigation and resolution (including disciplinary action) of alleged incidents of fraud

2. In what ways is the entity vulnerable to fraud? Consider:

    a. Employee defalcation

    b. Fraudulent financial reporting

3. What is management's process for identifying the risks of fraud in the entity?

4. Does the OIG get involved in discussions about fraud? If so, what do these discussions entail?

ASSESSMENT:

Policies related to antifraud programs and controls seem to be (mark the scale)

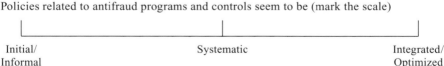

Initial/   Systematic   Integrated/
Informal   Optimized

Top-Level Financial Reporting Processes

1. How does the entity comply with the requirement that its senior management has an appropriate level of financial expertise?

    As a whole, do you believe that senior management possesses an appropriate level of expertise?

2. How does senior management stay current on financial reporting matters?

3. What is the process for structuring nonsystematic, nonroutine transactions?

Exhibit 6.8 Example Questions *(Continued)*

Top-Level Financial Reporting Processes (cont'd)

   a. What is the source driving these transactions; for example, are they necessary to:
   - Implement the entity's strategic plan?
   - Achieve planned results?

   b. At what point in the process does management receive input on the accounting treatment of these transactions?

   c. What factors does senior management consider when reviewing and approving these transactions?

4. What process does the entity follow for making its most significant accounting estimates?

   a. How is information relating to the underlying assumptions gathered?

   b. How do you know the information is reliable?

   c. What factors are considered when making significant assumptions about the estimate?

   d. How is senior management involved in the review and approval of significant estimates?

   In the agency's most recent financial reporting cycle, what were the most significant issues raised by senior management regarding the estimates of the estimation process?

5. Describe the conversations senior management and the OIG have had with the independent auditors regarding the quality of the entity's accounting principles?

   What actions did they take as a result of those discussions?

6. What is the process used by management to:

   a. Identify emerging accounting issues or other circumstances or events that may require a consideration of accounting policies?

   b. Choose appropriate accounting policies?

ASSESSMENT:

Policies related to top-level financial reporting processes seem to be (mark the scale)

Initial/ Informal	Systematic	Integrated/ Optimized

System-wide Monitoring

1. When applicable, how does management use the entity's automated compliance tool to monitor the effective operation of internal control?

   Does the entity's automated tool indicate whether the control was performed in both

   a. A timely manner?

   b. A proper fashion?

(continues)

Exhibit 6.8   Example Questions *(Continued)*

System-wide Monitoring (cont'd)
  2. What steps does management take to:
      a. Periodically evaluate the design of internal control policies and procedures?
      b. Understand the underlying causes for identified internal control deficiencies?
      c. Take appropriate corrective action in response to identified deficiencies?

ASSESSMENT:
Policies related to system-wide monitoring seem to be (mark the scale)

Initial/	Systematic	Integrated/
Informal		Optimized

Evaluating Responses

Your interview should be sufficient to allow you to form an initial impression about the effectiveness of the entity-level control policy. The form uses an abbreviated version of the Internal Control Reliability Model introduced in this chapter. Based on your interview, you should evaluate the policy according to the following scale:

- *Initial/Informal.* No awareness or only a limited awareness of the issue and how it affects internal control. Management's actions or process seems ad hoc and not well defined (or no action has even been taken). Attitude indicates a disinclination for change. Sees internal control as separate from the main business operations and someone else's responsibility.

- *Systematic.* Good understanding of the issue and how it contributes to internal control effectiveness. Processes seem to be well defined, and established criteria are used to guide decision making. Individual recognizes that internal controls are integral to the achievement of the entity's overall objectives. Acknowledges his or her oversight and control responsibilities. Interested in improving internal control.

- *Integrated/Optimized.* The individual's decision-making process routinely considers the internal control and financial reporting implications. Individual is actively involved in implementing and monitoring control effectiveness. Commitment to improvement of internal control is demonstrated through action.

Appendix 6D
Guidance for Designing a Computer General Controls Review

The purpose of this matrix (Exhibit 6.9) is to help you design a computer general controls review. This matrix is built on the COBIT framework, which was described in Chapter 2. The contents of the matrix have been adopted from *IT Control Objectives for Sarbanes-Oxley,* published by the Information Systems Audit and Control Association (ISACA) and available as a free download from their website at www. isaca.org. Additional, more extensive guidance can also be obtained from the GAO's Federal Information System Controls Audit Manual (FISCAM).

Note that, given the size and complexity of most federal agencies, the performance of the review and evaluation of results is best performed by an IT specialist.

Exhibit 6.9   Guidance for Designing a Computer General Controls Review

Control Objective	Example Controls
Planning and Organization	
Define a strategic plan.	• IT strategies are aligned with overall business objectives. • Feedback from users is used to monitor quality of planning process. • IT planning committee includes IT personnel, users, and senior management. • IT plans are communicated across the organization. • IT management communicates activities, challenges, and risks with senior management.
Define the information architecture.	• IT management has defined controls relating to the capture, processing, and reporting of information relevant for all financial statement assertions for all significant accounts and disclosures. • Information is classified in accordance with company security and privacy policies. • Security levels for each data classification are defined, implemented, and maintained.
Define the IT organization and relationships.	• IT personnel have adequate knowledge and experience. • Key systems and data are identified. • The roles and responsibilities of IT personnel are defined, documented, communicated, and understood. • Delegation of authority and responsibility to IT personnel is appropriate. • Appropriate segregation of duties is established and maintained.

(continues)

Exhibit 6.9   Guidance for Designing a Computer General Controls
                   Review *(Continued)*

Control Objective	Example Controls
Planning and Organization (cont'd) Define the IT organization and relationships.	• IT management monitors personnel to ensure that they perform *only* their assigned tasks. • IT management regularly evaluates staff performance. • IT management establishes and communicates policies to protect the entity's information-based assets. • IT management communicates all significant IT events or failures to senior management and the board.
Communicate management aims and direction.	• IT policies and procedures are documented and communicated. • Policies and procedures are periodically reviewed and modified as necessary. • IT management assesses compliance with established policies and procedures, investigates deviations, and takes appropriate corrective action.
Manage human resources.	• When IT personnel change or leave their jobs, controls are in place to ensure continued control effectiveness. • IT management supports a culture of continuous learning. • The IT organization supports the entity's overall culture and code of conduct.
Ensure compliance with external requirements.	• Changes to external reporting requirements are monitored, and changes to IT systems are made, as necessary. • Internal events that affect reporting requirements are identified, considered, and incorporated into IT policies and procedures, as required.
Assess risks.	• The entity's risk assessment process includes the consideration of information-related risks, including technology reliability, information integrity, and IT personnel. • The IT organization maintains a risk assessment process that is aligned with the entity's overall risk assessment process.

Exhibit 6.9　Guidance for Designing a Computer General Controls
Review *(Continued)*

Control Objective	Example Controls
Planning and Organization (cont'd)	
	• The IT organization performs a comprehensive security assessment for all significant systems and locations.
Manage quality.	• All significant IT processes and activities are documented.
	• Documentation is regularly updated and maintained.
	• The IT organization has developed a plan to maintain the quality of all IT activities.
	• Documentation standards are developed, communicated, and reinforced through training.
	• Data integrity, ownership, and responsibilities have been communicated to data owners, who have acknowledged their responsibilities.
Acquisition and Implementation	
Acquire and maintain application software.	• The IT organization's systems development lifecycle considers
	– Security
	– Availability
	– Processing integrity
	– Application controls that address all relevant financial statement assertions
	• The IT acquisition process is aligned with the entity's overall strategy.
	• Software is acquired in accordance with the overall IT planning process.
	• Controls exist over the installation of new and modified software.
Acquire and maintain technology infrastructure.	• Controls exist to ensure that infrastructure changes such as systems software and network devices are controlled during implementation and maintenance.
Develop and maintain procedures.	• User reference and support manuals are prepared as part of every information system development or modification project.
	• System documentation is adequate to ensure long-term sustainability of the system.

(continues)

Exhibit 6.9 Guidance for Designing a Computer General Controls
            Review *(Continued)*

Control Objective	Example Controls
Acquisition and Implementation (cont'd)	
Install and accredit systems.	• All significant changes in technology are tested.
	• Test procedures include
	– Unit, system, integration, and user acceptance
	– Load and stress testing
	– Interfaces with other systems
	– Data conversion.
Manage changes.	• Formal change management procedures exist for all changes as well as system or supplier maintenance.
	• The override of established procedures for system changes in emergency situations is identified and controlled.
	• Users are included in the design, selection, and testing of new or modified software.
	• Change management standards establish a structured approach to the timely change to systems and applications.
	• The IT organization monitors systems and applications to determine that they are performing as designed and meet the needs of the users.
Delivery and Support	
Define and manage service levels.	• IT management establishes vendor management policies, which are used to select vendors for outsourced services.
	• IT management defines key performance indicators to manage service level agreements.
Manage third-party service levels.	• The selection process for third-party service providers includes an assessment of capabilities to deliver the required service and the provider's financial viability.
	• Third-party service contracts include provisions that address the risks, security controls, and procedures for information systems and networks.

Exhibit 6.9   Guidance for Designing a Computer General Controls
Review *(Continued)*

Control Objective	Example Controls
Delivery and Support (cont'd)	<ul><li>The entity's business continuity controls consider risks related to continuity of service from third-party service providers. Escrow contracts exist where appropriate.</li><li>Contracts with third-party service providers are executed before any work is initiated.</li><li>Third-party service levels are monitored regularly and reported to IT management.</li><li>The monitoring of third-party service providers includes a regular review of security, availability, and processing integrity.</li></ul>
Manage performance and capacity.	<ul><li>Performance and capacity levels of the IT system are monitored.</li><li>Appropriate responses are taken when performance and capacity measures are less than optimal.</li><li>IT system design and implementation activities include performance and capacity planning.</li></ul>
Ensure continuous service.	<ul><li>IT management has established a business continuity framework and plan that is aligned with the company's overall business plan.</li><li>The continuity plan is tested at least annually, all deficiencies are corrected, and personnel responsible for the plan are adequately trained.</li><li>The continuity plan is updated whenever new risks are identified.</li><li>Offsite storage and recovery facilities are tested at least annually.</li><li>Company management has formally assessed the impact of systems failure on the financial reporting and disclosure process.</li><li>Management has defined the system recovery procedures necessary to ensure the timely reporting of financial information.</li></ul>

(continues)

Exhibit 6.9   Guidance for Designing a Computer General Controls
                  Review *(Continued)*

Control Objective	Example Controls
Delivery and Support (cont'd)	
Ensure systems security.	• IT management has developed a security plan, which is regularly updated and maintained.
	• All users are authenticated to the system as a means to ensure the validity of transactions.
	• Control policies and procedures are established to maintain the effectiveness of authentication and access mechanisms.
	• Control policies and procedures exist relating to requesting, establishing, issuing, suspending, and closing user accounts.
	• Where appropriate, controls exist to ensure that transactions cannot be denied by either party and that the origin of receipt, proof of submission, and receipt of transactions cannot be repudiated.
	• Where appropriate, controls such as firewalls exist to prevent unauthorized access to the network.
	• IT management regularly performs security assessments, which are used to update the IT security plan.
	• The IT security administrator monitors and logs security activity, and identifies and reports all security violations.
Educate and train users.	• The entity identifies and documents the training needs of all personnel using IT services.
	• Education and training programs include ethical conduct, system security practices, confidentiality standards, integrity standards, and security responsibilities.
Manage the configuration.	• Only authorized software is permitted to be used by employees.
	• System infrastructure is properly configured to prevent unauthorized access.
	• Application software and data storage systems are properly configured to provision access based on an individual's demonstrated need.

Exhibit 6.9   Guidance for Designing a Computer General Controls
Review *(Continued)*

Control Objective	Example Controls
Delivery amd Support (cont'd)	• Procedures have been established across the entire organization to protect the IT systems from computer viruses. • Software and network infrastructure are periodically tested to ensure that it is properly configured.
Manage problems and incidents.	• All operational events that are not part of the standard operation are recorded, analyzed, and resolved in a timely manner. • Emergency program changes are approved, tested, documented, and monitored. • The problem management system allows for the tracing from incident to underlying cause.
Manage data.	• Data processing controls address the completeness and accuracy of transaction processing, authorization, and validity. • Data input is checked for accuracy and validity. • Errors are identified, reported, and resolved in a consistent and authorized manner. • IT management has established policies and procedures for the handling, distribution, and retention of data and reporting output. • Sensitive information is protected during its storage and transmission. • The company has established retention periods and storage terms for data, programs, reports messages, and documents. • Data retention policies comply with all applicable laws and regulations. • The contents of a media library containing sensitive data are physically protected and periodically accounted for. • Data and programs are backed up. • The restoration process and the quality of backup media are tested periodically.

(continues)

Exhibit 6.9   Guidance for Designing a Computer General Controls
                  Review *(Continued)*

Control Objective	Example Controls
Delivery and Support (cont'd)	
Manage data.	• Changes to data structures are authorized, made in accordance with design specifications, and implemented in a timely manner. • Changes to data structures are evaluated to their effect on the financial reporting process.
Manage facilities.	• Physical access to facilities is restricted and controlled. • Physical facilities are equipped with adequate environmental controls.
Manage operations.	• Management has established and documented standard procedures for IT operations. • Processing continuity is maintained during operator shift changes. • Metrics are used to manage the daily activities of the IT department. • Sufficient system event data is retained to enable the reconstruction, review, and examination of the time sequences of processing.
Monitoring	
Monitor the processes.	• IT management measures IT activities against well-defined benchmarks. • Processes exist to identify IT weaknesses and take appropriate remedial action.
Assess internal control adequacy.	• IT controls are monitored regularly, and deficiencies are reported to senior management.
Obtain independent assurance.	• The IT organization uses independent reviews to provide assurance over significant IT services and activities.

Notes

1. This model has been adapted from the "capabilities maturity model" for software development, which was developed by the computer software community with stewardship and resources provided by the Software Engineering Institute. The model provides a basis

for judging the capabilities of a software development process and also identifies key practices that are required to further the maturity of this process.

Since its introduction, the maturity model approach has been adopted by COBIT as a way to assess the effectiveness of IT-related controls. More recently, several public accounting firms have recommended this type of approach to their clients as a means to assess overall internal control effectiveness. It is anticipated that a capabilities maturity model approach will ultimately gain wide acceptance within the independent auditor community as a means of evaluating management's assertion about the effectiveness of its internal control.

2. Arlene Fink and Jacqueline Kosecoff, *How to Conduct Surveys: A Step-by-Step Guide* (Thousand Oaks, CA: Sage Publications, 1998).

3. J. W. Harmeyer, S. P. Golden, and G. E. Summers, Conducting Internal Audit Interviews (Altamonte Springs, FL: Institute of Internal Auditors Research Foundation, 1994). Cited in *Audit Enquiry: Seeking More Reliable Evidence from Audit Enquiry,* a research report published by the Canadian Institute of Chartered Accountants, Toronto, Ontario, 2000.

4. *Audit Enquiry: Seeking More Reliable Evidence from Audit Enquiry,* a research report published by the Canadian Institute of Chartered Accountants, Toronto, Ontario, 2000, 6.

Chapter 7

Testing and Evaluating Activity-Level Controls

Chapter Summary

- Evaluate effectiveness of design of activity-level controls.
- Design tests of operating effectiveness.
- Provide guidance on the effective performance of various types of tests.
- Evaluate the results of tests.

INTRODUCTION

The objective of tests of activity-level controls is the same as the objective for testing entity-level controls. As described in Chapter 6, the testing of internal controls is necessary in order to support management's assertion about its effectiveness. To be effective, the tests should have:

- Clearly stated objectives
- A design that is appropriate to achieve those objectives
- A scope that is comprehensive enough to draw a reliable conclusion.

ASSESSING AND EVALUATING THE EFFECTIVENESS OF DESIGN

Activity-level controls are effective when they can provide reasonable assurance that material financial statement errors will be prevented or detected in a timely fashion. Assessing design effectiveness will require a review and evaluation of the documentation described in Chapter 5 to determine whether the system, as described, is capable of providing that level of assurance. To conduct the assessment, it is important to consider:

- The general types of errors that could occur
- The points in the processing stream at which errors may be introduced.

Once there is an understanding of what could go wrong and where, one must then look to see whether the system, as designed, adequately addresses these potential errors and error points. Again we emphasize that, although it is possible to evaluate the design of internal controls, in practice, we can only evaluate or make assertions about internal control after we have tested the operational effectiveness of the controls.

Financial Statement Assertions and Controls

The auditing literature uses a framework based on financial statement "assertions" to understand and identify potential misstatements. This same framework can be used to define activity-level control objectives.

Assertions are the representations of management that are embodied in the entity's financial statements. These assertions may be either explicit or implicit. For example, the balance sheet line item that reads "Fund Balance with Treasury .... $ xx,xxx" is an explicit assertion that all of the agency's Fund Balances with Treasury at the balance sheet date totaled the stated amount. *Implicit* assertions include the following:

- The agency has the right to spend the balances (within constraints that may have been imposed by Congress and the Office of Management and Budget [OMB], which are described in the notes to the financial statements)
- The stated amount includes *all* the agency's balances with Treasury
- The accounts included in the total are valid agency accounts that exist at the Department of Treasury.

The auditing literature describes the following financial statement assertions:

- Existence (of assets or liabilities) or occurrence (of transactions)
- Valuation or measurement of the amounts reported in the financial statements
- Completeness of the financial statements
- Rights (to reported assets) and obligations to pay (for reported liabilities representing goods or services received by the agency)
- Presentation and disclosure of the amounts and captions in the financial statements

In an effectively designed system, activity-level control objectives (and the related controls) will exist to ensure that each financial statement assertion is free of material misstatement. Exhibit 7.1 summarizes the link between financial statement assertions and control objectives.

The Committee of Sponsoring Organizations of the Treadway Commission (COSO) report describes example control objectives and related activities for the business process activities in the entity's value chain.

Information-Processing Streams

Chapter 5 describes the fundamental characteristics of an information-processing stream. Within this stream, errors can be introduced at the following points:

- The system boundary where events or transactions are initially identified, authorized, and captured
- The update and maintenance of databases, master files, or other electronic storage systems that are accessed by one or more applications

Exhibit 7.1 Linking Financial Statement Assertions to Control Objectives

Assertion	Description	Control Objectives
Existence	Reported assets and liabilities exist at the reporting date.	• Only properly authorized assets and liabilities are recorded. • Assets are safeguarded and protected from unauthorized use or disposition. • Accountability for assets is maintained.
Occurrence	Reported transactions or events took place during the reporting period.	• Proper cutoff between accounting periods. • Fictitious, unauthorized, or duplicate transactions are detected and prevented from being recorded.
Valuation or Measurement	Assets, liabilities, transactions, and events are recorded at their proper amount.	• Assets and liabilities are initially recorded at the appropriate amount. • Recoverability of assets and valuation of liabilities are assessed periodically. • Transactions are recorded at correct amounts.
Completeness	The financial statements include *all* the assets and liabilities of the entity and the effect of its transactions during the reporting period.	• All authorized, valid transactions are reported in the financial statements. • Proper cutoff between accounting periods.
Rights and Obligations	The entity has the rights to use reported assets and is obligated to settle reported liabilities.	• Entity has legal title to assets. • Proper authorization for the assignment of rights or encumbrance of assets. • Only the obligations of the entity are reported or disclosed.
Presentation and Disclosure	Items are properly classified, described, and disclosed in the financial statements.	• Financial statements are fairly presented in accordance with GAAP. • Disclosure is adequate and not misleading.

- The processing points in the stream at which information is manipulated or processed, for example:
  - Matched with other data
  - Combined with other data
  - Used as part of a calculation
  - Posted to the general ledger, subsidiary ledger, or other accounting records

Errors can be introduced whenever information is changed or otherwise processed. As a result, testwork should focus on the identification of these points in the information stream.

OPERATING EFFECTIVENESS

Test Design Considerations

Tests of application-level controls should allow for the gathering of sufficient evidential matter to support conclusions about the effectiveness of internal control. To be "sufficient," the evidence should be persuasive or convincing. A preponderance of the evidence gathered should support the conclusion, however, the evidence does not have to be incontrovertible in order to support the conclusion.

Tests of operating effectiveness should be designed to determine:

- How the control procedure was performed
- The consistency with which it was applied
- By whom it was applied

Nature, Timing, and Extent of Tests

Nature.   It is first necessary to determine the types of tests that will be performed. Will they include conducting inquiries, observing controls being performed, or reperforming certain control procedures? The nature of the tests performed depends on the type of control procedure being tested and whether its performance is documented.

Typically, a combination of one or more controls will be tested in order to gather evidence about its operating effectiveness. It is unlikely that one test would provide enough evidence to support a conclusion. For example, suppose the operation of a control procedure, such as an edit check on the electronic input of information, were observed. The control appears to be functioning properly, but it is impossible to know that the control was in place and operating effectively throughout the entire reporting period. This observation will have to be supplemented with other procedures, such as inquiry.

When determining the nature of the tests to be performed to support conclusions, consider that a representation on controls most likely will be formed by the congruence and consistency of the evidence gathered from *several* sources and types of tests.

Timing. Much like the Sarbanes-Oxley Act, revised OMB Circular A-123 mandates a reporting on the effectiveness of internal control as of a point in time, namely, June 30 or year-end for federal agencies (depending on whether the auditors are issuing an opinion on internal controls). Practically speaking, however, many of the tests will be performed in advance of the reporting date. When this is the case, it is important to consider the need to perform additional tests to establish the effectiveness of the control procedure from the time the tests were performed until June 30 or year-end, as appropriate. For example, if the effectiveness of Fund Balances with Treasury reconciliations is tested as of June 30 and the reporting date is September 30 (because the auditor is issuing an opinion on internal controls), one should consider performing tests to cover the period from June 30 through September 30. These tests may *not* require a repeat of the detailed tests performed at June 30 for the subsequent three-month period. If the effectiveness of the control procedure is established at June 30, a conclusion about the effectiveness of the control at the reporting date can be supported indirectly through the consideration of entity-level controls and other procedures such as:

- The effectiveness of personnel-related controls such as the training and supervision of personnel who perform control procedures. For example, are the people performing the Fund Balance with Treasury reconciliations adequately supervised, and was their work reviewed during the last quarter of the year?

- The effectiveness of risk identification and management controls, including change management. For example, would management be able to identify changes in the entity's business or its circumstances that would affect the continued effectiveness of Fund Balance with Treasury reconciliations as a control procedure?

- The effectiveness of the monitoring component of the entity's internal control.

- Inquiries of personnel to determine what changes, if any, occurred during the period that would affect the performance of controls.

- Repeating the procedures performed earlier in the year, focusing primarily on elements of the control procedure that have changed during the period. For example, if the entity were issued new appropriated funds or if new personnel were performing certain reconciliations, tests would be focused on those accounts and individuals.

Computer Application Controls. As described in Chapter 6, the COSO report describes two different levels of computer controls—general and application specific. Application controls are the structure, policies, and procedures that apply to separate, individual business process application systems. They include both the automated control procedures (i.e., those routines contained within the computer program) and the policies and procedures associated with user activities, such as the manual follow-up required to investigate potential errors identified during processing.

As with all other control procedures, computer application controls should be designed to achieve specified control objectives, which in turn are driven by the risks to achieving certain business objectives. In general, the objectives of a computer application are to ensure that:

- Transactions are appropriately authorized and recorded.
- Data remains complete, accurate, and valid during its input, update, and storage.
- Output files and reports are distributed and made available only to authorized users.

Specific application-level controls should address the risks to achieving these objectives. Exhibit 7.2 provides examples of computer application control objectives and related controls.

The way computer control objectives are met will depend on the types of technologies used by the entity. For example, the specific control procedures used to control access to an online, real-time database will be different from those procedures related to access of a "flat file" stored on a disk.

Exhibit 7.2   Example Computer Application Control Objectives and Controls

Control Objective	Control Activity
Authorization	
All application users are appropriately identified and authenticated.	• Passwords and personal identification numbers. • "Nonrepudiation" that prevents senders and receivers of information from denying that they sent or received the information. • Emerging technologies such as digital certificates or smart cards.
Access to the application and related data files is restricted to authorized users for authorized purposes.	• Logical access control system restricts access to the application and data to authorized users. • Firewalls protect application and data from unauthorized use. • Terminals automatically disconnect from the system when not used after a specified period of time. • Computer equipment is located in physically secure locations.
All data is authorized before entering the application.	• Critical input information is tested against predefined criteria. All exceptions are reviewed by an individual with the proper authority to approve them. • Paper-based information is reviewed and approved prior to input.

Exhibit 7.2 Example Computer Application Control Objectives and Controls
(Continued)

Control Objective	Control Activity
Completeness	
All authorized data enters and is processed by the application.	• Transactions are numbered prior to entry; sequence is checked periodically. • Control totals, hash totals, and record counts ensure that all data is processed. • Transaction data is matched with data in a master or suspense file. Unmatched items from both the transaction data and master or suspense files are reported for investigation.
Accuracy	
Data entry design features contribute to data accuracy.	• Preformatted screens and menu-driven input. • Electronic input of information.
Data validation and editing are performed to identify erroneous data.	• Automated validation and edit checks.
Erroneous data is captured, reported, investigated, and corrected.	• Suspense files capture and control errors. • Suspense files are regularly reviewed and items are appropriately resolved.
Confidentiality	
Access to application output is restricted to authorized users.	• Access to confidential information is limited to authorized individuals consistent with the entity's confidentiality policies. • Data encryption technologies protect the transmission of user authentication, verification, and confidential information.

An Information Technology (IT) controls specialist most likely will be needed to understand the risks involved in various technologies and the related activity-level controls.

Considering the Results of Entity-Level Tests. As described in Chapter 6, entity-level controls affect the operational effectiveness of activity-level controls. For example, the entity may have thorough, well-designed controls to ensure a proper accounts payable cut-off at year-end (activity-level control). If they do a poor job of communicating and monitoring the performance of the people responsible for performing the procedure (an entity-level control centering, not only on accounting personnel, but also on individuals responsible for authorizing payment), then ultimately the control will lack full effectiveness. When designing activity-level tests, conclusions about the effectiveness of entity-level controls should be used in two ways. First, plan activity-level tests to gather first-hand information about the effectiveness of entity-level controls. Use this information to (hopefully) corroborate earlier assessments of entity-level control effectiveness.

For example, when making inquiries of an individual about the control procedures he or she performs, consider expanding the inquiry to include questions about entity-level controls. Examples of inquiries that go beyond understanding activity-level control procedures include the following:

- If changes to your procedures were required, how would they be communicated?
- What kind of on-the-job or formal classroom training do you receive? Do you find it helpful?
- How closely is your work supervised?
- If any problems or errors that you can't fix are identified, do you ever get the impression that they are either ignored or "made to go away" without being adequately addressed?

To help create a questioning strategy or to formulate individual questions, it is often helpful to refer to the Employee Summary of Corporate Culture and Personnel Policies, included in Appendix 6B. By asking these or similar questions in an interview setting, the opportunity to ask follow-up questions that will allow for a more in-depth understanding of the operating entity-level controls is obtained. Thus, activity-level control testing provides an excellent opportunity to confirm initial assessments of entity-level control effectiveness.

The second way entity-level controls affect the design of activity-level controls is in the scope of testwork. As described in Chapter 6, weaknesses in entity-level controls should lead to the expansion of the scope of activity-level testing. Conversely, strengths in entity-level controls may allow for a reduction in the scope of activity-level tests.

For example, consider two separate federal agencies, both involved in similar activities, such as providing reimbursable services to other federal agencies. Reimbursable Revenue is a significant activity, and it is clear that revenue recognition is a critical accounting policy. However, their entity-level controls have significant differences, as indicated in Exhibit 7.3.

In the case of Agency A, it would be important to expand the scope of activity-level testwork for processing revenue transactions. For example, if tests included transaction testing, the sample size would need to be increased. Inquiries might be made of more individuals or people who otherwise would not have been considered for interviewing. The expansion might even include divisions or locations that otherwise would not have been considered. For Agency B, the opposite is true.

Additionally, the relative strength of entity-level controls should be considered when planning the timing of procedures. With Agency B, at which entity-level controls are strong, activity-level controls may be tested well in advance of the reporting date and reliance could be placed on entity-level controls to draw a conclusion

Exhibit 7.3 Example Entity-Level Controls

Agency A	Agency B
• Management performance is evaluated solely on the $ volume of reimbursable agreements "earned" by the agency.	• Management performance is evaluated on a "balanced scorecard" concept that considers volume along with customer satisfaction and quality of the goods or services delivered by the Agency.
• Allocation of scarce budgetary resources such as full-time employees and physical space is also based on the $ volume of reimbursable agreements generated by each Program Manager.	• Culture built on product/service innovation and improvement as well as quality customer service.
• Communication and training of employees is generally poor.	• Formal training methods for communicating policies and acceptable behavior.
• Oversight and supervision are lax.	• Effective oversight and supervision.

about operating effectiveness at the reporting date. For Agency A, a different strategy would most likely have to be adopted, for example, testing the controls closer to the reporting date or reperforming a limited number of activity-level tests near the reporting date.

Shared Activities.   Some activities in an agency are performed centrally and affect several different financial account balances. For example, disbursements affect not only Fund Balances with Treasury, but also accounts payable and payroll. The most common types of shared activities include:

- Cash disbursements
- Payroll
- Data processing
- Fund control
- Cash receipts

When designing activity-level tests, it is important to coordinate tests of shared activities with tests of individual processing streams. For example, plan on testing disbursements only once, not several times for each different processing stream that includes cash disbursements.

Types of Tests

Inquiry and Focus Groups.   Formal inquiries of entity personnel—either individually or as part of a focus group—can be a reliable source of evidence about the operating effectiveness of application-level controls. Inquiries can serve two main purposes:

- To confirm an understanding of the design of the control (what should happen)
- To identify exceptions to the entity's stated control procedures (what *really* happens)

Confirming Control Design.   Chapter 5 describes a process for documenting the design of activity-level controls. Typically, this process consists primarily of a review of documentation (such as policies and procedures manuals) and limited inquiries of high-level individuals or those in the accounting department. To confirm this understanding of the processing stream and control procedures, inquiries should be expanded to include federal program managers and operating personnel and those responsible for performing the control. To help in conducting the discussion, it is often helpful to use a flowchart of the information-processing stream, as described in Chapter 5, as a guide.

When conducting these inquiries, consider the following:

- Focus first on what *should* happen and whether understandings of the control procedure are consistent. This strategy accomplishes a number of important objectives:

  - It provides a baseline understanding of the procedure that everyone can agree on. It helps to start with everyone "on the same page." Exceptions to the norm can be discussed later.

  - If the employees' understanding of what should happen varies significantly from what is documented, that may indicate a weakness in entity-level controls. For example, it may be found that a weakness in the entity's hiring or training policies is the cause of the lack of understanding of what should happen. This weakness may have implications for the operating effectiveness of other application-level controls.

  - Differences between documentation and the employee's understanding of the procedures also may indicate that the implementation or use of the entity's automated documentation tool was poorly planned or executed. For example, documentation of a new control may have been created without informing operating personnel of the change.

- Ask open-ended questions. Open-ended questions get people talking and allow them to *volunteer information*. The results of inquiries are more reliable when individuals volunteer information that is consistent with documentation rather than simply confirming an understanding of a direct statement.

- Focus on how the procedure is applied and documented. As described earlier, operating effectiveness is determined by how the procedure was applied, the consistency with which it was applied and by whom (i.e., whether the person performing the control has other, conflicting duties). The last two elements will be the subject of inquiries to identify exceptions to the stated policy. Questions about what somebody does or how he or she documents control performance (e.g., by initialing a source document) typically are less threatening than questions related to consistency ("under what circumstances do you *not* follow the required procedure?") or possible incompatible functions.

- Interviewers should share their findings and observations with each other. Research indicates that the effectiveness of inquiry as an evidence-gathering technique improves when Project Team members debrief the results.

- Ask "what could go wrong?" Interviewees will easily understand a line of questioning that starts with "Tell me what could go wrong in processing this information" followed by "What do you do to make sure those errors don't occur?"

Toward that end, consider using the financial statement assertions model to frame questions. As described previously, one way to organize an understanding of activity-level controls is to link them to financial statement assertions. These assertions can be used to formulate questions. For example, "What procedures do you perform to make sure that you capture all the transactions?" is related to the completeness assertion.

- Consider the difference between processes and controls. Chapter 5 draws a distinction between processes and controls. A process changes or manipulates the information in the stream. Processes introduce the possibility of error. Controls detect errors or prevent them from occurring during the processing of information. Inquiries should confirm the earlier understanding of *both* the steps involved in processing the information and the related controls.

The duties of an individual employee may include the processing of information (e.g., the manual input of data into the computer system or the preparation of source documents), control procedures (e.g., the performance of a reconciliation or the follow-up on items identified in an exception report), or both. In making inquiries, it is important to remain cognizant of the distinction between processes and controls and the responsibilities of the individual being interviewed.

Appendix 7B provides example questions that can be used to gather evidence relating to the design effectiveness of internal control.

Identify Exceptions.   In every entity, there will be differences between the agency's stated procedures and what individuals actually do in the course of everyday work. The existence of differences is normal. In testing the effectiveness of application-level controls, these differences should be anticipated, and procedures should be planned to identify them and assess how they affect the effectiveness of activity-level controls. Differences between what *should* happen and what *really* happens can arise from:

- The existence of transactions that were not contemplated in the design of the system
- Different applications of the procedure according to operating division or component, location, or differences between the people executing operating and control tasks

- Changes in personnel or in their assigned responsibilities during the period under review
- Practical, field-level "workarounds" as a way to satisfy other objectives, such as bypassing a control to respond to customer needs better or achieve a specific performance measurement or objective

Once both parties have reached a common understanding of the agency's stated procedures, it is important to discuss the circumstances that result in a variation from these procedures. When making these inquiries, consider the following:

- *Don't make value judgments.* In any organization, the information that flows through a processing stream will follow the path of least resistance. Controls that are seen as barriers to the processing of legitimate transactions that meet the agency's overall objectives may be bypassed. The employee may not be at fault. More importantly, if the interviewee feels judged by the interviewer, he or she will be less inclined to participate productively in the information-gathering process, and the interview will lose effectiveness.
- *Separate information gathering from evaluation.* Remember that this phase of inquiry is a two-step process:

  1. Identify the exceptions to the stated policy.
  2. Assess the effect that these have on operating effectiveness.

Keep these two objectives separate. Be careful not to perform the evaluation prematurely, before having gathered all the necessary information. When performing inquiries, remember that the only objective is to gather information—the evaluation will be performed after the inquiries have been completed.

- *Use hypothetical or indirect questions to probe sensitive areas.* Many interviewees will feel uncomfortable describing how they circumvent agency policies or how they have incompatible duties that could leave the agency vulnerable to fraud. To gather this type of information, use indirect questioning techniques that do not confront the employee directly or otherwise put him or her on the defensive. For example, questions can be prefaced with qualifying statements, such as:

  ○ "If a situation arose in which . . ."
  ○ "Suppose that . . ."
  ○ "If someone wanted to . . ."

- *Ask them directly about their opinion of control effectiveness.* The overall objective of the inquiry is to gather information to assess the effectiveness of controls. The opinions of those who perform the control procedures on a daily basis are important. Ask them to share those opinions. Do they think the controls are effective? Why or why not?

Qualifications of Employees.   As described earlier, assessing the operating effectiveness of control activities requires a consideration of who performs such activities. Inquiries should determine whether the interviewee is qualified to perform the required procedures. To be "qualified," the individual should have the necessary skills, training, and experience, and should have no incompatible functions.

Exhibit 7.4 in Appendix 7B provides example inquiries that can help in assessing the operating effectiveness of internal control procedures.

Focus Groups. As a supplement to, or perhaps instead of interviewing people individually, one may wish to facilitate a group discussion about the entity's activity level control activities and their effectiveness. The purpose of the group discussion would be the same as a discussion with individuals: to confirm the initial understanding of control design and to gather information about operating effectiveness. However, the advantages of conducting a group discussion include the following:

- *See the whole process.* It may be possible to convene a group of individuals who represent every step in the processing stream, from the initiation of the transaction through its posting in the general ledger. A group discussion that includes these members will help to illuminate how the entire process fits together.

- *Foster communication and understanding.* In conducting a group discussion, individuals in the agency who may not interact together on a regular basis will be brought together and engaged in a discussion about operating procedures and controls. By participating in this process, employees will gain a greater understanding of their responsibilities and how these fit into the larger picture. This improved understanding among employees will allow the project to provide value to the agency that goes beyond mere compliance.

To conduct a group discussion, follow these steps:

1. Review the documentation of the processing stream and determine who should be invited to participate. Groups of five to ten people usually work the best—everyone can make a meaningful contribution to the conversation without things getting out of hand. Try to make sure that someone is present who has experience with every process, control, document, or electronic file described in the documentation of the processing stream.

2. Prepare a flowchart of the process on a large piece of paper. Use stickies to document processes and control points. The group discussion will be highly interactive, and the participants will have the opportunity to change the original flowchart to provide a more accurate description of what really happens in the process. Therefore, the flowchart should be prepared in a way that allows the group to work with it easily. Low tech, high touch works the best.

3. Assemble the group and explain:
   - The purpose of the discussion, as described previously
   - The process—participants will discuss how the process really works and will be free to describe what happens by modifying the flowchart
   - How long the discussion will take—usually one to two hours is the longest that a group discussion of this nature can remain productive. If more time is needed, it is better to conduct more sessions rather than have longer sessions.

4. Post the flowchart on the wall and walk the participants through interpretations of the process.

5. Using the questioning strategies and example questions provided in Appendix 7B, facilitate a discussion among the participants. As described earlier:

   ○ First, reach an understanding about what should happen.

   ○ Next, identify those instances in which exceptions exist (what really happens).

   ○ Throughout the discussion, encourage the participants to change the flow-chart as necessary so that it reflects what they have said.

   Here are some tips for facilitating the group discussion:

- Keep people focused on the flow of information, not on the flow of documents.

- Have the boundaries of the processing stream well defined. Make sure people understand that the information flowing into the financial statements is the primary concern. Also, when discussing how information is prepared, the discussion should be limited to what the agency does *internally,* not on how third parties may prepare information that the agency uses. (How the agency *reviews or otherwise controls* the information provided from external sources will, however, be discussed.)

- Participants will probably disagree on certain matters. That is normal, and an expectation should be set that differences of opinion are acceptable. In facilitating the discussion, try to probe and gain a better understanding of the source of these differences.

- Whenever possible, try to *quantify* what is learned about the process. For example, ask questions that begin with "How often do you encounter . . . ?" or "About what percentage of transactions . . . ?"

- Try to build consensus. Before drawing any conclusions about the process and related controls, make sure there is a consensus among group members. Conclusions should not be drawn if significant differences exist among members of the group. At some level, agreement should be sought on these issues.

Tests of Transactions.   Some control procedures allow for the selection of sample transactions that were recorded during the period and:

- An examination of the documentation indicating that the control procedure was performed

- Reperforming of the procedure to determine that the control was performed properly

   For example, the process for recording inventory purchases may require:

- Physically matching a paper-based warehouse receiving report with an approved purchase order

- Determining that the purchase order was properly approved, as indicated by a signature

- Determining that the vendor is an approved vendor
- Observing evidence (e.g., checkmarks, initials) that warehouse personnel counted the goods received.

To test the effectiveness of this control procedure one could:

- Examine documentation that the control was performed and:
  - Documents were matched
  - Purchase orders were signed
  - Receiving reports were marked.
- Determine that the control was performed properly and:
  - Purchase orders and receiving reports are for the same transaction
  - Vendor is an approved vendor
  - Signer of the purchase order has the authority to approve the transaction.

Computer application controls may also lend themselves to similar testing techniques. For example, suppose that purchased personal property is accompanied by a bar code that identifies the property received and the quantities. The bar code is scanned and the information is matched electronically to purchase order files and approved vendor master files. Unmatched transactions are placed in a suspense file for subsequent follow-up. (As indicated previously, the computer application control consists of *both* the programmed elements of the control and the manual follow-up of identified errors.) To test the effectiveness of this control one could:

- Prepare a file of test transactions and run through the system to determine that all errors are identified.
- Review the resolution of the suspense account items performed throughout the period to determine that they were resolved properly.

When performing tests of transactions, issues related to scope will have to be addressed—how many items to test. Suggestions for considering the scope of tests were provided earlier in this chapter.

Before performing tests of transactions, it is important to define what will be considered a control procedure error. When the evidence that a procedure was performed is documented (e.g., an initial or signature), the lack of documentation (a missing signature) should be considered an error in the operation of the control. That is, in order for a documented control to be considered properly performed, *both* of the following must be true:

- Documentation indicates that the control procedure was performed.
- Reperformance of the procedure indicates it was performed properly.

Reconciliations.   Reconciliations are a common control procedure, for example, Fund Balances with Treasury reconciliations or the reconciliation of the general ledger account total to a subsidiary ledger. In some instances, a well-designed reconciliation can provide an effective control over most of a processing stream. Testing the effectiveness of a reconciliation is similar to tests of transactions:

- Review documentation that the test was performed on a timely basis throughout the period.
- Reperform the test to determine that all reconciling items were identified properly.
- Investigate the resolution of significant reconciling items.

Observation.   The application of some control procedures, such as computer input controls like edit checks, may be observable. A physical inventory count also lends itself to observation as a means of assessing effectiveness. For a control performed only occasionally, such as a physical count, it may be possible to observe the control each time it is performed. For controls that are performed continuously for large volumes of transactions, observations will need to be supplemented with other tests, such as:

- Inquiry
- Tests of entity-level controls

EVALUATING TEST RESULTS

The results of tests of activity-level controls should support conclusions about their operating effectiveness. If testing revealed no deviations or deficiencies in the performance of control procedures, then one should be able to conclude that the control is operating effectively (assuming that the scope of the testwork, as discussed earlier in this chapter, was sufficient).

When testwork reveals deficiencies in either the design or operating effectiveness of a control procedure, it is important to exercise judgment in order to reach a conclusion about control effectiveness. Chapter 8 provides guidance on the factors that should be considered when making this judgment. (See the sections titled "The Nature of Internal Control Deficiencies" and "Making Judgments about the Severity of Internal Control Deficiencies.")

Ultimately, the effectiveness of internal control *as a whole* is what is being considered. When one is evaluating activity-level controls, the effectiveness of the entire information-processing stream should be considered, not just individual control procedures in isolation.

DOCUMENTATION OF TEST PROCEDURES AND RESULTS

As described in Chapter 6, it is important to document the test procedures performed and the results of those tests. Chapter 6 provides guidance on what should be included in the documentation related to tests of entity-level controls, and that guidance is applicable to tests of activity-level controls as well.

COORDINATING WITH THE INDEPENDENT AUDITORS AND THE OIG

Determining the nature, timing, and extent of tests is a significant decision. Whether or not separate opinions on internal controls and/or management assertions will be issued by the independent auditors, the independent auditors and/or the Office of the Inspector General (OIG) are a valuable and experienced source for validating the testing approach. If the independent auditors determine that tests were not sufficient to support the evaluation of the effectiveness of controls, then additional testwork should be required. The scope of additional tests may be significant, and the performance of these tests could delay the preparation of the required report.

For these reasons, it is important to review planned procedures with the independent auditors and the OIG before conducting a significant portion of the tests. Describe how these procedures build on the assessment of entity-level controls. Consider discussing how the testing strategy relates to the various financial statement assertions. Periodically, as the tests are performed and results received and evaluated, consider discussing the progress of the tests with the auditors to confirm that the original plan is still sufficient for their purposes.

Always remember that the auditors are required to evaluate internal controls as part of their execution of a financial statement audit, regardless of whether a separate opinion is being issued on controls or management's assertion on controls. Both COSO and the revised OMB Circular A-123 identify monitoring as a key component/standard of internal control. The periodic assessment of internal controls pursuant to the Federal Managers' Financial Integrity Act of 1982 (FMFIA) and OMB Circular A-123 requirements is an essential element of the monitoring standard/component. Thus, if the scope, testing, and other procedures are not considered sufficient, the auditors may conclude that there is a significant deficiency in internal controls, or even that a material weakness exists and must be reported.

Therefore, an ongoing dialogue with the independent auditors and the OIG should be established to reach a consensus on matters such as the following:

- The nature and extent of planned procedures and whether these are considered sufficient to draw a reliable conclusion.

- The circumstances under which the planned nature and extent of the procedures should be modified.

- The planned timing of tests and whether this timing will allow for drawing conclusions about the design and operating effectiveness of activity-level controls as of June 30 or year-end.

- The nature and extent of procedures that may be required to update conclusions about effectiveness from the time procedures are performed until year-end. (Note that if material weaknesses are uncovered after June 30 or year-end, but before the issuance of the Performance and Accountability Report (PAR), the assurance statement is required to be revised accordingly).

- The results of tests and the tentative and final conclusions reached regarding the effectiveness of activity-level controls.

- How the test procedures and results will be documented.

- The general type of deviations or conditions that might be considered significant deficiencies or material weaknesses.

- The corrective actions and possible reporting implications required to respond to the identification of significant deficiencies or material weaknesses.

Appendix 7A

Action Plan: Documentation

The following action plan is intended to help you implement the suggestions contained in this chapter for testing and evaluating activity-level controls.

1. Design Tests

Plan the nature, timing, and extent of tests necessary to draw a conclusion about the operating effectiveness of internal control as of year-end. For example:

- Consider the nature of possible errors that may occur in the information-processing stream.
  - Consider using the financial statement assertions framework to help you identify potential errors.

- Consider the control activities that are expected to exist based on your review of:
  - The entity's internal control documentation
  - The example control activities provided by COSO or others

- Consider the results of entity-level tests.

- Determine the combination of testing techniques that will be used to assess the operating effectiveness of each significant entity-level control. Consider:
  - Computer application controls
  - Inquiries and focus groups
  - Tests of transactions
  - Tests of reconciliations
  - Direct observation

2. Perform and Document Tests

Perform the planned tests. Update as necessary to support a conclusion about operating effectiveness as of June 30 or year-end. Document the procedures performed and the test results.

3. Assess Test Results

Evaluate the effectiveness of activity-level controls based on the results of your test-work. For example:

- Determine whether activity-level controls are functioning at a level that will prevent or detect material financial statement misstatements in a timely manner.
- Identify weaknesses in activity-level controls.
- Respond to identified weaknesses by taking corrective action.

4. Coordinate with the Independent Auditors

Establish an ongoing dialogue with the independent auditors that allows you to reach a consensus on the following:

- The nature and extent of your planned procedures and whether these are considered sufficient to draw a reliable conclusion
- The circumstances under which the planned nature and extent of the procedures should be modified
- The planned timing of your tests and whether this timing will allow you to draw conclusions about the design and operating effectiveness of activity-level controls as of year-end
- The nature and extent of procedures that may be required to update your conclusions about effectiveness from the time your procedures are performed until year-end
- The results of your tests and the tentative and final conclusions reached regarding the effectiveness of activity-level controls
- How the test procedures and results will be documented
- The general type of deviations or conditions that might be considered significant deficiencies or material weaknesses
- The corrective actions and possible reporting implications required to respond to the identification of significant deficiencies or material weaknesses

---

Appendix 7B

Example Inquiries

Exhibit 7.4   Example Inquiries

Design Effectiveness

- What documents or electronic files are necessary for you to perform your job? From whom do you receive the document? How do you access the electronic information? (Process)
- In what ways do you add to, combine, manipulate, or change the data you receive? (Process)

(continues)

Exhibit 7.4   Example Inquiries *(Continued)*

Design Effectiveness

- What happens to a file or document when you are finished with it? (Process)

- When you discover errors, how are they corrected? (Process)

- What checks do you perform on the information you use to make sure it is accurate? (Accuracy control)

- How do you know that you receive all the transactions you should receive? How do you make sure that you process everything you receive and that some transactions are not accidentally dropped from the process? (Completeness control)

- When you are processing the information, what steps do you take to make sure that no errors are introduced into the system? What controls are built into the system itself? (Completeness, accuracy controls)

- What signatures or other types of documentation are required before you process a transaction? How do you know that the transactions presented to you for processing are valid? (Existence, authorization control)

Operating Effectiveness

Your inquiries of operating effectiveness should be directed toward gathering information about two broad areas: the consistency with which the control procedure was applied and the qualifications of the person who performed the control. You also should consider asking employees for their opinion about the operating effectiveness of controls.

Consistency

- What kinds of situations do you encounter for which agency policies or procedures do not exist? How often do you encounter these situations?
  - If you encountered a situation or transaction for which no written policy existed, what would you do? How likely is it that you would encounter such a situation? What would it be? (Indirect)

- In what ways are written policies and procedures inefficient or otherwise "do not make sense"? How do you work around these policies? How often do you have to do this?
  - If you were in charge of designing policies and procedures, what changes would you make to improve their efficiency? (Indirect)

- Although it might not be written, when is it "okay" not to follow written policies exactly? How do you know it is "okay"?

- Do you think that others in the agency with the same job functions as yours perform the job in the same way? If differences exist, what are they? What causes these differences?

- Have you performed the procedures every day since the last annual evaluation of internal control effectiveness? Who took your place when you were not available to perform the procedures?

- Have there been any changes to the procedures since the last annual evaluation of internal control effectiveness?

Exhibit 7.4   Example Inquiries *(Continued)*

Qualifications of Personnel

- Do you feel adequately trained to perform your duties?
  - If you could design the training for your position, what topics would you be sure to include? How did you learn these things? How long did it take you to learn them? What else would you like to be trained in that would help you do your job better?
- Incompatible responsibilities exist when one individual is in a position where they must both process data (for example, prepare invoices, or post the general ledger) AND check their own work for errors AND no one checks their work. Have you observed situations like that in your department?
  - Suppose that someone were inclined to deliberately create an error in the reporting process, for example, by introducing a fictitious or unauthorized transaction. How would they do it without getting caught? (Indirect)
  - Which agency assets are most vulnerable to employee theft? How could these assets "disappear" without someone finding out? (Indirect)

Assessment of Effectiveness

- Overall, how effective is your system at preventing or detecting and correcting errors? Consider the reliability of your system. If you had to give it a letter grade, what grade would you give it? What recommendations would you make to improve the system?
  - Suppose that you leave the agency, and shortly after you leave, you learn that there was a major error in the agency's financial statements relating to your division/location. What is that error? Why it was never detected? (Indirect)

Chapter 8

Reporting

Chapter Summary

- Describe and explain the requirements for management's quarterly and annual reports on internal control.
- Guidance for reporting significant deficiencies and material weaknesses in internal control.
- Reporting when internal control deficiencies have been corrected during the period.
- Management reporting on internal control.

REPORTING REQUIREMENTS

This chapter summarizes and compares the certifications regarding internal control that are required for the federal government under the revised Office of Management and Budget (OMB) Circular A-123 and for publicly traded private entities as required by the Securities and Exchange Commission (SEC).

OMB Circular A-123 Guidance

As noted in Chapter 1, pursuant to Section VI of the revised Circular, management is to provide the following assurances in its Performance and Accountability Report (PAR):

- *Statement of Assurance.* The statement of assurance represents the agency head's informed judgment as to the overall adequacy and effectiveness of internal control within the agency.

- *Statement of Assurance for Internal Control over Financial Reporting.* Management is required to provide a separate assurance of the effectiveness of the internal controls over financial reporting. This assurance is a subset of the overall Statement of Assurance and is based on the results of management's assessment conducted in accordance with the requirements in Appendix A of OMB Circular A-123.

Sample Assurance Statements taken from the *Implementation Guide* are shown as Exhibits 8.1 through 8.3.

Also, as noted in Chapter 1, there are currently no external interim reporting requirements; however, the revised Circular makes it very clear that internal control issues are not a once-a-year requirement. In fact, the Circular emphasizes the need

Exhibit 8.1 Illustrative Template for a Statement of Assurance

---

Statement of Assurance

The [Agency's] management is responsible for establishing and maintaining effective internal control and financial management systems that meet the objectives of the Federal Managers' Financial Integrity Act (FMFIA). The [Agency] conducted its assessment of the effectiveness of internal control over the effectiveness and efficiency of operations and compliance with applicable laws and regulations in accordance with OMB Circular A-123, *Management's Responsibility for Internal Control.* Based on the results of this evaluation, the [Agency] can provide reasonable assurance that its internal control over the effectiveness and efficiency of operations and compliance with applicable laws and regulations as of September 30, 2xxx was operating effectively and no material weaknesses were found in the design or operation of the internal controls.

In addition, the [Agency] conducted its assessment of the effectiveness of internal control over financial reporting, which includes safeguarding of assets and compliance with applicable laws and regulations, in accordance with the requirements of Appendix A of OMB Circular A-123. Based on the results of this evaluation, the [Agency] can provide reasonable assurance that its internal control over financial reporting as of June 30, 2xxx was operating effectively and no material weaknesses were found in the design or operation of the internal control over financial reporting.

Agency Head Signature

Date

Source: Implementation Guide for OMB Circular A-123, Appendix A.

Exhibit 8.2 Illustrative Template for a Qualified Statement of Assurance

---

Statement of Qualified Assurance

The [Agency's] management is responsible for establishing and maintaining effective internal control and financial management systems that meet the objectives of the Federal Manager's Financial Integrity Act (FMFIA). The [Agency] is able to provided a qualified statement of assurance that the internal controls and financial management systems meet the objectives of FMFIA, with the exception of [number] material weakness(es) and [number] non-conformance(s). The details of the exception(s) are provided in Exhibit [xx].

The [Agency] conducted its assessment of the effectiveness of internal control over the effectiveness and efficiency of operations and compliance with applicable laws and regulations in accordance with OMB Circular A-123, *Management's Responsibility for Internal Control.* Based on the results of this evaluation, the [Agency] identified [number] material weakness(es) in its internal control over the effectiveness and efficiency of operations and compliance with applicable laws and regulations as of September 30, 2xxx. Other than the exceptions noted in Exhibit [xx], the internal controls were operating effectively and no other material weaknesses were found in the design or operation of the internal controls.

Exhibit 8.2 Illustrative Template for a Qualified Statement of Assurance
(Continued)

In addition, the [Agency] conducted its assessment of the effectiveness of internal control over financial reporting, which includes safeguarding of assets and compliance with applicable laws and regulations, in accordance with the requirements of Appendix A of OMB Circular A-123. Based on the results of this evaluation, the [Agency] identified [number] material weakness(es) in its internal control over financial reporting as of June 30, 2xxx. Other than the exceptions noted in Exhibit [xx], the internal controls were operating effectively and no other material weaknesses were found in the design or operation of the internal control over financial reporting.

Agency Head Signature

Date

Source: Implementation Guide for OMB Circular A-123, Appendix A.

Exhibit 8.3 Illustrative Template When an Entity Cannot Provide a Statement of Assurance

Statement of No Assurance

The [Agency's] management is responsible for establishing and maintaining effective internal control and financial management systems that meet the objectives of the Federal Manager's Financial Integrity Act (FMFIA). The [Agency] is unable to provide assurance that the internal controls and financial management systems meet the objectives of FMFIA, due to the [number] material weakness(es) and [number] non-conformances(s) listed in Exhibit [xx].

The [Agency] conducted its assessment of the effectiveness of internal control in accordance with OMB Circular A-123, *Management's Responsibility for Internal Control.* Based on the results of this evaluation, the [Agency] identified [number] material weakness(es) in its internal control over the effectiveness and efficiency of operations and compliance with applicable laws and regulations as of September 30, 2xxx. Other than the exceptions noted in Exhibit [xx], the internal controls were operating effectively and no other material weaknesses were found in the design or operation of the internal controls.

In addition, the [Agency] conducted its assessment of the effectiveness of internal control over financial reporting, which includes safeguarding of assets and compliance with applicable laws and regulations, in accordance with the requirements of Appendix A of OMB Circular A-123. The [Agency] did not fully implement the requirements included in OMB Circular A-123 and therefore cannot provide assurance that its internal control over financial reporting as of June 30, 2xxx was operating effectively. A summary of actions the [Agency] will take to comply with the OMB Circular A-123 requirements is included in Exhibit [xx].

Agency Head Signature

Date

Source: Implementation Guide for OMB Circular A-123, Appendix A.

Exhibit 8.4   Corrective Action Framework

Corrective Action Document	Stakeholder Group	Corrective Action Timeframe	Measure
Executive Summary	• OMB • Agency Management	• Long-term • Annual	• Final Compliance Indicator(s) / Target(s)
Corrective Action Plan Management Summary	• OMB • Agency Senior Management Council	• Long-term • Annual • Short-term	• Mid-term Compliance Indicator(s) / Target(s)
Detailed Corrective Action Plan	• OMB • Agency Senior Management Council • Agency Personnel	• Long-term • Annual • Short-term	• Short-term Compliance Indicator(s) / Target(s)

Source: Implementation Guide for OMB Circular A-123 Appendix A.

for continuous monitoring of corrective plans, and the *Implementation Guide* proposes a Corrective Action Framework, which is shown in Exhibit 8.4. In addition, the revised OMB Circular A-123 indicates that the OMB reserves the right to require additional reports in connection with corrective action.

The *Implementation Guide* proposes that the corrective action plan should list the action to be taken by agency personnel and should include the following:

• A summary description of the deficiency

• The year first identified

• The targeted corrective action date (the date of audit follow-up)

• The agency official responsible for monitoring progress

• The indicators, statistics, or metrics used to gauge resolution progress (in advance of audit follow-up) to validate the resolution of the deficiency

• The quantifiable target or otherwise qualitative characteristic (e.g., milestone) that reports how resolution activities are progressing

In addition, the *Implementation Guide* proposes the following documentation and report issuance guidance:

• The PAR-corrective action executive summary captures and reports activities from an annual timeframe.

• The management summary captures and reports activities from a quarterly timeframe.

• The detailed corrective action plan captures and reports activities from (at a minimum) a monthly timeframe.

Reporting weaknesses and deficiencies in internal control are still in a development stage, and it is anticipated that additional guidance will be forthcoming from the President's Council on Integrity and Efficiency (PCIE) and the Chief Financial

Officers (CFO) Council as well as the OMB. Regardless of the form the guidance ultimately takes, the Guide proposes a very useful model for monitoring, reporting, and resolving internal control weaknesses.

Required Disclosures

Revised OMB Circular A-123 identifies the following requirements in connection with the assurance statement:

- A statement of management's responsibility for establishing and maintaining adequate internal control over financial reporting for the agency
- A statement identifying the OMB Circular A-123, *Management's Responsibility for Internal Control,* as the framework used by management to conduct the assessment of the effectiveness of the agency's internal control over financial reporting
- An assessment of the effectiveness of the agency's internal control over financial reporting as of June 30, including an explicit conclusion as to whether the internal controls over financial reporting are effective
- If a material weakness is discovered by June 30, but corrected by September 30, a statement identifying the material weakness, the corrective action taken, and that it has been resolved by September 30
- If a material weakness is discovered after June 30, but prior to September 30, the statement identifying the material weaknesses should be updated to include the subsequently identified material weakness

As noted earlier, the agency is required to issue one of three possible statements of assurance (see Exhibits 8.1 through 8.3). In addition, federal financial managers should be aware of the following requirements:

- If one or more material weaknesses are present, management cannot conclude that its agency's internal controls over financial reporting are effective. A separate discussion in this chapter provides practical guidance (currently used in connection with Sarbanes-Oxley compliance) on determining whether an internal control deficiency is a material weakness.
- An exception to the above can be made if material weaknesses existing at June 30 had been corrected.

SEC Rules

Under SEC rules, an entity's annual report on Form10K must include:[1]

- *Management's annual report on internal control over financial reporting.* Provide a report on the entity's internal control over financial reporting that contains:
  - A statement of management's responsibilities for establishing and maintaining adequate internal control over financial reporting.

- ○ A statement identifying the framework used by management to evaluate the effectiveness of the entity's internal control over financial reporting.
- ○ Management's assessment of the effectiveness of the entity's internal control over financial reporting as of the end of the most recent fiscal year, including a statement as to whether internal control over financial reporting is effective. This discussion must include disclosure of any material weakness in the entity's internal control over financial reporting identified by management. Management is not permitted to conclude that the registrant's internal control over financial reporting is effective if there are one or more material weaknesses in the entity's internal control over financial reporting.
- ○ A statement that the registered public accounting firm that audited the financial statements included in the annual report has issued an attestation report on management's assessment of the registrant's internal control over financial reporting.

- *Attestation report of the registered public accounting firm.* Provide the registered public accounting firm's attestation report on management's assessment of the entity's internal control over financial reporting.
- *Changes in internal control over financial reporting.* Disclose any change in the entity's internal control over financial reporting that has materially affected, or is reasonably likely to materially affect, the entity's internal control over financial reporting.

The entity's annual report filed with the SEC also should include management's fourth-quarter report on the effectiveness of the entity's disclosure controls and procedures.

Exhibit 8.5 provides an example report that complies with SEC reporting requirements. Note that this example includes a paragraph that describes the inherent limitations of internal control systems. This paragraph is *not* required by SEC rules but has been included for illustrative purposes. Key provisions of these annual reporting requirements that merit further discussion include:

- *Management's statement of effectiveness.* Under guidance provided by the SEC, management must state whether internal control is functioning effectively. Negative assurance, in which management states "nothing has come to its attention that would lead it to believe that internal control was not functioning effectively" is not acceptable.[2]
- *Material weakness in internal control.* Management is required to disclose any material weakness in the entity's internal control. Furthermore, the existence of one or more material weaknesses precludes management from concluding that its internal control is effective.
- *"As of" reporting.* Management assesses the effectiveness of internal control *as of* the end of the fiscal year, rather than throughout the reporting period. This reporting requirement has significant implications for the reporting of material weaknesses that were identified and corrected during the period.

Exhibit 8.5   Example Management's Report on Internal Control over
                 Financial Reporting

The management of XYZ is responsible for establishing and maintaining adequate internal control over financial reporting. The internal control system has been designed to provide reasonable assurance to the company's management and board of directors regarding the preparation and fair presentation of the company's published financial statements.

All internal control systems, no matter how well designed, have inherent limitations. Therefore, even those systems determined to be effective can provide only reasonable assurance with respect to financial statement preparation and presentation.[a]

The management of XYZ has assessed the effectiveness of the company's internal control over financial reporting as of December 31, 20XX. To make this assessment, we used the criteria for effective internal control over financial reporting described in *Internal Control—Integrated Framework,* issued by the Committee of Sponsoring Organizations of the Treadway Commission. Based on our assessment, we believe that, as of December 31, 20XX, the Company's internal control over financial reporting met those criteria.

Our independent auditors have issued an attestation report on our assessment of the Company's internal control over financial reporting. This report can be found on page XX.

---

a. This statement regarding the inherent limitation of internal control is *not* required by the SEC rules. It has been included in this example report solely for illustrative purposes.

Required Disclosure in SEC Filings

Management's annual report on internal control is required to disclose any material weakness in internal control. Except for the requirement that the entity disclose any change to internal control that has materially affected or is reasonably likely to materially affect the entity's internal control, the rules do not prescribe any format or other requirements for the disclosure.

However, in practice, it is common for the disclosure to include:

- The fact that management has identified a material weakness in its internal control over financial reporting
- A definition of or reference to the definition of *material weakness*
- The actions taken by management to correct the deficiency

Appendix 8A includes several examples of the disclosure of a material weakness. Exhibit 8.6 provides an example of how management's required report on internal control could be modified to report a material weakness.

Note that except for the independent audit requirement, annual disclosure rules on Form 10K are similar to those of revised OMB Circular A-123. As is the case with federal agencies, management cannot conclude that internal controls over financial reporting are effective if one or more material weaknesses are present.

Exhibit 8.6 Example Management's Report on Internal Control over Financial
Reporting

(Introductory paragraph. See Exhibit 8.5)

(Optional inherent limitations paragraph. See Exhibit 8.5)

A material weakness in internal control is a significant deficiency or an aggregation
of significant deficiencies that preclude the entity's internal control from providing
reasonable assurance that material misstatements in the financial statements will be
prevented or detected on a timely basis by employees in the normal course of performing
their assigned functions. A significant deficiency is an internal control deficiency in
a significant control or an aggregation of such deficiencies that could result in a
misstatement of the financial statements that is more than inconsequential.

The management of XYZ has assessed the effectiveness of the company's internal control
over financial reporting as of December 31, 20xx, and this assessment identified the
following material weakness in the company's internal control over financial reporting.

(Describe material weakness)

To make our assessment of internal control over financial reporting, we used the criteria
described in *Internal Control—Integrated Framework,* issued by the Committee of
Sponsoring Organizations of the Treadway Commission. Except for the effect of the
material weakness described in the preceding paragraph, we believe that, as of December
31, 20xx, the company's internal control over financial reporting met those criteria.

Our independent auditors have issued an attestation report on our assessment of the
company's internal control over financial reporting. You can find this report on page xx.

IDENTIFYING AND DEFINING MATERIAL WEAKNESSES AND SIGNIFICANT DEFICIENCIES

The discussions that follow are designed to provide practical guidance to federal
managers involved in identifying and reporting material weaknesses and significant
deficiencies.

The Nature of Internal Control Deficiencies

Deficiencies in internal control can arise in one of the following two ways:

1. *Design deficiency.* A design deficiency exists when either:
    *   A control necessary to achieve a control objective does not exist, or
    *   A control policy or procedure exists but it is not designed in a way that will
        ensure that the control objective is met even if the procedure operates as
        designed.
2. *Operating deficiency.* An operating deficiency exists either:
    *   When a properly designed control is not operating as designed, or
    *   The person performing the procedure does not possess the necessary author-
        ity or qualifications to perform the control effectively.

Exhibit 8.7   Internal Control Deficiencies

Internal control deficiencies adversely affect the entity's ability to record, process, summarize, and report data consistent with management's assertions in the financial statements.

As indicated in Exhibit 8.7, internal control deficiencies range from inconsequential to material weakness. Note that the three levels of deficiency are placed in a continuum. If a deficiency is not inconsequential, then it is, at a minimum, significant.

At issue is where one should "draw the line," that is, at what point is a deficiency no longer inconsequential, and when does a significant deficiency become a material weakness?

The auditing literature defines material weakness in Statement on Auditing Standards (SAS) No. 60, *Communication of Internal Control Related Matters Noted in an Audit* (AU Section 325). For entities subject to Sarbanes-Oxley, the Public Company Accounting Oversight Board (PCAOB) *Auditing Standard No. 2* supersedes SAS No. 60. Under the new standard, the following definitions apply:

- A *significant deficiency* is a control deficiency, or combination of control deficiencies, that adversely affects the company's ability to initiate, authorize, record, process, or report external financial data reliably in accordance with generally accepted accounting principles such that there is more than a remote likelihood that a misstatement of the company's annual or interim financial statements that is more than inconsequential will not be prevented or detected.

- A *material weakness* is a significant deficiency, or combination of significant deficiencies, that results in a more than remote likelihood that a material misstatement of the annual or interim financial statements will not be prevented or detected.

- As noted in Chapter 1, Exhibit 1.4, revised OMB Circular A-123 has adopted the definition of control deficiency, reportable condition, and material weakness set forth in PCAOB's *Auditing Standard No. 2*. Federal financial managers should find the above guidance useful in assessing the magnitude of control deficiencies.

Making Judgments about the Severity of Internal Control Deficiencies

Determining whether an internal control deficiency is more than inconsequential is, at its core, a risk assessment process in which management should consider:

- *Likelihood,* that is, the chance that the deficiency could result in a financial statement misstatement. When assessing likelihood, consider:
  - The susceptibility of the related assets or liability to loss or fraud.

- ○ The subjectivity, complexity, or extent of judgment required to determine the amount involved.
- ○ The nature of the accounts, processes, or disclosures; for example, suspense accounts and accounts requiring estimates involve greater risk.
- ○ The relative importance of the control and whether the overall control objective is achieved by other control activities or a combination of control activities.
- ○ If the deficiency is an operating deficiency, the frequency of the operating failure rate; for example, numerous or repeated failures in the operation of a control would be more likely considered a significant deficiency than failures that are considered isolated occurrences.
- ○ Whether the control is automated and, therefore, could be expected to perform consistently over time.
- *Significance,* that is, the magnitude of potential misstatements resulting from the deficiency. When assessing significance, consider:
  - ○ The nature of the account balance or total of transactions affected by the deficiency and the financial statement assertions involved.
  - ○ Whether the deficiency relates to an entity-level or activity-level control. Because entity-level controls can affect many account balances, classes of transactions, or financial statement assertions, weaknesses in entity-level controls that seem relatively insignificant by themselves could result in material financial statement misstatements.
  - ○ The volume of activity in the account balance or class of transactions exposed to the deficiency that has occurred in the current period, or that is expected in future periods.

When evaluating the significance or magnitude of a potential misstatement, keep in mind that the significance of the misstatement depends on the *potential* for misstatement, not on whether a misstatement actually has occurred.

Considering the Results of the Independent Audit

When one is assessing the relative significance of an entity's internal control deficiencies, it is helpful to consider the results of the entity's most recent independent audit. A material misstatement detected by the independent auditor's procedures that was not first identified by the entity itself normally is indicative of the existence of a material weakness in internal control. However, the converse is not necessarily true. The absence of a material misstatement does not, in and of itself, allow management to conclude that no material weaknesses exist in the entity's internal control.

Example Internal Control Deficiencies

Exhibit 8.8 provides examples of possible significant internal control deficiencies.[3]

Exhibit 8.8 Eamples of Significant Deficiencies in Internal Control

Deficiencies in internal control design	• Inadequate overall internal control design • Absence of appropriate segregation of duties consistent with appropriate control objectives • Absence of appropriate reviews and approvals of transactions, accounting entries, or systems output • Inadequate procedures for appropriately assessing and applying accounting principles • Inadequate provisions for the safeguarding of assets • Absence of other controls considered appropriate for the type and level of transaction activity • Evidence that a system fails to provide complete and accurate output that is consistent with objectives and current needs because of design flaws
Failures in the operation of internal control	• Evidence of failure of identified controls in preventing or detecting misstatements of accounting information • Evidence that a system fails to provide complete and accurate output consistent with the entity's control objectives because of the misapplication of controls • Evidence of failure to safeguard assets from loss, damage, or misappropriation • Evidence of intentional override of internal control by those in authority to the detriment of the overall objectives of the system • Evidence of failure to perform tasks that are part of internal control, such as reconciliations not prepared or not timely prepared • Evidence of willful wrongdoing by employees or management • Evidence of manipulation, falsification, or alteration of accounting records or supporting documents • Evidence of intentional misapplication of accounting principles • Evidence of misrepresentation by client personnel to the auditor • Evidence that employees or management lack the qualifications and training to fulfill their assigned functions
Others	• Absence of a sufficient level of control consciousness within the organization • Failure to follow up and correct previously identified internal control deficiencies • Evidence of significant or extensive undisclosed related-party transactions • Evidence of undue bias or lack of objectivity by those responsible for accounting decisions

"Drawing the Line": PCAOB Guidance

The PCAOB has issued *Auditing Standard No. 2* on internal control reporting. The standard provides additional guidance on determining whether an exception noted during testing is an internal control deficiency and, if so, whether the deficiency is "significant" or rises to the level of "material weakness." We believe this guidance will assist federal managers in the evaluation of internal control deficiencies and the determination of whether they constitute a material weakness.

First, the standard recognizes that "exceptions" may be identified in testwork; for example, a control procedure was performed improperly. The auditor's first consideration is whether the exception is an isolated incident or indicative of an internal control deficiency. In making this determination, the proposed standard states that:

> When [you] identify exceptions to the entity's prescribed control procedures, [you] should determine, using professional skepticism, the effect of the exception on the nature and extent of additional testing that may be appropriate or necessary and on the operating effectiveness of the control being tested. A conclusion that an identi-fied exception does not represent an internal control deficiency is appropriate only if evidence beyond what [you] had initially planned and beyond inquiry supports that conclusion.

If it is determined that an internal control deficiency exists, the next step is to decide whether the deficiency is "significant." To make this decision, the standard provides the following guidance:

> When evaluating the significance of a deficiency in internal control over financial reporting, [you] also should determine the level of detail and degree of assurance that would satisfy prudent officials in the conduct of their own affairs that they have rea-sonable assurance that transactions are recorded as necessary to permit the prepa-ration of financial statements in conformity with generally accepted accounting principles. If [you] determine that the deficiency would prevent prudent officials in the conduct of their own affairs from concluding that they have reasonable assurance, then [you] should consider the deficiency to be at least a significant deficiency. Having determined in this manner that a deficiency represents a significant deficiency, [you] must further evaluate the deficiency to determine whether individually, or in combination with other deficiencies, the deficiency is a material weakness.

The standard goes on to state that certain deficiencies are, at a minimum, sig-nificant deficiencies in internal control. These de facto significant deficiencies are deficiencies in the following areas:

- Controls over the selection and application of accounting policies that are in conformity with generally accepted accounting principles
- Antifraud programs and controls
- Controls over nonroutine and nonsystematic transactions
- Controls over the period-end financial reporting process, including controls over procedures used to enter transaction totals into the general ledger; initiate, record,

and process journal entries into the general ledger; and record recurring and nonrecurring adjustments to the financial statements

Additionally, the standard states that certain circumstances should be regarded as at least a significant deficiency and a strong indicator that a material weakness exists. These circumstances are:

- Restatement of previously issued financial statements to reflect the correction of a misstatement.

- Identification by the auditor of a material misstatement in financial statements in the current period that was not initially identified by the entity's internal control over financial reporting (this is a strong indicator of a material weakness even if management subsequently corrects the misstatement).

- Oversight of the entity's external financial reporting and internal control over financial reporting by the entity's audit committee is ineffective (in this regard, the standard presents factors to evaluate whether the audit committee is ineffective in paragraphs 55 through 59 of the standard).

- For larger, more complex entities, the internal review/audit function or the risk assessment function is ineffective.

- For complex entities in highly regulated industries, an ineffective regulatory compliance function (to the extent that potential violations of laws and regulations could materially affect financial reporting).

- Identification of fraud of any magnitude on the part of senior management.

- Significant deficiencies that have been communicated to management and the audit committee remain uncorrected after some reasonable period of time.

- An ineffective control environment.

"As Of" Reporting Implications

OMB and SEC rules require management to report on the effectiveness of internal control *as of* a point in time, rather than during a given period. This distinction is important for several reasons, including:

- *Extent of testing.* Reporting on controls at a point in time will require testing of controls that is considerably *less* extensive than the testing required for reporting on the effectiveness of controls over a period of time. Testing strategies and the extent of tests are covered in more detail in Chapters 6 and 7.

- *Correction of deficiencies.* Point-in-time reporting is more conducive to the identification and correction of deficiencies. This is because the correction of a deficiency early in the reporting period may allow management to conclude that internal control is functioning effectively *at the end of the period.* For example, if a material weakness is identified early in the year (e.g., as a result of monitoring related internal controls) and management took immediate and effective corrective action, management would (if no other weaknesses are present) be able to assert that internal controls over financial reporting were effective as of

June 30. The results would be slightly different for a publicly traded company, pursuant to SEC rules, in that corrective action would require disclosure in the entity's first-quarter 10Q, since it would be a change in internal control that would have a material effect on internal control. Going forward, assuming that the corrective actions were successful, the entity may be able to conclude that controls are effective at subsequent reporting dates. Should the OMB require interim reporting on internal controls (e.g., for inclusion with the quarterly financials currently required), it is likely that the SEC practice discussed above would be followed.

Correction of Deficiencies.   For management to conclude that an identified control deficiency has been remediated successfully, the corrected control must be in place and operating effectively for a period of time that is sufficient to draw a reliable conclusion about its effectiveness. Determining what constitutes a "sufficient period of time" will require management to exercise its judgment. Matters to be considered when making this determination include:

- *Nature of the control objective.* The nature of the control objective being addressed should be considered. For example, some control objectives are transaction oriented, narrowly focused, and have a direct effect on the financial statements. A reconciliation and the matching of vendor invoices to an approved vendor list are examples of controls that meet these types of objectives. Other control objectives are control environment oriented, affect the entity broadly, and have only an indirect effect on the financial statements. Management's "tone at the top" and the entity's hiring and training practices are examples of these types of controls.

In general, because of their indirect effect on the financial statements and their ability to influence the effectiveness of other controls, corrections to environmentally oriented controls should be in place and operating effectively for a much *longer* period of time than corrections to controls that are more transaction based. That is, it will take longer to determine whether a change in management's attitude is having its desired effect on internal control performance than it will to determine whether a new reconciliation procedure is being performed properly.

- *Nature of the correction.* Some corrections may be programmed into the entity's information-processing system. For example, to correct a control deficiency, the entity may reprogram its system to generate an exception report. Assuming that the entity has effective computer general controls, a computer application should perform the same task consistently for an indefinite period of time. Thus, the reprogrammed application may be operational for a relatively short period of time before a reliable conclusion can be drawn about its effectiveness.

In contrast, suppose that a *person* is required to investigate and properly resolve the items identified on an exception report. Unlike a computer application, the performance of an individual will vary. For this reason, a correction that depends on people (rather than a computer system) should be operating effectively for a relatively long period of time before a reliable conclusion is reached.

- *Frequency of the corrected control procedure.* Some control procedures are performed frequently, for example, the authentication of credit card information for all online customers who purchase goods. Other procedures are performed less frequently, for example, account reconciliations. When control procedures are performed frequently, it takes less time to gather enough sample transactions to draw a reliable conclusion. For a credit card authorization, the control procedure may be performed thousands of times in just a few days. However, if an account reconciliation is performed only once a month, the control may need to be in place for several months before there would be enough evidence to assess its effectiveness.

Ultimately, taking steps to correct a control deficiency and then waiting a certain amount of time is not sufficient for management to conclude that the deficiency no longer exists. New controls must be tested, and the evidence from these tests must be sufficient to enable management to reach a conclusion about their effectiveness.

EXPANDED REPORTING ON MANAGEMENT'S RESPONSIBILITIES FOR INTERNAL CONTROL

Although OMB Circular A-123 did not go into effect until fiscal year 2006, certain agencies voluntarily elected to comply early, and still others have elected to comply with the requirements of Sarbanes-Oxley.

"Live" examples of the application of Sarbanes-Oxley, however, will provide additional information to enable federal agencies to comply with the revised reporting requirements. As a result, the remaining sections of this chapter, as well as Appendix 8A, discuss practices currently followed in the commercial sector.

Although it is not required, many entities include management reports relating to internal control in their annual reports to shareholders. Typically, these reports are located in close proximity to the entity's financial statements. These optional reports to shareholders are *not* usually designed to comply with SEC reporting requirements.

The Committee of Sponsoring Organizations of the Treadway Commission (COSO) has provided guidelines on the preparation of these optional internal control reports to shareholders. These guidelines attempt to achieve a balance between two competing needs: conformity and flexibility. On the one hand, consistency in reporting between entities enhances communication between the entity and its shareholders. On the other hand, "boilerplate" language may not be meaningful — management needs the flexibility to emphasize certain matters or to communicate in a certain style.

The COSO guidance, although directly addressing commercial applications, provides a sound standard for best practices to be followed by federal financial managers. With this in mind, COSO recommends that a report to shareholders on internal control include:

- *The category of controls being addressed.* Typically, management limits its reporting to internal control over financial reporting and will not address operational or compliance-related controls.

- *A statement about the inherent limitations of internal control systems.* It is helpful to remind readers of the limitations of internal control, although some judgment is required to determine the extent of this discussion.

- *A statement about the existence of mechanisms for system monitoring and responding to identified control deficiencies.* Shareholders desire some information that will help them assess whether and for how long an entity's internal control will continue to be effective. For this reason, statements about monitoring and the correction of identified deficiencies are useful.

- *A frame of reference for reporting.* Identification of the criteria against which the internal control system is measured.

- *A conclusion on the effectiveness of internal control.* A statement that management is responsible for establishing effective internal control usually is not sufficient unless management draws a conclusion as to whether those responsibilities have been met.

- *The date as of which the conclusion of effectiveness is made.*

- *The names of the report signers.*

Exhibit 8.9 is an illustrative report provided by COSO.

In addition to the internal control matters recommended by COSO, some entities choose to include the following in their internal control reports to shareholders:

- *Statement of responsibility.* It is relatively common for management to describe its responsibilities relating to the design and maintenance of effective internal control.

- *Audit committee.* Statements about the audit committee usually include a description of the committee's role and its duties.

- *Communication of written policies.* The entity may wish to describe its processes for documenting its internal control policies and procedures and communicating these policies to employees.

- *Organizational relationships.* These comments focus on the delegation of responsibility and establishment of appropriate reporting relationships within the system of internal control.

- *Personnel.* In some circumstances, the entity may choose to highlight its personnel policies, such as hiring, retention, training, or compensation, and how these policies contribute to effective internal control.

- *Code of conduct.* Discussions of the entity's code of conduct may include one or more of the following:
  - A brief description of major elements of the code
  - How the code is communicated
  - How compliance with the code is monitored and enforced

- *Internal audit.* Usually, these statements are limited to a simple description of the role that internal audit plays in the overall system of internal control.

Exhibit 8.9   Example Report on Internal Control in an Annual Report to Shareholders[a, b, c]

Internal Control System

XYZ Company maintains a system of internal control over financial reporting, which is designed to provide reasonable assurance to the company's management and board of directors regarding the preparation of reliable published financial statements. The system contains self-monitoring mechanisms, and actions are taken to correct deficiencies as they are identified. Even an effective internal control system, no matter how well designed, has inherent limitations—including the possibility of the circumvention or overriding of controls—and therefore can provide only reasonable assurance with respect to financial statement preparation. Further, because of changes in conditions, internal control system effectiveness may vary over time.

The Company assessed its internal control system as of December 31, 20XX, in relation to criteria for effective internal control over financial reporting described in *Internal Control—Integrated Framework* issued by the Committee of Sponsoring Organizations of the Treadway Commission. Based on this assessment, the company believes that, as of December 31, 20XX, its system of internal control over financial reporting met those criteria.

XYZ Company

by _____
Signature (CEO)

by _____
Signature (CFO/Chief Accounting Officer)

Date

---

a. *Internal Control—Integrated Framework,* by the Committee of Sponsoring Organizations of the Treadway Commission, published by the AICPA, 1994, p. 139.

b. The COSO report notes that "the wording of this illustrative report is provided as a guide, which may be particularly useful to managements with little or no experience with reporting on internal control. The illustrative report's wording is not intended as an absolute standard—managements may modify or expand on its contents."

c. This example report is an optional report on internal control that the company may include in its annual report to shareholders. It is not intended to comply with the SEC's required internal control report.

Appendix 8A contains several examples of these optional reports on internal control included in the entity's annual report to shareholders.

Responsibility for Financial Reporting

Management may wish to report on matters other than internal control to its shareholders. These matters may include:

- Management's responsibility for preparing the financial statements

Exhibit 8.10   Example Report on Management's Responsibility for
Financial Reporting in an Annual Report to Shareholders

Financial Statements

XYZ Company is responsible for the preparation, integrity and fair presentation of its
published financial statements. The financial statements, presented on pages xx to yy,
have been prepared in accordance with generally accepted accounting principles and,
as such, include amounts based on judgments and estimates made by management.
The company also prepared the other information included in the annual report and is
responsible for its accuracy and consistency with the financial statements.

The financial statements have been audited by the independent accounting firm,
ABC & Co., which was given unrestricted access to all financial records and related
data, including minutes of all meetings of stockholders, the board of directors and
committees of the board. The company believes that all representations made to the
independent auditors during their audit were valid and appropriate. ABC & Co.'s
audit report is presented on page xx.

Source: Internal Control—Integrated Framework, p. 140.

- The use of estimates and judgments in the preparation of the financial statements
- The responsibility of the independent auditors

When the entity elects to include this information in its report, it should do so
in a way that is separate from the discussion and conclusions on internal control.
It is not necessary for the entity to have two reports—rather, it can combine a report
on financial reporting with a discussion of internal control, as long as the combined
report is clear. For example, this might be achieved by separate headings that identify the two elements of the combined report.

Exhibit 8.10 is an illustrative report of management's responsibility for financial reporting.

COORDINATING WITH THE INDEPENDENT AUDITORS AND LEGAL COUNSEL

The independent auditors should be consulted during the drafting of report(s) on
internal control over financial reporting. It is during this time that consensus should
be reached on the following matters:

- Contents of the report(s), including:
    - Completeness and whether the contents satisfy federal reporting requirements
    - Possible deletion of material that is not required
- Report language
- Definition of "significant deficiency" and "material weakness" provided by the
  most current auditing standards

- Disclosure of material weaknesses that exist at the reporting date
- The nonreporting of material weaknesses that existed and were reported at an interim period but have subsequently been remediated

---

Appendix 8A
Examples of Current Private Industry Practices

Since revised OMB Circular A-123 related reports will not be available until after the completion of fiscal year 2006, there are currently no live examples of A-123 related reports. As a result, the following examples were taken from the commercial sector for illustrative purposes. These illustrations will provide guidance to federal financial managers in the following areas:

- Disclosures of material weaknesses
- Reports on management's responsibilities for reporting and internal control

DISCLOSURES OF MATERIAL WEAKNESSES

Argonaut Technologies, Inc.
Selected Disclosures in
12/31/04 10K

Item 9a.   Controls and Procedures

Evaluation of Disclosure Controls and Procedures.   Our management, including our Chief Executive Officer (CEO) and our Chief Financial Officer (CFO), are responsible for evaluating and attesting as to the effectiveness of the design and operation of our disclosure controls and procedures as of the end of the period covered by this Annual Report on Form 10-K as required by Rule 13a-15 under the Securities Exchange Act of 1934. In connection with the audit of our consolidated financial statements for the year ended December 31, 2004, our independent registered public accounting firm, Ernst & Young LLP, reported to our audit committee the identification of a " material weakness" (under the standards established by the Public Company Accounting Oversight Board) in our internal controls. Based on that evaluation, our management, including the CEO and CFO, concluded that as of December 31, 2004, our disclosure controls were not effective to ensure that that information about us required to be disclosed by us was recorded, processed, summarized and reported as required by applicable Securities and Exchange Commission rules and forms.

The material weakness identified related to: (1) the failure to retain supporting documentation in our records relating to certain items, (2) a lack of sufficient accuracy in certain of our records and accounting entries, (3) the failure to timely reconcile certain accounts and (4) the failure to timely record certain expenses incurred in 2004.

Management believes that many of the items cited in connection with the material weakness determination were due to employee turnover in our finance department and the focus of our remaining resources on the pending sale of substantially all of our assets to Biotage AB. In response to the material weakness, we began instituting a number of corrective actions to insure that the financial information and other disclosures included in future reports are complete and accurate in all material respects. Those actions included increasing internal review time in our finance department as well as utilizing additional third-party accounting experts and temporary staffing, when needed.

Rockford Corp.
Selected Disclosures in
12/31/04 10K

Item 9a. Controls and Procedures

Evaluation of Disclosure Controls and Procedures.   Rockford's principal executive officer and principal financial officer are responsible for establishing and maintaining adequate internal control over its financial reporting. They have reviewed Rockford's disclosure controls and procedures as at December 31, 2004 in order to comply with the SEC's requirements for certification of this Form 10-K. Rockford is a non-accelerated filer and, accordingly, it is required to comply with the SEC's enhanced requirements for certification and attestation of internal control over financial reporting for its Form 10-K for its fiscal year ending December 31, 2006.

Rockford is currently evaluating what changes will be needed to meet the enhanced reporting relating to internal controls required by the Sarbanes-Oxley Act and subsequent SEC regulations. Rockford is currently in the process of establishing an enhanced internal control process. Rockford did not make any substantial changes in its internal review of Rockford's financial reporting during 2004, other than the correction of the matters discussed below.

Based on their review of Rockford's disclosure controls and policies, Rockford's principal executive officer and principal financial officer concluded that its disclosure controls and procedures were deficient as discussed below.

Material Weaknesses of Disclosure Controls and Procedures

Preparation of Annual Report for the Year Ended December 31, 2004. Rockford has concluded, in connection with the preparation of this Annual Report, that it was subject to a material weakness in its disclosure controls and procedures, in that the internal controls were not sufficient to ensure the information required to be disclosed in Rockford's reports was accurate and was recorded, processed, summarized and reported within the requisite time periods. Deficiencies resulted from substantial management and staff turnover, particularly in the general accounting and finance areas, during the fourth quarter of 2004 and first quarter of 2005. This turnover caused a loss of operations and process knowledge that interfered with the preparation of this Annual Report.

In connection with the preparation of Rockford's consolidated financial statements for the year ended December 31, 2004, significant internal control deficiencies became evident to management. In the aggregate, a material weakness resulted from control deficiencies that included inadequate staffing and supervision, leading to the untimely identification and resolution of certain accounting matters; failure to perform timely reviews, substantiation and evaluation of certain general ledger account balances; and lack of procedures or expertise needed to prepare all required disclosures. A material weakness is a significant deficiency in one or more of the internal control components that alone or in the aggregate precludes the internal controls from reducing to an appropriate low level the risk that material misstatements in the financial statements will not be prevented or detected on a timely basis.

Rockford's registered public accounting firm, Ernst & Young LLP, advised management and the audit committee of the board of directors that the financial reporting deficiencies described above are considered to be a material weakness in Rockford's internal controls which constitutes a reportable condition under standards established by the American Institute of Certified Public Accountants. The Audit Committee, board of directors, management, and Ernst & Young discussed these weaknesses and Rockford has assigned the highest priority to their correction. Even before the discussion of the material weakness, Rockford was actively seeking to hire appropriate replacement personnel who could restore the required expertise lost as a result of turnover in 2004 and 2005. Rockford plans in the first half of 2005 to add financial resources and expertise, both through internal hiring and using outside consultants, that will provide hands-on oversight of the monthly financial closing, data analysis, and account reconciliation. Management and the audit committee are committed to addressing and resolving the weaknesses fully and believe that additional financial resources and expertise will correct the material weakness.

Accounts Payable Reconciliation for the Year Ended December 31, 2003.

During the first quarter of 2004, Rockford identified a material weakness in procedures for reconciling accounts payable at the end of each reporting period. The material weakness arose as a result of a reconciliation process that failed to reconcile the accounts payable module of Rockford's Oracle information system, which includes all pending invoices, with the general ledger accounts payable. Before the first quarter of 2004, the reconciliation process for each period focused on the general ledger balances and did not reconcile the general ledger to the Oracle accounts payable module. Timing issues resulting from the approval process for accounts payable caused the general ledger accounts payable not to reflect all of the accounts payable that had been entered into the accounts payable module in Oracle. The reconciliation process did not identify this discrepancy. As a result, the general ledger and financial statements did not reflect all of the accounts payable that the Oracle module showed at the end of each period nor did they reflect certain corresponding assets.

Rockford reviewed its financial statements for prior periods and believes that the reconciliation failures did not have a material effect on reported earnings in any quarter for the last four fiscal years, going back through fiscal 2000. As a result, Rockford did not restate results for any prior periods. Rockford also concluded that the underlying business processes were properly using the Oracle payables module and that, upon approval through normal business processes, the payables shown in the Oracle payables module were being paid in accordance with their terms and reflected in the general ledger and financial statements.

For the first quarter of 2004, and going forward, Rockford implemented additional reconciliation procedures to assure that the accounts payable reported on the general ledger reconcile to the information contained in the Oracle accounts payable module for the end of each period reported. As at March 31, 2004, the balance sheet reflected an increase in accounts payable of $4.7 million, an increase in inventory in-transit of $3.7 million, and an increase in other assets or offsets to other accrual accounts of $0.5 million as a result of this reconciliation. The after tax impact on operating results for the quarter was $0.3 million, or $0.03 per share. Rockford believes each of these items reflects a one-time adjustment and that going forward the reconciliation process will not have a material impact on results of operations.

Rockford's independent registered public accounting firm, Ernst & Young LLP, advised management and the audit committee of the board of directors that the reconciliation failure described above is considered to be a material weakness in Rockford's internal controls and constitutes a reportable condition under standards established by the American Institute of Certified Public Accountants. The audit committee, board of directors, management, and Ernst & Young discussed this weakness. Rockford assigned the highest priority to the correction of this weakness and implemented new reconciliation procedures effective with the first quarter 2004 closing. Management and the audit committee are committed to addressing and resolving this weakness fully and believe that the new reconciliation process has corrected this weakness. Rockford believes the weakness resulted from a failure to identify and fully understand the interaction between different parts of the Oracle information system, rather than from a failure in the ability or intent of Rockford's personnel, and has taken steps to correct these failures. Rockford continues to evaluate other parts of the Oracle system, but has not identified and does not expect to find other significant weaknesses in Rockford's understanding of the system that will have as significant an effect on Rockford's financial reporting efforts.

Systemax
Selected Disclosures in
12/31/04 10K

Item 9A. Controls and Procedures

Management's Assessment.   Management has determined that, as of the December 31, 2004 measurement date, there were deficiencies in both the design and the effectiveness of our internal control over financial reporting. Management has assessed these deficiencies and determined that there were eight material weaknesses in Loudeye's internal control over financial reporting. As a result of our assessment that material weaknesses in our internal control over financial reporting existed as of December 31, 2004, management has concluded that our internal control over financial reporting was not effective as of December 31, 2004. The existence of a material weakness or weaknesses is an indication that there is a more than remote likelihood that a material misstatement of our financial statements will not be prevented or detected in a future period. Moss Adams LLP has issued an attestation report concurring with management's assessment of Loudeye's internal control over financial reporting which appears in this annual report in Item 8 "Financial Statements."

We first reported material weaknesses in our internal control over financial reporting in August 2004. We have included in the disclosure below all material weaknesses we have identified to date.

Management and our audit committee have assigned a high priority to the short- and long-term improvement of our internal control over financial reporting.

We have listed below the nature of the material weaknesses we have identified, the steps we are taking to remediate these material weaknesses and when we expect to have the material weaknesses remediated.

Deficiencies pertaining to insufficiently skilled personnel and a lack of human resources within our finance and accounting reporting functions. As described above, we first identified this material weakness in August 2004. During 2004 we experienced complete turnover of the personnel in our finance and accounting department. The lack of appropriately skilled personnel could result in material misstatements to financial statements not being detected in a timely manner.

- *Remediation.* During the fourth quarter of 2004, we filled four of five (two with temporary personnel) then existing positions within our accounting and finance department and created and filled three new positions in our accounting and finance departments. As a result, our accounting and finance staff consists of significantly more personnel with more accounting experience than was the case during the second and third quarters of 2004. However, as all planned personnel were not hired as of December 31, 2004, our remediation efforts were not complete as of the December 31, 2004 measurement date.

  During the first quarter of 2005, we hired two permanent employees to replace the temporary personnel and filled the fifth existing position.

  Although our Overpeer and OD2 subsidiaries were outside the scope of our assessment of our internal control over financial reporting as of December 31, 2004, we have already identified a potential need to hire additional qualified personnel for our finance and accounting function at OD2.

- *Timing.* With the completion of our hiring efforts during the first quarter of 2005, we believe as of the date of this report that we have remediated this material weakness.

Insufficient oversight of financially significant processes and systems, including deficiencies relating to monitoring and oversight of the work performed by our finance and accounting personnel. As described above, we first identified this material weakness in August 2004. Due primarily to the lack of human resources in our accounting and finance department during most of 2004, we noted deficiencies related to insufficient review and approval and documentation of the review and approval of the work being performed by employees within our accounting and finance department relating to the following matters:

- All journal entries.
- Periodic reconciliations of subledgers, balance sheet and income statement accounts.
- Payroll and employee benefit related processing and accounting.
- Royalty related tracking, reporting, and accounting.
- Processes related to the invoicing of customers and the processing of credits to customers.
- Processes related to the purchasing of and the payment for goods and services received.
- Accrual of expenses.
- Documents supporting the monthly, quarterly, and annual consolidation and general ledger closing process.
- Periodic financial reporting.

As a result, Loudeye does not have sufficient internal control over financial reporting to ensure underlying transactions are being appropriately and timely accounted for, which could lead to material misstatements in the financial statements not being detected in a timely manner.

- *Remediation.* In the fourth quarter 2004, we began to implement new controls and procedures designed to ensure proper oversight of work performed by employees in our accounting and finance functions. As of December 31, 2004, these efforts were not complete or sufficiently integrated into our existing control environment.

In the first quarter 2005, our remediation efforts have continued, aided by the additional staff we have hired within our accounting and finance department. For example, we have established new reconciliation, review, and documentation requirements for finance and accounting employees to ensure that:

- Journal entries, including the appropriate supporting documentation, are reviewed, approved, and documented prior to being posted to the general ledger.
    - Sub ledgers, balance sheet, and income statement accounts are periodically reconciled, including the clearing of any reconciling items, and reviewed and approved in a timely manner.
    - Payroll and employee benefit calculations, payments, and related journal entries are reviewed, approved, and documented prior to posting in the general ledger.

- ○ Royalty related tracking, reporting and accounting is reviewed, approved and documented in a timely manner.
- ○ System generated reports, invoicing support, and credit requests are reviewed, approved, and documented prior to posting to the general ledger.
- ○ Invoices received for goods and services are properly approved and invoice coding is reviewed, approved, and documented prior to posting to the general ledger.
- ○ Open purchase orders are periodically reviewed, investigated as necessary, and documented. Support and the basis for accruals of amounts in the general ledger is reviewed, approved, and documented prior to posting to the general ledger.
- ○ Documents supporting the monthly, quarterly and annual consolidation and general ledger closing process are reviewed, approved and documented as part of the periodic closing process. Income statement and balance sheet accounts are reviewed approved and documented monthly using actual to budget and/or actual to prior period actual comparisons.
- ○ Supporting working papers and documentation for financial data included in all financial reports are reviewed, approved and documented. Final signed copies of SEC filings are retained.
- *Timing.* We are continuing to remediate these deficiencies and anticipate completing our remediation efforts during the second and third quarters of 2005.

Deficiencies pertaining to the lack of controls or ineffectively designed controls. We noted that there are an insufficient number of effectively designed controls or there are ineffectively designed controls to ensure that:

- All revenue transactions occurred, are accurately calculated in accordance with the terms of the applicable contract, are processed properly and are accurately reflected in the proper period in the general ledger.
- All royalty transactions occurred, are accurately calculated in accordance with the terms of the applicable contract, are processed properly and are accurately reflected in the proper period in the general ledger.
- All revenue transactions are properly authorized before entry into the general ledger.

As a result, adjustments to our revenue and royalty accounts and financial statements could occur.

- *Remediation.* We did not complete any significant remediation efforts with respect to this material weakness during the year ended December 31, 2004. Beginning in March 2005, we focused our remediation efforts with respect to these deficiencies on designing automated systems for tracking, reporting, and recording revenue generating transactions and associated royalty obligations.
- *Timing.* We are continuing to remediate these deficiencies and anticipate completing our remediation efforts during the second and third quarters of 2005.

Deficiencies in our general computer controls relating to financially significant applications and business processes, including application-level design and documentation deficiencies. As a result of these deficiencies, we were unable to rely upon general computer controls to perform as expected over time and we were unable to demonstrate through testing that our internal controls that depend upon general computer controls were operating effectively. We identified design deficiencies in our general computer controls including:

- Insufficient approval and testing processes for internally developed software integrated into financially significant business processes.
- Insufficient password management and unauthorized sharing of passwords.
- Insufficient physical access controls that could allow unauthorized access to our general computer controls.

We also identified deficiencies relating to documentation of our general computer controls including:

- Insufficient formal documentation of the approval and testing process of internally developed software integrated into financially significant business processes and changes to those programs.
- Insufficient formal documentation to support system usage and maintenance.
- Insufficient formal documentation to support the design effectiveness of financially significant general computer controls, such as the controls surrounding the capturing and reporting of data from our music sample service or our encoding services.

Examples of the control objectives with respect to which we were not able to demonstrate that our existing control activities were operating effectively as a result of deficiencies in our information technology general controls include:

- The proper capture, input, validation and processing of all data related to customer invoicing and revenue recognition.
- The proper capture, input, validation and processing of all data related to the calculation, tracking, reporting and recording of royalties.
- The proper processing of data related to fixed asset additions and deletions and the calculation of periodic depreciation expense.

As a result, errors in our financial statements that have not been prevented or detected by our information technology and general computer controls could occur.

- *Remediation.* In the fourth quarter 2004, we began to document controls and procedures designed to ensure proper oversight of work performed by employees in our information technology operations and program and development functions. We began work to ensure that:
  - A software development lifecycle (SDLC) methodology is documented and controls relevant to testing and approvals are implemented as designed.

- ○ A "change management" process is documented and controls relating to approvals are implemented as designed.
- ○ Controls are implemented for managing security and physical access to systems, data, and applications that support financial reporting.
- ○ Access policy and controls include a periodic review by management of access privileges.
- ○ Transaction flows for applications that capture and report financial data are properly documented.

- *Timing.* As of December 31, 2004, our remediation efforts were not complete, and during the first quarter of 2005 we continued to document controls and procedures designed to ensure proper oversight of work performed by employees in our information technology operations and program and development functions.

We are continuing to remediate these deficiencies and anticipate completing our remediation efforts during the second quarter and third quarter of 2005.

Deficiencies relating to insufficient analysis, documentation and review of the selection and application of generally accepted accounting principles, or GAAP, to significant non-routine transactions, including the preparation of financial statement disclosures relating thereto. We first identified this material weakness as it relates to significant non-routine transactions in August 2004 in connection with completing our quarterly report on Form 10-Q for the quarter ended June 30, 2004 and the accounting treatment relating to our acquisition of OD2. See the discussion above under the heading "—Material Weaknesses Identified Prior to December 31, 2004."

In addition, during the preparation of our financial statements for the year ended December 31, 2004, we made revisions of classification with regard to expenses incurred during the years ended December 31, 2003 and 2002. Such revisions of classification had no impact on net loss, stockholders' equity or cash flows as previously reported. These revisions of classification are consistent with this material weakness and related to the following:

- *Regent Fees.* We revised our classification of $878,000 relating to service fees paid to Regent Pacific Management Corporation during the year ended December 31, 2003, from special charges—other to general and administrative expense in the current presentation as we determined that these expenses were not restructuring charges in accordance with FAS 146 and were more appropriately classified as general and administrative expense.
- *Amortization of Intangible Assets.* We revised our classification of amortization of acquired technology and capitalized software costs totaling approximately $269,000 in 2003 and $1.3 million in 2002 from operating expenses — amortization of intangibles to cost of revenue in the current presentation as we determined that these expenses were more appropriately classified as cost of revenue in accordance with FAS 86 and related accounting literature.
- *Impairment of Intangible Assets.* We revised our classification of impairment charges related to acquired technology and capitalized software costs totaling

approximately $601,000 in 2003 and $694,000 in 2002 from operating expenses — special charges — other to cost of revenue in the current presentation as we determined that these charges were more appropriately classified as cost of revenue in accordance with FAS 86 and related accounting literature.

As a result, Loudeye does not have sufficient internal control over financial reporting to ensure that underlying non-routine transactions are appropriately and timely accounted for in the general ledger.

- *Remediation.* During the fourth quarter 2004, we filled four of five (two with temporary personnel) then existing positions within our accounting and finance department and created and filled three new positions in our accounting and finance departments. During the first quarter 2005, we hired two permanent employees to replace the temporary personnel and filled the fifth position. As a result, our accounting and finance staff consists of significantly more personnel with more accounting experience than was the case during the second and third quarters of 2004.

  We have also implemented processes by which the classification of expenses, significant revenue related and non-routine transactions are reviewed for application of GAAP by accounting and finance personnel with appropriate subject matter expertise, by members of senior management, and, where appropriate by our audit committee or our board of directors. However, because we had not filled all of the vacancies in our accounting and finance department as of December 31, 2004, our remediation efforts with respect to this material weakness were not complete as of the December 31, 2004 measurement date.

- *Timing.* We completed our hiring efforts during the first quarter 2005. We will continue to monitor our remediation efforts with respect to this material weakness.

Failure to appropriately assess and monitor the effectiveness of controls executed by third party service providers, and to adequately implement and/or maintain customer level controls related to the provision of services by third party service providers. We identified design deficiencies in our customer level controls including:

- Failure to provide timely written notification to third party service providers of changes in Loudeye authorized personnel that result from Loudeye employee terminations.

- Insufficient review and approval, and insufficient documentation of review and approval, of input reports prior to their submission to the service provider and of output reports received from service providers.

As a result, the information and reports from third-party service providers received and utilized by us may contain errors.

- *Remediation.* In the fourth quarter 2004, we began to implement new controls and procedures designed to ensure proper oversight of work performed by employees in our accounting and finance functions. As of December 31, 2004, these efforts were not complete.

In the first quarter 2005, our remediation efforts have continued, aided by the additional staff we have hired within our accounting and finance department. For example, we have established new reconciliation, review and documentation requirements for finance and accounting employees to ensure that, among other things, payroll and benefit related reports are reviewed and approved prior to submission to the third party provider and that output reports received from the service provider are also reviewed and approved. Additionally, we expect to put controls in place to ensure we provide timely written notification to third party service providers of changes in authorized Loudeye personnel.

- *Timing.* We are continuing to remediate these deficiencies and anticipate completing our remediation efforts during the second and third quarters of 2005.

Inadequate entity-level controls. As of December 31, 2004, we did not have effective entity-level controls with respect to our overall control environment and monitoring efforts as defined in the COSO framework. The pervasive nature of the material weaknesses in our internal control over financial reporting in itself constitutes a material weakness. We failed to systematically communicate entity-wide policies and procedures and to uniformly and consistently communicate the importance of controls. We also had failed to implement processes to ensure periodic monitoring of our internal control activities. As a result, management concluded that there are deficiencies in the design and execution of our entity-level controls that constitute a material weakness in our internal control over financial reporting and errors in our financial statements that have not been prevented by our entity-level controls could occur.

- *Remediation.* In the fourth quarter 2004, we began to implement new controls and procedures designed to ensure that entity-wide policies and procedures are systematically communicated and that documentation evidencing employees' receipt thereof is retained. In the first quarter 2005, we also began developing an ongoing monitoring system to facilitate continuous monitoring of our internal control over financial reporting.

- *Timing.* As of December 31, 2004, these efforts were not complete and we are continuing to remediate these deficiencies and anticipate completing our remediation efforts during the second and third quarter 2005.

Inability to demonstrate through testing that our internal control over financial reporting was effective as of December 31, 2004. We were unable to demonstrate through testing the effectiveness of our remediation efforts with respect to the material weaknesses described above. Our processes with respect to quarterly and annual controls, such as our control processes relating to general ledger close procedures and periodic financial reporting, were not fully implemented until the fourth quarter 2004. Although we believe these processes were designed effectively as of December 31, 2004, there was an insufficient sample base to enable us to demonstrate through testing that these controls were operating effectively as of December 31, 2004.

- *Remediation.* We have dedicated significant internal and external resources to our remediation efforts with respect to material weaknesses in our internal control over financial reporting as noted above. We expect to have a sufficient sampling base to enable us to test the effectiveness of our remediation efforts at future measurement dates and testing periods for our internal control over financial reporting.
- *Timing.* We are continuing to remediate these deficiencies and anticipate completing our remediation efforts during the third quarter 2005.

The steps described above, including the hiring of additional qualified accounting and finance personnel, are designed to ensure that management's evaluation of our internal control over financial reporting is thorough and complete and that a timely and appropriate remediation plan is implemented. Our audit committee is overseeing management's assessment and its implementation of a remediation plan and is prepared to take additional measures, where necessary, to ensure that management has the required resources in place to address known and not yet identified material weaknesses, significant control deficiencies and other control deficiencies. The effectiveness of the steps we have taken to date and the steps we are still in the process of completing is subject to continued management review, as well as audit committee oversight, and we may make additional changes to our internal controls and procedures. Although we have undertaken the foregoing initiatives, we cannot assure you that we will not in the future identify further material weaknesses or significant deficiencies in our internal control over financial reporting that have not previously been identified.

Management estimates that we will incur additional costs in connection with our remediation efforts including outside advisor fees and incremental personnel costs. Management estimates that these costs will aggregate approximately $1 million for the fiscal year ended December 31, 2005.

Except as disclosed above regarding remediation efforts we conducted in the fourth quarter 2004 with respect to known material weaknesses and deficiencies in our internal control over financial reporting, there were not any changes in our disclosure controls and procedures, including our internal control over financial reporting, during the quarter ended December 31, 2004, that had materially affected, or are reasonably likely to materially affect, our disclosure controls and procedures, including our internal control over financial reporting.

REPORTS ON MANAGEMENT'S RESPONSIBILITIES FOR REPORTING AND INTERNAL CONTROL

Sharper Image
Selected Disclosures in 1/31/05 10K

Management's Annual Report on Internal Control over Financial Reporting

The Company's management is responsible for establishing and maintaining adequate internal control over financial reporting as defined in Rules 13a-15(f) and 15d-15(f) under the Securities Exchange Act of 1934. The Company's internal control over financial reporting is a process designed to provide reasonable assurance regarding the reliability of financial reporting and the preparation of financial statements for external purposes in accordance with generally accepted accounting principles.

Because of its inherent limitations, internal control over financial reporting may not prevent or detect misstatements. Also, projections of any evaluation of effectiveness to future periods are subject to the risk that controls may become inadequate because of changes in conditions, or the degree of compliance with the policies or procedures may deteriorate.

Under the supervision of the Company's Chief Financial Officer and Controller, and with the participation of management, including the Chief Executive Officer and President, the Company conducted its assessment of the effectiveness of its internal control over financial reporting as of January 31, 2005. This evaluation was based on the framework in *Internal Control—Integrated Framework* issued by the Committee of Sponsoring Organizations of the Treadway Commission.

A material weakness is a control deficiency, or combination of control deficiencies, that results in more than a remote likelihood that a material misstatement of the annual or interim financial statements may not be prevented or detected. As of January 31, 2005, the Company failed to design and implement appropriate controls regarding its accounting and disclosure for accounts payable that resulted in an understatement of accounts payable and an overstatement of net income, as well as a corresponding overstatement of stockholders' equity, for each of the periods presented. Specifically, the Company failed to analyze and reconcile on a timely basis its liability for product received and yet to be invoiced. As a result, the Company was required to restate prior interim and annual financial statements. The impact of the restatement on the previously issued financial statements is described in Note B to the financial statements. This deficiency was concluded to be a material weakness due to the significance of the adjustment that also resulted in the restatement of previous financial statements. Because of the existence of the material weakness, management concluded that the Company did not maintain effective internal control over financial reporting as of January 31, 2005, based on criteria in *Internal Control—Integrated Framework*.

Pathmark
Selected Disclosures in
1/29/05 10K

Management's Annual Report on Internal Control over Financial Reporting

The management of Pathmark Stores, Inc. (Pathmark) is responsible for establishing and maintaining adequate internal control over financial reporting as defined in Rules 13a-15(f) under the Securities Exchange Act of 1934. Pathmark's internal control over financial reporting is designed to provide reasonable assurance regarding the reliability of financial reporting and the preparation of financial statements for external purposes in accordance with U.S. generally accepted accounting principles. Pathmark's internal control over financial reporting includes those policies and procedures that: (i) pertain to the maintenance of records that, in reasonable detail, accurately and fairly reflect the transactions and dispositions of the assets of Pathmark; (ii) provide reasonable assurance that transactions are recorded as necessary to permit preparation of financial statements in accordance with U.S. generally accepted accounting principles, and that receipts and expenditures of Pathmark are being made only in accordance with authorization of management and directors of Pathmark; and (iii) provide reasonable assurance regarding prevention or timely detection of unauthorized acquisition, use or disposition of Pathmark's assets that could have a material effect on the financial statements. Because of its inherent limitations, internal control over financial reporting may not prevent or detect misstatements. Also, projections of any evaluations of effectiveness to future periods are subject to the risk that controls may become inadequate because of the changes in conditions, or that the degree of compliance with the policies or procedures may deteriorate.

With the participation of Pathmark's Chief Executive Officer and the Chief Financial Officer, management assessed the effectiveness of Pathmark's internal control over financial reporting as of January 29, 2005. In making this assessment, management used criteria established in *Internal Control—Integrated Framework,* issued by the Committee of Sponsoring Organizations of the Treadway Commission (COSO). As a result of this assessment, management identified the following: (1) a material weakness existed in our year-end calculation of goodwill impairment, which resulted in a year-end audit adjustment affecting goodwill and the goodwill impairment charge; specifically, controls over the processes followed in calculating the fair market value of certain assets and liabilities were not effective to ensure that goodwill and the goodwill impairment charge were fairly stated in accordance with generally accepted accounting principles; and (2) a material weakness existed in our accounting for book overdrafts related to the right of offset of certain cash accounts, which resulted in a year-end audit adjustment affecting our cash and accounts payable accounts; specifically, there was a deficiency in the design of the Company's process of determining whether a right of offset exists related to the Company's overdrafts.

As defined by the Public Company Accounting Oversight Board's *Auditing Standard No. 2,* a material weakness is a control deficiency, or combination of control deficiencies, that resulted in more than a remote likelihood that a material misstatement of our annual or interim financial statements would not be prevented or detected. As a result of the aforementioned material weaknesses, our management has concluded that our internal control over financial reporting was not effective as of January 29, 2005.

Pathmark's independent auditor, Deloitte & Touche LLP, a registered public accounting firm, has issued an audit report on our management's assessment of our internal control over financial reporting. Their report follows.

Great West Life Assurance Company
Annual Form 40F
July 2, 2003

Management's Responsibility

The consolidated financial statements are the responsibility of management and are prepared in accordance with generally accepted accounting principles. The financial information contained elsewhere in the annual report is consistent with that in the consolidated financial statements. The financial statements necessarily include amounts that are based on management's best estimate due to dependency on subsequent events. These estimates are based on careful judgments and have been properly reflected in the financial statements. In the opinion of management, the accounting practices utilized are appropriate in the circumstances and the financial statements fairly reflect the financial position and results of operations of the Company within reasonable limits of materiality.

In carrying out its responsibilities, management maintains appropriate systems of internal and administrative controls designed to provide reasonable assurance that the financial information produced is relevant and reliable.

The consolidated financial statements were approved by the Board of Directors, which has overall responsibility for their contents. The Board of Directors is assisted with this responsibility by its Audit Committee, which consists entirely of Directors not involved in the daily operations of the Company. The function of the Audit Committee is to:

- Review the quarterly and annual financial statements and recommend them for approval to the Board of Directors.

- Review the systems of internal control and security.

- Recommend the appointment of the external auditors and their fee arrangements to the Board of Directors.

- Review other audit, accounting, financial and security matters as required.

In carrying out the above responsibilities, this Committee meets regularly with management, and with both the Company's external and internal auditors to approve the scope and timing of their respective audits, to review their findings and to satisfy itself that their responsibilities have been properly discharged. The Committee is readily accessible to the external and internal auditors.

The Board of Directors of The Great West Life Assurance Company, pursuant to Section 165(2)(i) of the Insurance Entities Act (Canada), appoints the Actuary who is:

- Responsible for ensuring that the assumptions and methods used in the valuation of policy liabilities are in accordance with accepted actuarial practice, applicable legislation, and associated regulations or directives.

- Required to provide an opinion regarding the appropriateness of the policy liabilities at the balance sheet date to meet all policyholder obligations of the Company. Examination of supporting data for accuracy and completeness, and analysis of Company assets for their ability to support the amount of policy liabilities, are important elements of the work required to form this opinion.
- Required each year to analyze the financial condition of the Company and prepare a report for the Board of Directors. The analysis tests the capital adequacy of the Company until December 31, 2003, under adverse economic and business conditions.

Deloitte & Touche LLP Chartered Accountants, as the Company's appointed external auditors, have audited the consolidated financial statements. The Auditors' Report to the Shareholders is presented following the financial statements. Their opinion is based upon an examination conducted in accordance with generally accepted auditing standards, performing such tests and other procedures as they consider necessary in order to obtain reasonable assurance that the consolidated financial statements are free of material misstatement and present fairly the financial position and results of operations of the Company in accordance with generally accepted accounting principles.

Symons International
Annual 10-K
June 3, 2003

Management's Responsibility

Management recognizes its responsibility for conducting the Company's affairs in the best interests of all its shareholders. The consolidated financial statements and related information in this Annual Report are the responsibility of management. The consolidated financial statements have been prepared in accordance with generally accepted accounting principles, which involve the use of judgment and estimates in applying the accounting principles selected. Other financial information in this Annual Report is consistent with that in the consolidated financial statements.

The Company maintains a system of internal controls, which is designed to provide reasonable assurance that accounting records are reliable and to safeguard the Company's assets. The independent accounting firm of BDO Seidman, LLP has audited and reported on the Company's consolidated financial statements for 2002, 2001, and 2000. Their opinion is based upon audits conducted by them in accordance with generally accepted auditing standards to obtain assurance that the consolidated financial statements are free of material misstatements.

The Board of Directors, two members of which include outside directors, meets with the independent external auditors and management representatives to review the internal accounting controls, the consolidated financial statements and other financial reporting matters. In addition to having unrestricted access to the books and records of the Company, the independent external auditors also have unrestricted access to the Board of Directors.

Kimberly-Clark
Annual Report
February 18, 2003

The management of Kimberly-Clark Corporation is responsible for conducting all aspects of the business, including the preparation of the consolidated financial statements in this annual report. The consolidated financial statements have been prepared using generally accepted accounting principles considered appropriate in the circumstances to present fairly the Corporation's consolidated financial position, results of operations and cash flows on a consistent basis. Management also has prepared the other information in this annual report and is responsible for its accuracy and consistency with the consolidated financial statements.

As can be expected in a complex and dynamic business environment, some financial statement amounts are based on management's estimates and judgments. Even though estimates and judgments are used, measures have been taken to provide reasonable assurance of the integrity and reliability of the financial information contained in this annual report. These measures include an effective control-oriented environment in which the internal audit function plays an important role, an Audit Committee of the board of directors that oversees the financial reporting process, and independent audits.

One characteristic of a control-oriented environment is a system of internal control over financial reporting and over safeguarding of assets against unauthorized acquisition, use or disposition, designed to provide reasonable assurance to management and the board of directors regarding preparation of reliable published financial statements and such asset safeguarding. The system is supported with written policies and procedures, contains self-monitoring mechanisms and is audited by the internal audit function. Appropriate actions are taken by management to correct deficiencies as they are identified. All internal control systems have inherent limitations, including the possibility of circumvention and overriding of controls, and, therefore, can provide only reasonable assurance as to financial statement preparation and such asset safeguarding.

The Corporation also has adopted a code of conduct that, among other things, contains policies for conducting business affairs in a lawful and ethical manner everyplace in which it does business, for avoiding potential conflicts of interest and for preserving confidentiality of information and business ideas. Internal controls have been implemented to provide reasonable assurance that the code of conduct is followed.

The consolidated financial statements have been audited by the independent accounting firm, Deloitte & Touche LLP. During their audits, independent auditors were given unrestricted access to all financial records and related data, including minutes of all meetings of stockholders and the board of directors and all committees of the board. Management believes that all representations made to the independent auditors during their audits were valid and appropriate.

During the audits conducted by both the independent auditors and the internal audit function, management received recommendations to strengthen or modify internal controls in response to developments and changes. Management has adopted, or is in the process of adopting, all recommendations that are cost effective.

The Corporation has assessed its internal control system as of December 31, 2002, in relation to criteria for effective internal control over financial reporting described in "Internal Control—Integrated Framework" issued by the Committee of Sponsoring Organizations of the Treadway Commission.

Based on this assessment, management believes that, as of December 31, 2002, its system of internal control over the preparation of its published interim and annual consolidated financial statements and over safeguarding of assets against unauthorized acquisition, use, or disposition met those criteria.

American General Finance Inc.
Quarterly 10Q
July 30, 2003

Report of Management's Responsibility

The Company's management is responsible for the integrity and fair presentation of our condensed consolidated financial statements and all other financial information presented in this report. We prepared our condensed consolidated financial statements using accounting principles generally accepted in the United States (GAAP). We made estimates and assumptions that affect amounts recorded in the financial statements and disclosures of contingent assets and liabilities.

The Company's management is responsible for establishing and maintaining an internal control structure and procedures for financial reporting. These systems are designed to provide reasonable assurance that assets are safeguarded from loss or unauthorized use, that transactions are recorded according to GAAP under management's direction, and that financial records are reliable to prepare financial statements. We support the internal control structure with careful selection, training and development of qualified personnel. The Company's employees are subject to AIG's Code of Conduct designed to assure that all employees perform their duties with honesty and integrity. We do not allow loans to executive officers. The systems include a documented organizational structure, policies, and procedures that we communicate throughout the Company. Our internal auditors report directly to AIG to strengthen independence. They continually monitor the operation of our internal controls and report their findings to the Company's management and AIG's internal audit department. We take prompt action to correct control deficiencies and address opportunities for improving the system. The Company's management assesses the adequacy of our internal control structure quarterly. Based on these assessments, management has concluded that the internal control structure and the procedures for financial reporting have functioned effectively and that the condensed consolidated financial statements fairly present our consolidated financial position and the results of our operations for the periods presented.

Pepsico, Inc.

Management's Responsibility for Financial Statements

To Our Shareholders:

Management is responsible for the reliability of the consolidated financial statements and related notes. The financial statements were prepared in conformity with generally accepted accounting principles and include amounts based upon our estimates and assumptions, as required. The financial statements have been audited by our independent auditors, KPMG LLP, who were given free access to all financial records and related data, including minutes of the meetings of the Board of Directors and Committees of the Board. We believe that our representations to the independent auditors are valid and appropriate.

Management maintains a system of internal controls designed to provide reasonable assurance as to the reliability of the financial statements, as well as to safeguard assets from unauthorized use or disposition. The system is supported by formal policies and procedures, including an active Code of Conduct program intended to ensure employees adhere to the highest standards of personal and professional integrity. Our internal audit function monitors and reports on the adequacy of and compliance with the internal control system, and appropriate actions are taken to address significant control deficiencies and other opportunities for improving the system as they are identified. The Audit Committee of the Board of Directors consists solely of directors who are not salaried employees and who are, in the opinion of the Board of Directors, free from any relationship that would interfere with the exercise of independent judgment as a committee member.

The Committee meets during the year with representatives of management, including internal auditors and the independent auditors to review our financial reporting process and our controls to safeguard assets. Both our independent auditors and internal auditors have free access to the Audit Committee.

Although no cost-effective internal control system will preclude all errors and irregularities, we believe our controls as of December 28, 2002, provide reasonable assurance that the financial statements are reliable and that our assets are reasonably safeguarded.

Notes

1. See Regulation S-K, Item 308 (17 CFR §229.308).
2. See footnote 62 to the SEC's final rule, "Management's Reports on Internal Control over Financial Reporting and Certification of Disclosure in Exchange Act Periodic Reports" (release numbers 33-8238 and 34-47986).
3. These example deficiencies are provided in the auditing literature. See the American Institute of Certified Public Accountants (AICPA), *Professional Standards,* AU Sec 325.21.

Index

A

Accountability of Tax Dollars Act, 94
Accounting for Direct Loans and Loan Guarantees, 67
Accounting manuals, 153–154
Accounting principles:
  selection/application of, 128–130
Action plan, 45–46
Activity-level controls, 135, 138
  assessment of, 176
  documentation of, 154–157
  evaluating effectiveness of, 239–242
  planning tests of, 211–212
  significant, 132
  test result evaluation for, 254
  tests of, 242–254
Activity-level significant control objectives, 131–133
Act of 1789, 7
AGA (Association of Government Accountants), vii
Agencies:
  and control activities, 65
  FFMIA requirements for, 9
  mission documentation of, 152
Agency personnel, 98
AICPA standards, 27–28
American General Finance, Inc., 296
An Audit of Internal Control over Financial Reporting Performed in Conjunction with an Audit of Financial Statements, see PCAOB *Auditing Standard No. 2*
Annual audit requirements, 94
Annual budget, 97–98
Annual reporting:
  required by CFO Act, 8
  under revised Circular A-123, 17–18
  under Sarbanes-Oxley Act, 18–19
  under SOX, 1–2
  submitted to SEC, 1–2
Anti-fraud programs, 137
  employees survey for, 187–188
  for entity-level control objectives, 124–126
  evaluating, 126
Application controls, 6, 73
Application-level controls, 198–199

Argonaut Technologies, Inc., 279–280
"As of" reporting, 266, 273–274
Assertions, financial statement, 240, 241
Assessment team, 39–45
  documentation by, 78
  and management meetings, 41–43
  members of, 100–101
  pre-project evaluation considerations for, 39–41
  project scope/work arrangement clarification by, 43–45
Association of Government Accountants (AGA), vii
Attestation Report of the Registered Public Accounting Firm, 18
Audit committee:
  control responsibilities of, 119
  evaluating, 118
"audit gap," 27–29
Audit guidance:
  of OMB, 6–7
Audit guidelines:
  issued with OMB, 6–7
Auditing Standard No. 2, see PCAOB *Auditing Standard No. 2*
Auditor(s):
  independent, *see* Independent auditors
  objective of, in PCAOB *Auditing Standard No. 2,* 29
  opinion formation of, 29
Auditor's report:
  on internal controls, 22–26
  for publicly listed corporations, 3
Audits:
  expansion of, in CFO Act, 28
  independent, 270
  integrated, 4
Authority, 58–59
Automated compliance tools, 176–183
  and automated control procedures, 182
  and automated testing of controls, 181
  for documentation of significant controls, 149, 176–183
  implementation of, 177–178
  value of, 183
Automated control procedures, 182
Automated documentation tool, 175

Automated testing, 181
Availability (term), 74
Available evidence, 200

B

Bazerman, Max H., 124
Belief systems, 116
Board of directors, 119
Bottom-up approach, 35
Budget, annual, 97–98
Budget and Accounting Act of 1921, 7
*Budget and Accounting Procedures Act of
   1950,* 7–8
Business activities, 82
Business process activities:
  identifying, 70
  in Internal Control—Integrated
    Framework, 69–73
Business strategy, 42

C

Canadian Institute of Chartered
   Accountants, 210
Centers for Disease Control and Prevention,
   73
CEO, *see* Chief executive officers
Certifications:
  of management, 20–21
  subcertification, 22
CFO Act, *see* Chief Financial Officers Act
   of 1990
CFO Council (Chief Financial Officers
   Council), 11–14
CFOs, *see* Chief financial officers
Champy, James, 132
*Changes in Internal Control over Financial
   Reporting,* 19
Chief executive officers (CEOs):
  control responsibilities of, 119
  and internal control over financial
    reporting, 18
Chief financial officers (CFOs), 18
Chief Financial Officers Act of 1990 (CFO
   Act), 8–9
  agencies of, 11
  annual audit requirements of, 94
  and annual reporting, 8
  audit expansion in, 28
  audit guidelines, issued with OMB, 6–7
Chief Financial Officers Council (CFO
   Council), 11
Circular A-123, *see* OMB Circular A-123

COBIT, *see* Control Objectives for
   Information and Related Technology
   framework
Code of conduct, 152
Collusion, 53
Committee of Sponsoring Organizations of
   the Treadway Commissions (COSO),
   vii, 5
  controls identified by, 6
  Framework, see Internal Control—
    Integrated Framework
  internal control definition of, 51–52
  internal controls definition in, 5–6
Communication, 54, 56
  as component of internal control, 6
  formal, 68
Competence, 58
Compliance (term), 75
Compliance tools, automated, 176–183
Comptroller General, 7, 8
Computer application controls, 243–245
  examples, 244–245
  and flowcharting, 163
Computer general controls, 228–236
  designing, 228–236
  as entity-level control objectives, 120–121
Computer general controls review, 207,
   229–236
Conduct, code of, 152
Confidentiality, 75
*Consideration of Fraud in a Financial
   Statement Audit,* 124–125
Consistency, 122, 123
Consultants:
  outside, 46
Control(s):
  activity-level, 176, 211–212
  alignment of, 120
  application, 6, 73
  application-level, 198–199
  automated testing of, 181
  computer application, 243–245
  defined, 166
  documentation of, 150, 151, 155
  entity-level, 176, 247
  general, 6
  identified by COSO *Framework,* 6
  internal, 51–52
  IT-related, 75
  levels of, 53–54
  logical access, 180
  significant, 83
Control activities, 54, 55, 64–66
  characteristics of, 65

as component of internal control, 6
  integration with, 67
  types of, 65–66
Control criteria, 49–60
  and control activities, 64–66
  and control environment, 56–60
  disclosure of, 77–80
  and information and communication
    system, 66–68
  and Internal Control—Integrated
    Framework, 50–56
  and monitoring, 68–69
  need for, 49
  over information technology systems,
    73–77
  and risk assessment process, 60–64
Control deficiency, 85, 87
Control design:
  confirming, 248–249
  evaluation, 171–174
  testing, 13
Control environment, 5, 54–60
Control frameworks, 5
Control objectives:
  activity-level, 131–133
  entity-level, 115–130, 193–194
  related to organizational culture, 116
  significant, 113–145
Control Objectives for Information and
    Related Technology (COBIT)
    framework, 49, 74
  and general computer control objectives,
    119
  and information technology, 74
Control policies/procedures, 183–190
Control procedures, 51
Controls standards, 5–6
Control structures, 121–123
Control warehouse function, 178
Corporate culture, 136
  control policy/procedure linked to,
    183–184
  employees survey for, 216–219
Corporate governance, 151
Correction plans:
  in Implementation Guide, 13–14
  and OMB Circular A-123, 13–14
COSO, *see* Committee of Sponsoring
    Organizations of the Treadway
    Commissions
COSO *Framework, see* Internal Control—
    Integrated Framework
Credit Reform, 67
Critical success factors, 60

Culture:
  corporate, 136, 216–219
  defined, 115, 116
  organizational, 115–116
Customer (term), 70

D

Decisions, documenting, 103–104
Defense Logistics Agency, 72
Deficiencies:
  control, 85
  correction of, 274–275
  design, 268
  internal control, 69, 84–88, 268–275
  operating, 268
  reporting, 69
  significant, 32, 85, 269
  as term, 69
Deficiency, internal control, 32
Degree of interaction, 91
Department of Agriculture's Natural Finance
    Center, 72
Department of Education, 72
Department of Health and Human Services
    (DHHS), 73
Department of Homeland Security, 64
Design deficiency, 268
Design effectiveness, 199–200
Detective controls, 162
DHHS (Department of Health and Human
    Services), 73
Direct Loan Operation, 72
Disclosure(s):
  of material weakness, 32–33, 279–290
  required, 265, 267–268
Disclosure Committee, 93
Disclosure committees, 19–20
Disclosure controls and procedures, 16
  considerations for, 77–80
  defined, 77
  and FMFIA, 77
  internal control over financial reporting
    vs., 16
  and management, 16
  and materiality, 37
  quarterly reporting of, 19
  SEC definition of, 16
Dockery Act of 1894, 7
Documentation:
  action plan for, 174–176
  of activity-level control objectives,
    256–257
  of activity-level controls, 154–157

Documentation *(continued)*
    adequacy of, 149–151
    of agency mission, 152
    assessment of existing, 175
    by assessment team, 78
    automated tools for, 149, 176–183
    of controls, 31, 148–176
    of entity-level control policies and
        procedures, 151–154
    flowcharting as, 158–163
    importance of, 147–148
    independent auditors coordination of, 174
    internal control, 155–157
    internal control vs., 148
    matrixes as, 168–174
    narratives as, 163–167
    objective of, in assessment project,
        148–149
    and PCAOB *Auditing Standard* No. 2, 31
    of planning decisions, 107
    of policies, 65
    reasonable support for, 31
    requirements for, 154
    of significant control objectives, 38
    of test procedures and results, 254
Documents, key, 208

E

Effective monitoring, 147–148
Effectiveness:
    of activity-level controls, 239–242
    of entity-level controls, 193–194,
        199–200, 209–212
    evaluating, of internal control, 34, 37–38
    and financial reporting, 75
Efficiency, 75
Employees surveys, *see* Surveys, of
        employees
Engagement letter, 43, 44
Entity-level controls, 115–130, 134–135,
        193–237
    alignment with control structures,
        121–123
    anti-fraud programs for, 124–126
    and application-level controls, 198–199
    assessment of, 176
    computer controls as, 120–121
    and computer general controls, 228–236
    control areas of, 151
    coordination of, with independent
        auditors and OIG, 213
    documentation action plan for, 256–257
    documentation of, 151–154

    effectiveness of, 193–194, 199–200,
        209–212
    effect on financial statement accounts, 35
    examples of, 247
    inquiries of management regarding,
        222–228
    and internal control reliability model,
        195–200
    organizational culture as, 115–116
    personal policies as, 117–120
    risk identification for, 123–124
    survey tools for, 215–222
    and system-wide monitoring, 130
    testing and evaluation of, 194–195,
        213–215
    testing techniques for, 200–209
    test result considerations for, 245–247
    test result documentation for, 212–213
    and top-level financial reporting
        processes, 126–130
Entity personnel, 119
Ethics, 125–126
Ethics in Government Act of 1978, 152
Evaluation/assessment (of internal controls),
        33–45
    consultative approach to, 38–39
    phases for, 37–38
    SEC and PCAOB Guidelines for, 33,
        36–37
    structured approach to, 33, 34
    teams for, 101
    top-down approach for, 33, 35–36
Evidence, available, 200

F

Fair presentation, 62, 129–130
FAM (Financial Audit Manual), 212
FASAB (Federal Accounting Standards
        Advisory Board), 9
FDA (Food and Drug Administration), 73
Federal Accounting Standards Advisory
        Board (FASAB), 9
Federal Financial Management
        Improvement Act of 1996 (FFMIA),
        9–10
Federal government, internal controls in,
        6–10
Federal Loan Programs, 66–67
*Federal Managers' Financial Integrity Act of
        1982 (FMFIA):*
    and disclosure controls, 77
    establishment of, 8
    and OMB Circular A-123, 10

FFMIA, *see* Federal Financial Management Improvement Act of 1996
Finance officers, control responsibilities of, 119
Financial Audit Manual (FAM), 212
Financial management systems, 9
Financial Management Systems, OMB Circular A-127, 18
Financial reporting:
  confidentiality in, 75
  and effectiveness, 75
  efficiency of, 75
  primary qualities of, 74–75
  responsibility of, 277–278
Financial reporting processes:
  information system for, 68
  top-level, 126–130
Financial reporting regulations, vii
Financial significance, 88–89
Financial statement accounts, 35
Financial statement assertions, 240, 241
Flowcharting, 158–163
  and computer application controls, 163
  for information storage and retrieval, 162–163
  of preventative controls, vs. detective, 162
  for routine activity-level controls, 158
  strengths of, 158
  tips for, 158–161
  of transactions, vs. events, 161–162
  weaknesses of, 158
FMFIA, *see* Federal Managers' Financial Integrity Act of 1982
Focus groups, 251–252
Food and Drug Administration (FDA), 73
Foreign operations, 64
Form 10K, 18–19
Formal communication system, 68
the Framework, *see* Internal Control—Integrated Framework
Fraud:
  and OMB Circular A-123, 125
  PCAOB guidance for, 125
  SEC guidance for, 125
Free responses, 179

G

GAAP (generally accepted accounting principles), 129
GAAS, *see* Generally accepted auditing standards
GAO, *see* General Accounting Office; Government Accountability Office

GAO/PCIE Financial Audit Manual (FAM), 212
GAO reports, 98
GAO's *Financial Auditing Manual*, 169
GAO's Standards for Internal Control in the Federal Government ("Green Book"), 12
GAS *(Government Auditing Standards)*, 6
General Accounting Office (GAO), 6–8. *See also* Government Accountability Office
General computer control objectives:
  and COBIT framework, 119
  significant, 119–120
General computer controls, 136, 185–186, 206–207
General controls, 6, 73
Generally accepted accounting principles (GAAP), 129
Generally accepted auditing standards (GAAS), 23
GMRA (Government Management and Reform Act) of 1994, 94
Governance, corporate, 151
Government Accountability Office (GAO), 6, 212. *See also* General Accounting Office
Government Auditing Standards (GAS; Yellow Book standards), 6
Government Management and Reform Act of 1994 (GMRA), 94
Great West Life Assurance Company, 293–294
Green Book, 12
Guarantees, 44

H

Hammer, Michael, 132
Handbook, personnel, 152–153
History, congress and internal controls, 7–10
  and CFO Act, 8–9
  in 1800s and 1900s, 7–8
  and Federal Financial Management Improvement Act of 1996, 9–10
  in 1990s, 8
Honesty, 125–126
Human error, 53
Human resource management, 72
Human resource policies, 59–60, 152–153

I

Implementation Guide for OMB Circular A-123 (Implementation Guide), 11–14

Implementation Guide for OMB Circular A-123 (Implementation Guide) *(continued)*
  and correction plans, 13–14
  and matrix use, 169
Inbound logistics, 70, 71
Independent audits, 270
Independent auditor(s):
  and "audit gap," 27–29
  entity-level controls coordination with, 213
  internal controls reporting by, 3–4
  OIG coordination with, 102–103
  OMB requirements of, 22–26
  reliance on others, 32
  reporting coordination with legal counsel, 278–279
  reporting responsibilities of, 4, 22–29
  and significant control objectives, 134, 140, 142–145
  and SOX/PCAOB requirements, 26–27
  test coordination with, 255–256
  working with, 140, 142–145
Informal communication system, 68
Information gathering, 54, 56
  as component of internal control, 6
  for internal control assessment, 82–93
Information gathering matrix, 169–171
Information processing, 66, 90
Information-processing streams, 240, 242
Information Systems Audit and Control Association (ISACA), 49, 75, 77, 101
Information technology, and COBIT framework, 74
Information Technology Governance Institute (ITGI), 60, 75, 77, 101
Information technology systems, 73–77
Infrastructure, 72
Inherent risk, 84
Inquiries, of management, 204–206
  improving effectiveness with, 205–206
  purpose of, 204–205
  questions for, example, 223–228
  response evaluation of, 228
  use of, 222–223
Inquiry tests, 247–251, 257–259
Integrated agency accounting and financial management systems, 9
Integrated audit, 4
Integration, 67
Integrity (term), 74
Interaction, degree of, 91
Internal auditor(s), 119

Internal control(s):
  assessment, project planning for, *see* Internal control assessment
  auditor's report on, 22–26
  components of, 54–56
  congressional history involving, *see* History, congress and internal controls
  COSO definition of, 51–52
  COSO *Framework* definition of, 5–6
  defined, 14, 17
  definition of, by OMB Circular A-123, 14–15
  definition of, by Sarbanes-Oxley Act, 16–17
  documentation vs., 148
  evaluating, at entity level, 12
  evaluating, at process level, 12–13
  evaluating effectiveness of, 34, 37–38
  evaluation/assessment of, *see* Evaluation/assessment
  in federal government, 6–10
  independent auditors reporting of, 3–4
  management assessment of, 3, 14–17, 46–47
  management responsibility for, 10, 275–278
  material weakness in, 23, 266
  objectives of, 15
  PCAOB requirements for, 26–27
  reliability of, 147
  reports on management responsibility for, 290–297
  requirements of, by Sarbanes-Oxley Act, 26–27
  standards of, 15
Internal control assessment, 81–111
  action plan for, 105–107
  defined in OMB Circular A-123, 11–14
  documenting decisions in, 103–104
  and effectiveness of internal controls, 88–93
  focus areas for, 84–88
  information gathering for, 82–93
  information sources for, 93–99
  objectives for, 81–82
  and OIG coordination with independent auditors, 102–103
  questions for, 107–111
  significant control objectives affecting, 82–84
  term structuring for, 99–101
Internal control deficiencies, 32, 268–275
  assessing, 85
  defining, 84–88

examples of, 270–271
reporting, 69, 268–275
severity judgments on, 269–270
Internal control documentation, 155–157
Internal control effectiveness, 80
Internal Control in a Financial Statement Audit, see SAS No. 55, *Internal Control in a Financial Statement Audit*
Internal Control—Integrated Framework (the Framework), 5, 50–56
and business process activities, 69–73
and control environment, 56–60
controls identified by, 6
information and communication system in, 66–68
internal control components in, 138–139
internal controls definition in, 5–6
key characteristics of, 50–53
monitoring, 68–69
risk assessment process in, 60–64
and significant control objectives, 138–139
Internal control over financial reporting, 15
defined, 16
disclosure controls and procedures vs., 16
and materiality, 37
Internal control reliability model, 195–200
capabilities of, 197–198
and reliability levels, 195–197
Internal control report, 1–2, 23
Internal controls:
in COSO *Framework,* 138–139
effectiveness of, 88–93
reporting, 272
reporting, before Sarbanes-Oxley Act, 6
Intervention, management, 57
ISACA, *see* Information Systems Audit and Control Association
IT Control Objectives for Sarbanes-Oxley, 60, 75, 77, 101
Item 307, of SEC Regulation S-K, 19
ITGI, *see* Information Technology Governance Institute
IT processes, 75
IT-related controls, 75

K

Key business activities, 82
Key documents, reading/assessment of, 208
Kimberly-Clark, 295–296
Knowledge qualification, 21

L

Legal counsel, coordination with independent auditors, 278–279
Legislative Reorganization Act of 1947, 7
Letter, engagement, 43
Letter to employees, 215–216
Limitations, on contract, 44
Line managers, 78
Linkage, 122
Logical access controls, 180
Logistics:
inbound, 70, 71
outbound, 71

M

Main agreement, 44–45
Management:
control responsibilities of, 119
and disclosure controls and procedures, 16
inquiries of, *see* Inquiries, of management
internal control assessment by, 3, 14–17, 46–47
line managers, 78
psychology of, 124
responsibility for internal control, 10, 275–278, 290–297
responsibility for reporting internal control, 275–278
senior management, 67–68
and significant control objective assessment, 140, 141
Management Anti-Fraud Programs and Controls, 124–125
Management assessment process evaluation, 30–31
Management certifications, 20–21
Management Discussion and Analysis, 94–95
Management intervention, 57
Management meetings, 41–43
Management override, 53
Management's Annual Report on Internal Control over Financial Reporting, 18
Management's Discussion and Analysis (MD&A), 22
Management's Responsibility for Internal Control (Section II of OMB Circular A-123), 14
Marketing and sales, 71
Materiality, 37, 62
Material weakness, 32, 85, 269

Material weakness *(continued)*
  definition of, by OMB Circular A-123, 24–25
  disclosures of, examples, 279–290
  in internal control, 23, 266
  preliminary definition of, 106
  reporting requirements for, 86
Material weakness disclosures, 32–33, 279–290
Matrixes, 168–174
  and control design evaluation, 171–174
  information gathering matrix, 169–171
  preparing, 168–169
  strengths of, 168
  weaknesses of, 168
MD&A (Management's Discussion and Analysis), 22
Menu-driven responses, 179
Monitoring, 54, 56
  as component of internal control, 6
  and control criteria, 68–69
  effective, 147–148
  of internal control effectiveness, 80
  ongoing activities for, 69
  as significant control objectives, 130
  system-wide, 130, 138

N

Narrative documentation, 163–167
  of internal controls, example, 165–166
  preparing, 164–167
  as primary documentation, 164–167
  strengths of, 163–164
  as supplement documentation, 167
  weaknesses of, 164
National Commission on Fraudulent Financial Reporting, 50
National Institutes of Health, 73
Non-conformance:
  definition of, by OMB Circular A-123, 24–25, 87
  reporting requirements for, 87
Nonroutine information, 68
Norms, 115–116

O

Objective-driven approach, 52
Observation, 208–209
Observations, 254
OCFO (Office of the Chief Financial Officer), 100
OCFO accountants, 100

Office of Government Ethics (OGE), 152
Office of Government Ethics Reauthorization Act of 1988, 152
Office of Management and Budget (OMB), vii
  audit guidance of, 6–7
  audit guidelines issued with, 6–7
  OMB Bulletin 01-02, *Audit Requirements for Federal Financial Statements,* 23, 27–28
  OMB Circular A-123, *see* OMB Circular A-123
Office of Personnel Management (OPM), 152–153
Office of the Chief Financial Officer (OCFO), 100
Office of the Inspector General (OIG):
  coordination with independent auditors, 102–103
  OIG reports, 98
  test coordination with, 255–256
OGE (Office of Government Ethics), 152
OIG, *see* Office of the Inspector General
OMB, *see* Office of Management and Budget
OMB Bulletin 01-02, *Audit Requirements for Federal Financial Statements,* 23
  auditing requirements of, above AICPA standards, 27–28
  internal control report requirements outlined by, 23
OMB Circular A-127, *Financial Management Systems,* vii–viii, 10–14, 18
  annual reporting under, 17–18
  control deficiency definition of, 24
  and correction plans, 13–14
  first year of implementation of, 36
  and FMFIA, 10
  and fraud, 125
  guidance for reporting, 261–265
  independent auditors requirements by, 22–26
  internal control assessment process defined in, 11–14
  internal control definition by, 14–15
  material weakness definition of, 24–25
  non-conformance definition of, 24–25
  reportable conditions definition of, 24
  revised reporting requirements under, 17–18
  Section II of, 14
"One-size-fits-all" approach, 52
Open-ended phrases, 44

Operating deficiency, 268
Operating environment, 63
Operating style, 58
Operational effectiveness:
    design effectiveness vs., 199–200
    of significant control objectives, 38
    at transaction level, 13
Operational significance, 89
Operations, 71
Operations personnel, 100
OPM (Office of Personnel Management), 152–153
Organizational culture, 115–116
Organizational vulnerabilities, 124
Outbound logistics, 71
Outside consultants, 46
Override, by management, 53
Oversight agency activities, 91–93
Oversight process, 126

P

PAR, *see* Performance and Accountability Report
PAR (Performance and Accountability Report), 17
Pathmark, 291–292
Payroll, 90
PCAOB, *see* Public Company Accounting Oversight Board
PCAOB 2 Release No. 2004-001 (internal controls), 2
PCAOB *Auditing Standard* No. 2, 4–5, 29–33
    auditor's objective in, 29
    and documentation, 31
    and independent auditor's reliance on others, 32
    and integrated audit, 4
    management assessment process evaluation in, 30–31
    and management evaluation of significant control objectives, 140, 141
    material weakness disclosure under, 32–33
    and significant controls, 83–84
    testwork guidance in, 31–32
"PCAOB's Staff Questions and Answers Auditing Internal Control Over Financial Reporting June 23, 2004 Answer No. 7," 143–145
PCIE (President's Council on Integrity and Efficiency), 11
Pepsico, Inc., 297

Performance and Accountability Report (PAR), 17, 94–97
    financial section of, 96–97
    Management Discussion and Analysis section of, 94–95
    objectives of, 94
    performance section of, 95–96
Personnel, agency, 98
Personnel handbook, 152–153
Personnel issues, 63–64
Personnel policies, 59–60, 136
    control policy/procedure linked to, 184–186
    employees survey for, 216–219
    as entity-level control objectives, 117–120
Physical controls, 66
Pilot testing, of employee surveys, 203
Policies:
    documentation of, 65
    human resource, 152–153
    personnel, 184–186
Policies and procedures manuals (PPMs), 98
Policy (element), 64
PPMs (policies and procedures manuals), 98
"Predictable Surprises: The Disasters You Should Have Seen Coming," 124
President's Council on Integrity and Efficiency (PCIE), 11, 212
Preventative controls, detective vs., 162
Primary activities, 70–71
Problem solving, 42
Procedure (element), 64
Procedure(s) (element), 65
Procurement, 72
Project administration, 42–43, 181
Project planning, 37. *See also* Internal control assessment
Project Team, 12
Project team, 106
Proposals, 44
Public Company Accounting Oversight Board (PCAOB), vii
    2 Release No. 2004-001, 2
    and advice solicitation, 143–145
    fraud guidance by, 125
    guidelines for evaluation of internal controls, 33, 36–37
    internal control requirements, 26–27
    requirements for independent auditors, 26–27
    and significant controls, 83
Public Company Accounting Oversight Board *Auditing Standard* No. 2, *see* PCAOB *Auditing Standard* No. 2

Publicly listed corporations:
  auditor's report for, 3
  controls standard for, 5

Q

Qualitative information, 78
Quantitative information, 78
Quarterly reporting, 19
  of disclosure controls and procedures, 19
  under Sarbanes-Oxley Act, 19

R

Reasonable assurance, 52
Reconciliations, 253–254
*Reengineering the Corporation: A Manifesto
  for Business Revolution,* 132
Reliability:
  of internal control, 147
  levels of, 195–197
  as term, 62
Reportable conditions, 23
  definition of, by OMB Circular A-123, 24
  reporting requirements for, 86
Reporting, 69, 261–297
  "As of" reporting, 266, 273–274
  coordination of, with independent
    auditors and legal counsel, 278–279
  deficiencies, 69
  evaluation results, 13
  financial reporting, 277–278
  independent auditors' responsibilities for,
    22–29
  internal control deficiencies, 69
  and internal control deficiencies,
    268–275
  internal controls, 272
  on management responsibility for internal
    control, 275–278
  OMB Circular A-123 guidance for,
    261–265
  OMB Circular A-123 requirements for,
    17–18
  private industry practices for, examples,
    279–297
  quarterly, 19
  and required disclosures, 265, 267–268
  Sarbanes-Oxley Act requirements for,
    18–22
  SEC rules for, 265–267
Reporting requirements, 261–268
  for control deficiencies, 87
  for material weakness, 86

for non-conformance, 87
for reportable conditions, 86
Reports:
  auditor's, 3
  on management responsibility for internal
    control, 290–297
*Reports on the Processing of Transactions
  by Service Organizations,* 91
Required disclosures, 265, 267–268
Resource library, 181
Responsibilities:
  assignment of, 58–59
  clarifying, 44
Restructurings, 64
Risks:
  identification of, 62–63
  inherent, 84
  significant, 83
Risk assessment, 51, 54, 63
  as component of internal control, 5
  and control criteria, 60–64
  and documenting controls, 33
  integration with, 67
  link to process of, 65
Risk exposure, 89
Risk identification, 137
  employees survey for, 187
  for entity-level control objectives,
    123–124
Rockford Corp., 280–282
Routine activity-level controls, 158
Routine information, 68
Routine systematic processes, 126–127
Rule 13a-14(a), SEC, 20–21

S

Sale (term), 70
Sales and marketing, 71
Sarbanes-Oxley Act (SOX) of 2002:
  annual reporting under, 1–2, 18–19
  and control frameworks, 5
  and disclosure committees, 19–20
  history of, 1–2
  internal control definition by, 16–17
  internal control requirements, 26–27
  internal controls reporting before, 6
  management certifications required by,
    20–21
  quarterly reporting under, 19
  requirements for independent auditors,
    26–27
  revised reporting requirements under,
    18–22

Section 302 of, 20
Section 404 of, 2, 18, 92
Section 906 of, 20, 21
SAS No. 55, *Internal Control in a Financial Statement Audit,* 64, 68
SAS No. 69, *The Meaning of "Presents Fairly in Conformity with Generally Accepted Accounting Principles" in the Independent Auditor's Report,* 62
SAS No. 70, *Reports on the Processing of Transactions by Service Organizations,* 91
SAS No. 99, *Consideration of Fraud in a Financial Statement Audit,* 124–125
SEC, *see* Securities and Exchange Commission
SEC Regulation S-K, Item 307 of, 19
SEC Rule 13a-14(a), 20–21
Section 302 of Sarbanes-Oxley Act, 20
Section 404 of Sarbanes-Oxley Act, 2, 18, 92
Section 906 of Sarbanes-Oxley Act, 20, 21
Section II of OMB Circular A-123 *(Management's Responsibility for Internal Control),* 14
Securities and Exchange Commission (SEC):
annual reports submitted to, 1–2
disclosure controls and procedures definition by, 16
financial reporting regulations, vii
fraud guidance by, 125
guidelines for evaluation of internal controls, 33, 36–37
Item 307 of SEC Regulation S-K, 19
and management's internal control assessment, 3
rules for reporting, 265–267
SEC Rule 13a-14(a), 20–21
Segregation of duties, 66
Senior Assessment Team:
establishment of, 11–12
and evaluation results, 13–14
as key player in pre-execution, 41
role of, 78–79
Senior management, 67–68
Senior Management Council, 12
meeting with, in pre-project execution, 39–41
policies/processes of, 93
role of, 78
Service organizations, 90, 91
Services:
description of, 44
as primary activity, 71

Services exhibit, description of, 45
SFFAS No. 2, *Accounting for Direct Loans and Loan Guarantees,* 67
Sharper Image, 290–291
Significant activities, 65
Significant activity-level controls, 132
Significant controls, 83, 113–145
action plan for identifying, 134–135
activity-level, 131–133
affecting internal control assessment, 82–84
control policies/procedures linked to, 183–190
and COSO *Framework,* 138–139
design effectiveness of, 38
documentation of, 38
entity-level, 115–130
examples, 135–138
and independent auditors, 134, 140, 142–145
management evaluation of, 140, 141
monitoring as, 130
operating effectiveness of, 38
and PCAOB, 83
and PCAOB *Auditing Standard* No. 2, 83–84
understanding, 105
Significant deficiency, 32, 85, 269
Significant general computer control objectives, 119–120
Significant risks, 83
Socialization, 115–116
Standardized updating procedures, 180
"Standards for Ethical Conduct for Employees of the Executive Branch," 152
Standards for Internal Control in the Federal Government, 14
Statement of Assurance, 17, 261
Statement of Assurance for Internal Control over Financial Reporting, 17, 261
Statements of Federal Financial Accounting Standards (SFFAS) No. 2, *Accounting for Direct Loans and Loan Guarantees,* 67
Subcertification, 22
Support activities, 71–72
Surveys, of employees, 201–204
analyzing/reporting results of, 203–204
for anti-fraud programs, 187–188
for corporate culture and personnel policies, example, 216–219
evaluation of, 219–222
letter to employees preceding, example, 215–216

Surveys, of employees *(continued)*
pilot testing of, 203
questions for, 204
for risk identification, 187
sample selection for, 201–202
for system-wide monitoring, 190
timing of, 202–203
for top-level financial reporting
processes, 188–190
Survey tools, 215–222
Symons International, 294
Systematic processes, 126–127
Systemax, 282–290
System-wide monitoring, 138
employees survey for, 190
and entity-level control objectives, 130

T

Technical expertise, 42
Technical specialists, 100–101
Technology development, 72
Temptations, 57
10K, 18–19
Terms, structuring of, 99–101
Testing:
and available evidence, 200
control design, 13
and evaluation, 194–195
and general computer controls, 206–207
inquiries, of management, 204–206
observation, 208–209
and reading/assessment of key documents, 208
surveys, of employees, 201–204
teams for, 101
Tests:
of activity-level controls, 242–254
coordinating, with independent auditors and OIG, 255–256
focus groups, 251–252
inquiry, 247–251, 257–259
nature of, 242–243
observations, 254
reconciliations, 253–254
timing of, 243
of transactions, 252–253

The Meaning of "Presents Fairly in Conformity with Generally Accepted Accounting Principles" in the Independent Auditor's Report, 62
Top-down approach, 33
Top-level financial reporting processes, 137–138
consideration of, 127–128
employees survey for, 188–190
and entity-level control objectives, 126–130
nature of, 127
routine, systematic processes vs., 126–127
Top-level reviews, 65–66
Transaction data, 154
Transaction processing, 127
Transactions:
events vs., 161–162
tests of, 252–253
Treadway Commission, 5

U

Updating procedures, standardized, 180
U.S. Department of Treasury, 7

V

Value-chain methodology, 70–71
Value imbalance, 124
Values, 115

W

Watkins, Michael D., 124
Weakness, material, *see* Material weakness
Web sites, 98
Work product, ownership of, 44–45
Work programs, 181
Written agreement, 44

Y

Yellow Book standards *(Government Auditing Standards),* 6